KT-570-919

Overcoming Your Workplace Stress

Occupational stress affects millions of people every year and is not only costly to the individual – in terms of their mental and physical health – but also results in major costs for organizations due to workplace absence and loss of productivity. This cognitive behaviour therapy (CBT) based self-help guide will equip the user with the necessary tools and techniques to manage work related stress more effectively.

Divided into three parts, this book will help you to:

- understand occupational stress
- learn about a range of methods to reduce stress levels
- develop your own self-help plan.

Overcoming Your Workplace Stress is written in a straightforward, easy-to-follow style, allowing the reader to develop the necessary skills to become their own therapist.

Martin R. Bamber is a consultant clinical psychologist, Professional Head of Psychological Therapies for North Yorkshire and York NHS Primary Care Trust and Director of MRB Clinical Psychology Services Ltd, a private practice based in York, UK. He is also author of *CBT for Occupational Stress in Health Professionals* (Routledge).

BRITISH MEDICAL ASSOCIATION

0727244

Overcoming Your Workplace Stress

A CBT-based self-help guide

Martin R. Bamber

Routledge
Taylor & Francis Group

LONDON AND NEW YORK

First published 2011 by Routledge
27 Church Road, Hove, East Sussex BN3 2FA

Simultaneously published in the USA and Canada
by Routledge
711 Third Avenue, New York NY 10017 (8th Floor)

Routledge is an imprint of the Taylor & Francis Group, an Informa business

© 2011 Martin R. Bamber

All rights reserved. No part of this book may be reprinted or reproduced
or utilized in any form or by any electronic, mechanical, or other means,
now known or hereafter invented, including photocopying and recording,
or in any information storage or retrieval system, without permission in
writing from the publishers.

Trademark notice: Product or corporate names may be trademarks
or registered trademarks, and are used only for identification and
explanation without intent to infringe.

British Library Cataloguing in Publication Data
A catalogue record for this book is available from the British Library

Library of Congress Cataloging in Publication Data
Bamber, Martin R.
   Overcoming your workplace stress : a CBT-based self-help guide /
   Martin R. Bamber. — 1st ed.
     p. cm.
   Includes index.
   ISBN 978-0-415-55661-3 (hardback) — ISBN 978-0-415-67178-1
(pbk.) 1. Stress (Psychology) 2. Job stress. 3. Stress management—
Handbook, manuals, etc. 4. Cognitive therapy—Handbooks, manuals,
etc. I. Title.
   BF575.S75B295 2011
   158.7'2—dc22

                            2010050493

ISBN: 978–0–415–55661–3 (hbk)
ISBN: 978–0–415–67178–1 (pbk)
ISBN: 978–0–203–81422–2 (ebk)

Typeset in Times by RefineCatch Limited, Bungay, Suffolk
Printed and bound in Great Britain by TJ International Ltd, Padstow, Cornwall
Paperback cover design by Andrew Ward

This book is dedicated to my sister Jackie, who tragically lost a four year battle against cancer on 13 September 2010. You were a wonderful sister, Jackie, and you are missed so much by us all. May you rest in peace. It is also dedicated to my mother Barbara and her partner Gordon, who devoted much of their time to caring for Jackie during her illness.

Also to my brother Paul and my other sister Shirley, who have always shown their love and support for me over the years, and good old 'Uncle Peter', who has been an admirable role model for me throughout my formative years and provided the illustrations in Chapter 6 of this book.

Contents

PART III
Pulling it all together 191

Figures and tables

Figures

Tables

---

* Tables 1.1, 1.2, 2.1, 4.2, 6.1, 7.1, 9.1, 9.2, 9.3 and 11.1 are available to view and print from the following website: www.routledgementalhealth. com/9780415671781

About the author

Dr Martin Bamber, BA (Hons), RMN, MA, MPhil, DPsychol, CPsychol, AFBPsS, is a chartered consultant clinical psychologist. He completed his clinical psychology training at the University of Edinburgh in 1989. He presently holds the post of Professional Head of Psychological Therapies and County Wide Adult Cognitive Behavioural Therapy Services for North Yorkshire and York NHS Primary Care Trust. He has also worked as an assistant director on the University of Teesside Doctoral Training Programme and as a teaching fellow at the University of York in the Department of Psychology. He is currently honorary visiting lecturer in the School of Health and Social Care at the University of Teesside. He is founder and director of MRB Clinical Psychology Services Ltd, a private practice based in York. Previously, he worked as a clinical psychologist in occupational health for four years, during which time he had the privilege of setting up and developing an occupational health psychology service for staff employed by a number of NHS Trusts in Cleveland. It was during this time that the seeds of a number of ideas presented in this book were sown. More recently, he worked as a clinical psychologist in an occupational health service for NHS staff in York. His research interests are in the fields of psycho-neuro-immunology, occupational stress and innovative applications of cognitive behavioural therapy. He has published a number of articles in national and international journals and is the author of a book entitled *CBT for Occupational Stress in Health Professionals: Introducing a Schema-focused Approach*. He is an associate fellow of the British Psychological Society Division of Clinical Psychology, a member of the British Association for Behavioural and Cognitive Psychotherapies and a certified member of the International Society for Schema Therapy.

Dr Bamber can be contacted at the Psychological Therapies Service of North Yorkshire and York NHS Primary Care Trust, based at the Chantry Suite, Bootham Park Hospital, York YO30 7BY, UK, Email: martin.bamber@nyypct.nhs.uk

Preface

Over recent years we have all become exposed to the chill winds of a global economy. As the global banking crisis and the recent credit crunch have shown us, economies around the world are interdependent upon one another more than ever before. When one collapses, others tend to follow. Yet at the same time they are in competition with one another for their market share and are being faced with the constant drive to reduce inefficiencies and become more competitive in the marketplace. As well as the economic pressures, work organizations all around the world are being subjected to other pressures resulting from a sharp escalation of change, rapid technological advancement and the need to meet ever increasing customer expectations of cheap and high quality products. In order to survive in such a harsh and competitive economic environment, there has inevitably been an unrelenting pressure on employees to produce 'more for less'. One of the main consequences of this unrelenting pressure for individual employees is 'occupational stress'.

It is well documented that occupational stress has become a problem of pandemic proportions, costing world economies many billions of pounds each year through lost production due to sickness absence, retirement through ill health, litigation and poor work performance, and it is on the increase. It is estimated that staff account for between 50 and 80 per cent of organizational costs and if it is not addressed, occupational stress can have a devastating negative impact on profits. There are of course those cynics who argue that the solution to this problem is simple and that if you do not like your job or you are finding it too stressful, you should simply find alternative employment. After all, no job is worth suffering ill health for. However, for many employees, it is not that straightforward and there may be numerous reasons why they cannot just leave. For example, they may have invested many years' training to do the job, or may not be trained to do any other kind of work. They may be a victim of what is known as the 'golden handcuffs' dilemma, where the individual may hate the job but be trapped by it because they are unable to afford a drop in salary. Alternatively, in an employment market where jobs are scarce, or where unemployment is high, there may not be any suitable alternative employment to go to. The individual may also be tied to a particular geographical area through personal and family commitments and be unable to move around the country to find work. Thus, for many people, leaving the job is considered to be the last resort when all else has failed.

There is a growing acknowledgement among many employers that addressing occupational stress makes sense not only for humanitarian reasons but also on sound economic grounds. Despite this, access to workplace occupational health services and employee assistance programmes for many employees suffering from work related stress is patchy and inadequate, or non-existent. The harsh reality is that many employees are either left to fend for themselves or placed on unacceptably long waiting lists to receive help. The need to learn 'self-help' strategies for managing work related stress has never been more important than at the present time.

While many generic texts have been published over the years on 'managing stress', there have been relatively few specifically relating to 'managing occupational stress'. Unfortunately, of the literature that has focused on managing stress at work, much of it has consisted of rather simplistic explanations and overly standardized treatment interventions, which have largely ignored the conceptualization of stress as an interaction between the individual and their environment. They fail to acknowledge employees as complex human beings with emotions and motivations, who bring with them to the workplace their own history, past experiences, beliefs and attitudes, and idiosyncratic ways of coping and behaving. All of these personal factors interact with the work environment and play a crucial part in the development of occupational stress. Interventions aimed at tackling occupational stress need to be able to address this.

Another criticism of much of the self-help literature on this topic is that it tends to be written in a rather chatty or superficial style, which could be easily construed as a little patronizing to those who are suffering from occupational stress. Books are often written by life coaches who seem to promote the ideal that you can 'become whoever you want to be' and the 'sky is the limit'. This can be quite demotivating for someone suffering from stress who simply wants to be able to feel in control enough to manage a day's work. At the other extreme there are academic textbooks written by professionals for professionals, and there appears to be nothing currently in the literature that fills the middle ground. That is, a more serious, evidence-based selp-help manual for clients but which is not an academic textbook. Also while some books can be found which deal with specific aspects of managing stress in the workplace (e.g., time management or assertiveness at work), there does not appear to be any text which provides an overall approach to occupational stress management. This book aims to fill these gaps in the literature by providing a comprehensive coverage of a range of interventions to manage occupational stress based upon the clinically proven evidence-based techniques of cognitive behavioural therapy (CBT). Finally, this book is intended to be more than just a text that people read. It is intended to encourage individuals to take an analytical problem solving approach to the work stress they are experiencing and offers practical steps to tackle it. It is a self-help manual providing step-by-step advice, suggestions, case examples and practical tools and techniques for managing stress in the workplace. It is intended to help you not only to understand the causes and consequences of occupational stress but also to develop a detailed and comprehensive self-help programme. As far as I am aware, there are currently no other up-to-date comprehensive self-help texts available on this topic, which incorporate such a systematic and evidence-based approach to this problem.

This book is aimed at individuals who do not have a sophisticated knowledge or understanding of the subject of psychology. It is written in a simple and easy to read, user friendly and jargon free style, which is readily understandable to the interested lay person. It is deliberately free of the clutter of references throughout the text, as would typically be found in an academic text. The book will also be of interest to those who treat clients suffering from occupational stress, such as counsellors, psychologists and psychiatrists working in both mainstream mental health services and occupational health services. It could also be of use to those who care for people suffering from occupational stress, such as family and friends and those who have to manage its consequences in the workplace such as personnel managers and human resources workers.

The book is presented in three parts. Part I (Chapters 1 and 2) aims to promote your understanding of the concept of stress and outlines the main individual and environmental causes of stress. The consequences of occupational stress for the individual, the organization and the nation are also presented. Stress is conceptualized as being the result of an interaction between the individual and their environment. The central importance of the appraisal or meaning of an event or situation to the individual in the causation of stress is emphasized and an overview of the emotional and physiological changes triggered in the stress reaction is also presented.

Researchers in the field of occupational stress have developed a taxonomy of interventions. Three levels of interventions for managing work related stress more effectively have been identified, known as primary, secondary and tertiary level interventions. Primary level interventions aim to change the sources of stress in the work environment itself. It is acknowledged, however, that sometimes it is not possible to change the work environment either because it is uneconomical for the employer to do this, or because there are aspects of the job itself that are inherently stressful. Where this is the case and the sources of stress cannot be readily removed, secondary level interventions are considered to be more appropriate. Secondary level interventions aim to teach the employee a range of coping skills or strategies to help buffer them against an inherently stressful environment and to assist them to develop the confidence to look after themselves more effectively in situations that would in actual fact be stressful to anyone. Tertiary level interventions are aimed at more severe levels of clinical distress which are impacting on the individual's capacity to be productive in the work setting, or even to remain at work, and where secondary level interventions are assessed as being unlikely to be effective on their own. These involve more formal psychological therapy to assist the individual to return to their previous normal levels of productivity.

Part II of this book (Chapters 3 to 10) outlines a range of primary, secondary and tertiary level interventions for tackling occupational stress. In Chapter 3 a number of primary level interventions aimed at providing a healthy working environment are introduced. In Chapters 4 to 9 a range of secondary level interventions are presented. These include developing a healthy lifestyle, effective time management, assertiveness, interpersonal skills, relaxation training and cognitive coping skills aimed at changing the way that an individual relates to their environment. In Chapter 10 a number of tertiary level interventions aimed at helping the individual overcome the symptoms associated with stress syndromes are discussed.

In Part III of this book, the tools and techniques required to 'become your own therapist' are outlined in Chapter 11, and a step-by-step guide to enable you to develop your own self-help plan to overcome occupational stress is also provided. Finally, Chapter 12 is a summary of the main learning points from the book and outlines the main conclusions reached. Information on self-help resources and further reading on specific problem areas is provided in the Appendix.

Acknowledgements

I would like to thank everyone who has either indirectly or directly made a contribution to the writing of this book. This includes work colleagues past and present with whom I have shared my ideas, and also my patients, who have been the source of much of the clinical material contained in this book. I would also like to thank the publishers for giving me the opportunity to write this book and in particular the editorial team for their support and guidance through to its completion.

Part I

Understanding occupational stress

Chapter I

Occupational stress and its consequences

> In order that people may be happy in their work, these three things are
> needed: They must be fit for it. They must not do too much of it. And
> they must have a sense of success in it.
>
> (John Ruskin 1819–1900)

Normal stress

When reading the literature about stress it would be easy to conclude that
it has universally negative consequences and that it is something that
needs to be eradicated from all areas of our lives. However, it is important
to emphasize from the outset of this book that not all stress is bad for us.
A certain degree of stress is a natural, normal and unavoidable part of
everyday life. For example, most of us can relate to the stress we have
experienced when we have been about to take an exam, do our driving
test, or give a presentation to managers or colleagues at work. This is
known as positive stress, because it motivates us to do well and can
actually enhance our performance on the task in hand. With positive
stress the individual is motivated to meet the challenge and ultimately
experiences a sense of achievement at having successfully mastered it
(as acknowledged in the quote by John Ruskin above). This normal type
of stress does not have any lasting consequences and if successfully
managed, it can result in an increased sense of competence, fulfilment
and wellbeing. There is an evolutionary explanation for this kind of
stress in that our ancestors' reactions to perceived threats and dangers
had survival value. For example, in primitive society, hunter-gatherers
would on occasions risk their lives in the hunt for food or to defend their
community. In doing so, they would experience dangers which would
have triggered the body's stress response. This in turn would have

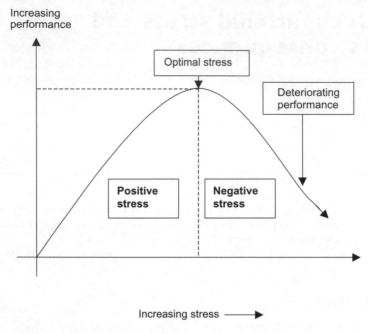

Figure 1.1 The stress–performance curve

prepared the individual for action, either to fight or to escape the threat. In modern societies and cultures, however, the stressors experienced are not usually life threatening in the way that they were for our ancestors, but they still trigger the stress response. The relationship between stress and performance is illustrated in Figure 1.1.

It can be seen on the left hand side of the graph in Figure 1.1 that low to moderate levels of stress actually serve to enhance performance until the optimal level is reached. However, once the level of stress exceeds the optimal level, there is a rather rapid and steep decline in performance and it is this that is described as negative stress.

The 'fight or flight' response

While it is not necessary for the purposes of this book to know the detailed anatomy of the brain, it is useful to know a little bit about the biological and chemical basis of what is known as the 'fight or flight' response to stress. Of particular relevance to discussion of the fight or flight response is the autonomic nervous system. This extends from the brain to most of the important organs of the body and consists of two parts, called the sympathetic and parasympathetic nervous systems. Also within the brain is a structure called the hypothalamus, which has two distinct segments that are linked to the autonomic nervous system (see Figure 1.2). One segment is concerned with bodily arousal and is linked to the sympathetic part and the other segment is concerned with the reduction of bodily arousal and is linked to the parasympathetic part of the autonomic nervous system. The hypothalamus thus forms the starting point of the two sections of the autonomic nervous system. The physical consequences of the activation of the two respective parts of the autonomic nervous system on the organs of the body are shown in Figure 1.2.

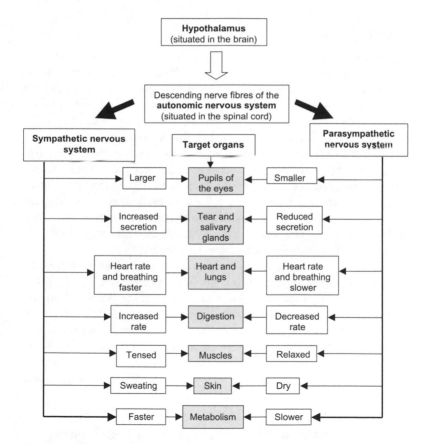

Figure 1.2 Diagrammatic representation of the structure and function of the autonomic nervous system

The pituitary gland is a structure linked to the hypothalamus by a small stalk and connected to it by both nerves and blood vessels. It is the 'master gland' of the body and produces a number of hormones which control the activity of other glands elsewhere in the body. The most important of these glands in relation to stress are the adrenal glands, which are situated in the kidneys and assist the body to cope with stress by producing hormones. When the brain interprets a situation as being stressful, it triggers the pituitary gland to produce chemical messengers which instruct the kidneys to release stress hormones called epinephrine and norepinephrine into the bloodstream. These stress hormones are pumped around the body and result in the fight–flight response.

Harmful stress

Under conditions of successful coping, the parasympathetic nervous system is suppressed. However, if the individual is not successful in overcoming the threat and the stress reaction continues without successful resolution for a prolonged period of time, the individual moves into a chronic phase. Examples of such chronic stressors include things like being stuck in a bad marriage, living in noisy or overcrowded conditions, and career or work related problems. In the chronic phase the para-sympathetic nervous system becomes overactivated, bodily systems are inhibited and there is decreased physiological arousal, as shown in Figure 1.2. This is achieved through the release by the kidneys of a different stress hormone called cortisol (which is also associated with depression). If the stress continues, the individual eventually becomes physically exhausted and ultimately can become depressed.

The model of stress described here is thus a two stage one characterized by acute and chronic phases. If the individual experiences high levels of stress (acute stress) for a short period of time, it is unlikely to do any lasting harm, but if it continues over a prolonged period of time (chronic stress), it not only has detrimental effects on their performance but also can have harmful longer-term physical and mental consequences. Some of the harmful physical and mental consequences of chronic, long-term, unmitigated stress for both the individual and the organization are reported below.

The consequences of harmful stress on the individual

Prolonged moderate levels of stress can lead to physical ailments such as headaches, backache, poor sleep, increased heart rate, raised blood pressure, dry mouth and throat, and indigestion. The individual may also experience a range of physical symptoms associated with anxiety, such as muscular pains, tremors, palpitations, diarrhoea, sweating, respiratory distress and feelings of dizziness. On an emotional level it can lead to feelings of anger and irritability, low mood and depression. Socially the individual may experience increased levels of marital and family conflicts, reflecting the stresses of the work situation that they take home with them. People under stress also tend to withdraw from supportive relationships; in the longer term this can lead to marital breakdown and social isolation. Mentally the individual may experience difficulties concentrating and remembering things, or may be prone to more negative thinking leading to increased feelings of self-blame and reduced feelings of self-confidence. Behavioural consequences of stress can include increased alcohol intake, increased smoking and drug use, overeating or loss of appetite, and less of an interest in sex. In the work context the individual may experience increased arguments and interpersonal conflicts, be less productive and more prone to accidents.

Prolonged high levels of unmitigated stress can lead to more serious physical health problems developing. For example, it has been found that digestive disorders and diabetes often follow prolonged high levels of stress. High and prolonged levels of stress can also compromise the effectiveness of the body's immune defences, making the immune system less effective. This allows diseases and infections which would normally be fought off by the immune system to take hold. Links have also been found between stress and coronary heart disease.

The consequences of harmful stress for the organization

'Occupational stress' is the term used to describe the stress experienced as a result of the job that one does. It is the common cold of the psychological world and has become a problem of pandemic proportions, affecting millions of people in every country across the world. This is due to the ever increasing pressures being placed on workplace organizations to adapt and change in order to become more efficient in the context of a highly competitive global economy. It is estimated that up to 40 per cent of all sickness absence from work is due to stress related symptoms, and this is costing employers and health insurance companies billions of pounds each year in lost productivity and health insurance claims. But the costs of occupational stress to employers are much broader than just those incurred through sickness absence. They include increased staff turnover, recruitment problems, low staff morale, decreased productivity, poor timekeeping, impaired decision making, increased industrial conflicts, increased accident rates, premature retirement due to ill health, redeployment, retraining, replacement costs, grievance procedures and litigation costs.

It is estimated that we spend on average at least one hundred thousand hours of our lives at work, so it is crucial that we find it a satisfying and rewarding place to be. Given the fact that we spend so much of our time at work and the serious consequences of chronic unmitigated stress, one might argue that if we are experiencing stress, we should remove ourselves from it. For example, we should leave a bad marriage, move out of poor living conditions or find another job. So why not just avoid the stress in the first place? The answer is that in reality it is often not that easy to simply walk away from the stress we are experiencing. With respect to leaving a marriage, there might be children involved, or with poor living conditions we may not be able to afford to pay for anything better. Similarly with employment there may be numerous reasons why we are unable to simply walk away from the job. We are thus left to find alternative ways to manage the stress we are experiencing.

Conceptualizing stress

Over the years numerous definitions and conceptualizations of stress have been cited in the literature. Some have taken the view that stress is caused solely by events or characteristics in the environment. Others have defined stress in terms of the response of the individual to the demands of their environment. However, these definitions cannot explain why it is that two individuals confronted by exactly the same situation can react very differently to it and consequently experience different levels of stress. Cognitive therapists argue that in many situations it is not the environment itself that causes stress but the individual's appraisal of the situation or event in their environment. It is of course not the intention here to imply that individuals are responsible for causing all of their own stress but simply to emphasize the importance of the meaning that we attach to situations as a factor which mediates between the environment and the level of stress experienced. Nor is it to deny that there are some environmental situations that may be objectively stressful for anyone.

In the work context, the saying 'one man's meat is another man's poison' summarizes this approach well, since two employees doing exactly the same job can, according to the model, appraise and experience the job in very different ways. One employee can appraise the job as being stressful whereas another employee can appraise it as being challenging and satisfying. There is a growing consensus among psychologists that stress is the result of an interaction (or transaction) between an individual's appraisal of their environment (i.e., the meaning that they attach to it) and the actual environment itself. This is known as the transactional model of stress.

The 'camera analogy'

Aaron T. Beck, who is considered by many to be the father of cognitive therapy, used a camera analogy to describe the interaction of the individual with their environment. He likened an individual's construction of a particular situation or event to taking a snapshot. When taking a photograph of a particular event or situation, the existing settings of the camera (e.g., lens, focus, speed and aperture settings) all determine what the eventual picture obtained will look like. For example, there may be some blurring or loss of detail due to inadequate focusing, or some distortion or magnification of the picture if a wide-angle or telephoto lens has been used. Likewise, a photograph taken with a soft focus sepia finish will convey a different message from a sharp focus black and white picture. In a similar way, Beck argued, the pre-existing 'cognitive settings' of an individual's mind will influence the way an event or situation in their environment is perceived. He called these pre-existing cognitive settings 'schemas'.

Schemas are stable structures that process incoming information to the brain in a similar way as the lens, focus, speed and aperture settings described in the camera analogy. They are formed by early life experiences and determine that individual's propensity to interpret situations in a particular way. For example, if the individual has experienced significant rejection in their childhood, they will be particularly sensitive to situations or events that signal rejection. Thus, a situation signalling rejection will result in activation of that schema and the individual will experience it as stressful. However, an individual who does not have the rejection schema will not interpret the situation as being stressful. Once the unhealthy schema is activated, the individual begins to feel and behave 'as if' they were in reality being rejected. Thus, schemas are at the core of stress reactions, because they provide the meaning of an event for the individual. If through the activation of their schemas an individual perceives that a threat is present, and the risk posed by that threat is greater than their resources for coping with it, the 'emergency response' is activated.

The emergency response

The emergency response consists of a sequence of cognitive, motivational, emotional, physiological and behavioural events, associated with a stress reaction and is outlined below.

Changes in thinking

The individual's capacity for rational, realistic and objective thinking becomes seriously disrupted. It is replaced by a more primitive mode of thinking, in which the individual makes more rigid, extreme, simplistic and one-sided judgements about things. These distortions in thinking can become so potent that they totally dominate the individual's consequent feelings and behaviours. There is also a tendency to 'frame' others who are perceived as a threat in terms of a few simple and extreme negative characteristics (polarized thinking). This, together with a greater tendency towards egocentricity (self-centred thinking), can result in increased interpersonal conflicts, as others around the stressed individual respond negatively to their selfish and hostile patterns of thinking.

Changes in motivation

'Behavioural inclinations' are activated during the emergency response. These are not actual behaviours but the precursors to behaviour and are best described as motivations. For example, as a result of an event triggering a schema, an individual may experience anger and the desire to attack someone. However, they may at the same time acknowledge that it is in their interests to suppress the behavioural inclination to hit someone because of the possible consequences (especially if that someone is their boss at work!). Similarly, a situation that arouses anxiety such as, for example, giving a presentation at work may lead to the behavioural inclination to run away and escape. However, the individual may decide to suppress this inclination because they realize that it would not do much for their career or promotion prospects if they did. Thus, behavioural motivations can be acted upon or suppressed and are the precursors of actual behaviours.

Changes in emotion

When the emergency response is triggered, the physiological arousal mechanism of the fight–flight response is initiated. A detailed description of this response has already been presented in this chapter (pp. 4–6), so will not be discussed again here in any detail: to summarize, the autonomic nervous system is activated and stress hormones are produced, leading to an emotional response in the individual. This emotional response can be one of anger, anxiety or depression.

Changes in behaviour

A behavioural strategy is ultimately chosen to deal with the perceived threat. The main behavioural strategies are the fight, flight and freeze responses, which correspond to the emotions of anger, anxiety and depression respectively. If the emotional response to the appraisal is extreme, the behavioural strategy chosen is likely to be equally extreme. For example, a very angry person may concede to the behavioural inclination to hit someone, a highly anxious person may concede to the behavioural inclination to escape from a situation, or a very depressed person may concede to the behavioural inclination to stay in bed.

The development of stress syndromes

Prolonged exposure to situations or events perceived as stressful, without any successful resolution, will result in the emergency response becoming chronically activated and can lead to the development of a stress syndrome. Three stress syndromes have been identified, namely the hostility syndrome, which is characterized by feelings of chronic anger and the desire to fight perceived injustices, the fear or anxiety syndrome, which is characterized by chronic feelings of anxiety and the desire to flee, escape and avoid perceived dangers and threats, and the depression syndrome, which is characterized by feelings of sadness, a negative view of self, the world and the future and the desire to withdraw, give up, surrender and accept defeat. The syndromes of anger and anxiety are associated with the first phase of the two stage model of stress described earlier in this chapter, and the depression syndrome is associated with the second phase of the model (p. 6).

Dispelling some myths about stress

To be in the best position to help yourself tackle stress, you need to have a good understanding of the stress concept generally. In order to do this there are a number of commonly held myths and misconceptions about stress which you may need to dispel. The quiz in Table 1.1 has been designed to test your knowledge and understanding of stress. It consists of a number of common assertions about stress, some of which will test what you read earlier in this chapter.

Table 1.1 A stress quiz

Please indicate next to each of the statements whether you believe it to be true (T) or false (F) by circling the letter.		
1. Stress is an inevitable and unavoidable consequence of modern life	T	F
2. Stress is a sign of weakness	T	F
3. Most people lead stress free lives	T	F
4. All stress is bad for us	T	F
5. The causes of stress are the same for everyone	T	F
6. The symptoms of stress are the same for everyone	T	F
7. The most popular techniques for reducing stress are the best ones	T	F
8. One can still be suffering from stress even if there are no symptoms	T	F
9. Minor symptoms of stress should be ignored	T	F
10. Combating workplace stress can actually save employers money	T	F
11. Taking time off work is the only solution	T	F
12. Being stressed at work must mean that I am important and indispensable	T	F
13. Occupational stress can be caused by having too little work to do	T	F
14. Stress is cured by working more	T	F
15. All occupational stress is the employer's fault	T	F
16. Home and work life are separate	T	F

Note: This table is available to view and print from the following website: www.routledge mentalhealth.com/9780415671781

Answers for the stress quiz (Table 1.1)

Statement 1

'Stress is an inevitable and unavoidable consequence of modern life' (Answer: False)

Although the causes of stress may be different in modern societies from those of our ancestors, stress has always been a part of life throughout history. It is unhelpful and wrong, however, to assume that it is an aspect of modern life that we simply have to put up with. You can do something about it and can plan your life so that it does not become overwhelming. Remember you were not born this way but acquired the stress somewhere along life's journey. It is possible to move away from being a highly stressed individual to a low stress one. However, in order for this change to be possible, it is a prerequisite that you believe that change can happen. If you do not believe that change is possible, it will not happen for you.

Statement 2

'Stress is a sign of weakness'
(Answer: False)

We are constantly bombarded in the media by stereotypes of strong men and superwomen, who claim that you can 'do it all' and 'have it all'. For example, the media image of the City business superwoman, 'queen of the square mile', 'power dressing millionaire mother of several children', who never misses a school prize giving, is enough to make any average woman feel inadequate if she believes the hype. Similarly, we hear stories of high flying chief executives and government ministers, who work exceptionally long hours, travel all over the world and yet still claim that they do their fair share of the household chores and childcare, changing nappies, tucking their children up in bed and reading them a story most nights. Perhaps they also find time to do a bit of DIY and pursue their hobbies when the children are asleep and of course they are no doubt the perfect partner and lover! If we are to believe these stereotypes, there are clearly people who appear to be able to have it all, do it all and apparently never show any signs of stress. The message portrayed is that stress is something for other mere mortals to struggle with. Stereotypes of 'superman' and 'superwoman' can make the average person struggling to meet all the mundane demands of home and work life feel just a tad inadequate.

This sense of weakness and inadequacy can be reinforced by unhelpful 'macho' management attitudes in the workplace. Such managers believe that being stressed is a sign of an inherent weakness in the individual employee. The saying 'If you can't stand the heat then stay out of the kitchen' sums up this attitude well. However, the reality is that anyone under sufficient pressure will begin to show signs of stress. Ask yourself, 'What would happen if my workload or targets were doubled tomorrow?' It is most unlikely that you would be able to cope. So the message here is that experiencing stress is not a sign of weakness but a normal response to excessive demands being placed on an individual. Do not believe all the hype about supermen and superwomen. Admittedly there may be a few exceptional people who can juggle many things without becoming stressed but they are not the norm. Also, when you scratch below the surface of claims made in the media about these people, you invariably find that they are supported by a small army of nannies, housekeepers, gardeners and other helpers who they are fortunate enough to be able to afford to employ. This is often accompanied by an extremely supportive, self-sacrificing partner and lots of extended family support. So, it is a myth that these individuals are doing it all on their own.

Statement 3

'Most people lead stress free lives'
(Answer: False)

When people are under stress, their thinking patterns change. They can become more self-centred and display more rigid, extreme and polarized thinking about others. One manifestation of this is the belief that everyone else around them is having a great time and it is only them who is suffering. However, in reality it is not possible to live a completely stress free life. Stress is no respecter of age, wealth, social group, status or position and no one is immune from stress. It can affect anyone from the pauper to the millionaire, the casual labourer to the highly skilled surgeon. Although the causes may differ between these groups, the consequences are just as distressing for everyone. Also, do not think that it is only those in work who experience stress. The incidence of stress in unemployed people is actually higher than for those in employment.

Another factor that may make people think that stress is less prevalent than it is really is the stigma attached to it. On the whole individuals still feel a sense of shame and are very reluctant to admit that they are suffering from stress. While they may be able to talk freely about a physical health problem such as a broken leg, they are much less likely to talk to others about their stress. This can reinforce the mistaken belief that most people live stress free lives.

Statement 4

'All stress is bad for us'
(Answer: False)

Not all stress is bad for us. There are some types of stress that are actually helpful to us. For example, low levels of stress can act as a motivator and improve our performance in challenging situations such as a job interview, exam, or giving a presentation in front of a group of people. This is known as normal, positive or optimal stress. Once the trigger to this kind of stress has passed, the body and mind return to their previous relaxed state. However, high levels of unmitigated stress over a long period of time can be harmful. So while some stress can be potentially harmful, not all stress is harmful. A guitar string analogy is an appropriate one to use here. If there is too little tension in the string, it cannot do its job, but if there is too much tension in the string, it will snap. A little bit of tension allows us to function at an optimal level but too much can be harmful. The normative levels of stress that we experience as part of everyday life are not bad for us.

Statement 5

'The causes of stress are the same for everyone'
(Answer: False)

Each individual has their own unique personality traits, capabilities, needs and coping strategies that they bring with them to any situation. As mentioned earlier in this chapter (pp. 8–9), they also possess their own idiosyncratic beliefs and attitudes which determine how they will interpret a situation that they are presented with. In most cases it is not the situation or event itself that causes stress but the meaning that it is given by the individual which determines whether they will experience stress. This is summed up by the saying 'one man's meat is another man's poison', meaning something which triggers stress in one individual may not do so in another individual. So, the causes of stress are not the same for everyone.

Statement 6

'The symptoms of stress are the same for everyone'
(Answer: False)

There are many manifestations of the stress response. It can produce a combination of one or more of a wide range of cognitive, behavioural, emotional and physical symptoms. For example, behaviourally one individual may drink more alcohol, whereas another may eat more, or experience sleep disturbance. Emotionally, one individual may experience anxiety and another experience anger or depression. Physical symptoms can also be numerous and varied, such as nausea, headaches, palpitations or muscular aches and pains. Cognitively, symptoms may include impairment in memory and concentration or indecisiveness for example. Because these are so numerous and varied, it is very unlikely that any two individuals are going to display exactly the same presentation of symptoms.

Statement 7

'The most popular techniques for reducing stress are the best ones' (Answer: False)

There are many different ways of reducing stress and every individual has their own unique way of tackling it. Techniques cannot be generically prescribed as if the individual were taking a particular medication. For example, one individual may find that having a hot bath, reading a good book and having a warm milky drink is the best way of relaxing for them, while another individual may find that a good workout at the gym or a hard game of squash does the same for them and the idea of a hot bath and reading a book may simply not appeal to them. We all have different ways of relaxing, whether it is, for example, to go fishing, play golf or watch television, and we need to find the one that works for us. Someone who works in isolation may find having an active social life relaxing, whereas someone who is constantly working with people may long for isolation to help them 'recharge their batteries'. Each of us has different life situations, resources and reactions to stress and stress management packages need to be individually tailored to meet those different circumstances and needs. The best-known or most popular techniques are not necessarily the most effective ones and individuals need to find those that work for them personally.

Statement 8

'One can still be suffering from stress even if there are no symptoms' (Answer: True)

An individual can still be suffering from stress even if there are no identifiable symptoms. For example, the symptoms of stress can be masked by taking medication. While taking medication may be necessary in some circumstances, one of the downsides to taking it is that it can deprive the individual of valuable feedback. Physical and emotional messages can help the individual to identify what is actually causing their stress and realize the changes that they need to make to their situation in order to reduce the stress that they are experiencing. Without symptoms they are effectively working in the dark.

Statement 9

'Minor symptoms of stress should be ignored'
(Answer: False)

The emergence of physical and mental symptoms are our body and mind's way of informing us that something is not right with our situation. They are the early warning signs or the alarm signal that are telling us that changes need to be made to our situation. They should not be ignored and the causes of these symptoms should be explored. If they are addressed at the earliest opportunity, probably things can be nipped in the bud, and the root causes can be eliminated before the symptoms get the chance to become more severe and entrenched. So, minor symptoms should not be ignored.

Statement 10

'Combating workplace stress can actually save employers money'
(Answer: True)

The traditional wisdom is that one of the main reasons why employers do not do more to tackle workplace stress is that it is too financially costly to do so. As mentioned earlier in this chapter, stress is costing employers and health insurance companies billions of pounds each year in lost productivity, health insurance claims and other indirect ways such as increased industrial conflicts, accident rates, premature retirement due to ill health, grievance procedures and litigation costs. More recently the traditional wisdom has been challenged. It has been increasingly recognized that addressing occupational stress in the workforce makes sense not only on humanitarian grounds but also for sound economic reasons. The current state of thinking is that it is possible to achieve a balance between the costs and benefits of work, whereby the needs of both the organization and the individual can be successfully met, allowing the individual to remain healthy and motivated in their work, and at the same time allowing the organization to remain productive.

Statement 11

'Taking time off work is the only solution'
(Answer: False)

While it may be necessary to take some time off work initially to overcome one's symptoms, taking a long time off work is not necessarily always the best solution. It can in fact increase stress levels. The employee may worry about their job, what is happening to it in their absence or the backlog that they will have when they return to work. Also it is very easy to lose confidence if the circumstances in which the employee went on sick leave were particularly difficult or embarrassing. This can lead to an increased reluctance or avoidance of a return to work and increased self-doubt as the length of time away from work increases. The employee may then begin to wonder if they will ever be able to return to work. In many cases it is better if the employer can assist the employee with an earlier return to work and support them in staying at work to overcome the stressful situation. This might, for example, involve working part-time, doing light duties or being super-numerous for a period of time.

Statement 12

'Being stressed at work must mean that I am important and indispensable'
(Answer: False)

Do not kid yourself! No one is indispensable to an organization and if you believe that you are, you are deluding yourself. Everyone and every role within an organization is replaceable. It would be nice to think that 'I am crucial to the success of the company', or that 'No one can do the job as well as me'. However, the reality is that we are all cogs in the machine and most of us play a very small part in the running of it. There will always be someone else coming along who can do your job as well as you can. So, do not make the mistake of interpreting your stress as a sign of being important or irreplaceable.

Statement 13

'Occupational stress can be caused by having too little work to do'
(Answer: True)

Many people think that stress is caused only by work overload. While it is true that an excessive workload is a common cause of stress, it is a lesser known fact that having too little work to do, boredom and inactivity can for some people be just as stressful as having too much work to do. For example, it can lead to having too much time to think about everything that is wrong with the job and also make the individual feel that their input is unimportant and undervalued. The ideal balance of course is somewhere in the middle of the two extremes of work overload and work underload. Employees need a sufficient amount of work to make them feel challenged but not so much that they begin to feel stress.

Statement 14

'Stress is cured by working more'
(Answer: False)

Many people believe that stress is caused by falling behind at work and so one solution to this is to work even more hours to catch up with everything. The idea behind this is that once you have caught up with the backlog, you will then be able to relax and the stress will go away. In most cases, however, the idea that eventually everything will be sorted out and we will be completely up to date with everything is an illusion. The reality is that in most workplaces, there is simply too much work to do and there will always be a list of jobs waiting to be done. In fact if an employee rushes to get one piece of work completed more quickly, this will simply lead to them being given another job to do! So the answer to reducing stress does not lie in working more but in changing your reaction to falling behind at work. You need to work at a pace that you feel you can comfortably maintain and learn not to worry so much about the backlog.

Statement 15

'All occupational stress is the employer's fault'
(Answer: False)

The employer does have a duty of care to ensure that employees are able to work in a safe and healthy environment, are sufficiently trained to do the job, are given a manageable workload and are able to work in a relatively low stress environment. However, employees also have a responsibility to ensure that they remain fit for work. For example, employees are responsible for ensuring that they live a healthy lifestyle, eat properly, get sufficient sleep, do not drink to excess, keep fit and generally make sure that they are in good shape to do the job. They also have a responsibility to inform the employer if they are experiencing stress to the extent that they are not coping with the job. If the employee does not let the employer know that they are experiencing stress, it would be unreasonable to blame the employer for not acting to reduce it. If the employer is made aware, they have the opportunity to provide the employee with the support and assistance they need. Tackling occupational stress is necessarily a shared responsibility between employers and employees.

Statement 16

'Home and work life are separate'
(Answer: False)

While it may appear that work life and life outside of work are separate, this is not actually the case. Events at work can impact on home life and vice versa. For example, an employee who has a happy marriage, a good social support network and stable home life outside of work is likely to be in a better position to cope with a stressful work situation caused by a lack of support and social contact at work. The supports outside of work can act as a source of support which can buffer that individual against stress at work. However, someone who does not have these support networks in their personal life may be more vulnerable to experiencing stress at work. Also, if an employee is experiencing stress at work, they may become more irritable and moody with family, friends and acquaintances in their personal life. This in turn can lead to increased arguments and conflicts outside of work. Thus, it can be seen that home and work life can and often do impact on each other.

How well did you do in the quiz?

If you got 16 out of 16, well done! However, do not worry if you did not get full marks. What is important is that you learn from what you have read and that some of the myths surrounding occupational stress have been dispelled. Having tested your knowledge of stress, the next section in this chapter aims to help you identify how much stress you are currently experiencing.

How stressed are you?

Earlier in this chapter the physical, emotional, cognitive and behavioural signs and symptoms of stress in the individual were outlined (pp. 6–7). These have been summarized in the form of a checklist (Table 1.2). In order to identify the symptoms and the severity of the stress you are currently experiencing, you are requested to complete the checklist. You will notice that there are a number of physical symptoms listed. The assumption being made when you complete this checklist is that any medical causes of these symptoms have already been investigated and eliminated by your doctor. If this is not the case, it is important that you get these checked in the first instance by your doctor to exclude any medical condition. For example, it would be unwise to simply assume that breathlessness and palpitations are symptoms of stress without having this confirmed by your doctor. It is also important to be aware that this is not a sophisticated diagnostic tool but a checklist aimed at giving you an indication of how much stress and what symptoms you are experiencing at the present time.

A stress checklist

For each item presented in Table 1.2, please indicate on the 1 to 5 scale the symptoms and severity of the symptoms that you have been experiencing over the *past month* by ticking the appropriate box.

Scoring and interpreting the checklist (Table 1.2)

Each item on the checklist is rated from 1 to 5. A score of 1 on an item indicates that you have never experienced that symptom over the past month, whereas a score of 5 indicates that you have been experiencing that symptom constantly over the past month. The higher the score, the more severe the symptom (1 = Never; 2 = Seldom; 3 = Sometimes; 4 = Often; 5 = Always). If you scored between 47 and 93 this indicates that you are currently experiencing a low level of stress, a score between 94 and 140 indicates a moderate level of stress, a score between 141 and 187 indicates a high level of stress and a score of 188 or more indicates a very high level of stress.

Table 1.2 A stress checklist

Symptoms	Never	Seldom	Sometimes	Often	Always
Behaviours	1	2	3	4	5
Change in eating habits? (i.e., eating more or less)					
Eating on the run?					
Change in sleep pattern? (i.e., sleeping more or less)					
Increased consumption of alcohol?					
Smoking more than usual? (if applicable)					
Increased use of medication/drugs?					
Increased caffeine intake? (e.g., tea, coffee or cola drinks)					
Missing breaks at work?					
Taking work home with you?					
Rushing around and hurrying things more than usual?					
Trying to do several jobs at once?					
Having no time for rest or relaxation?					
Withdrawal from social contact with family and/or friends?					
Withdrawal from hobbies and interests?					
Loss of interest in sex?					
Reduced motivation generally?					
Physical symptoms					
Increased fatigue/tiredness?					
Indigestion?					
Feeling sick/nausea?					
Headaches?					
Aching muscles?					
Backache?					
Neck ache?					
Stomach ache?					
Dizziness?					
Difficulty breathing?					
Going to the toilet more frequently?					
Hot flushes/sweating?					
Palpitations?					

Symptoms	Never	Seldom	Sometimes	Often	Always
Emotional					
Being irritable more than usual?					
Feeling angry more than usual?					
Feeling anxious more than usual?					
Feeling panicky?					
Feeling low in mood?					
Experienced feelings of failure?					
Experienced feelings of hopelessness?					
Enjoying things less than usual?					
Over-sensitive to comments and criticism?					
Feeling emotionally drained and exhausted?					
Feeling emotionally cut-off/numb?					
Cognitive					
More indecisive than usual?					
Finding it difficult to concentrate?					
Difficulty remembering something?					
Experienced thoughts of guilt/self-blame?					
Thinking more pessimistic/negative?					
Found your mind racing?					
Loss of confidence/low self-esteem?					

Note: This table is available to view and print from the following website: www.routledge
mentalhealth.com/9780415671781

Summary

The aim of this chapter was to improve your understanding of the stress concept. The distinction between normal and harmful stress was made and the consequences of long-term unmitigated stress for the individual and the organization were outlined. The physical, cognitive, emotional and behavioural aspects of the emergency response were introduced and the importance of the interpretation or meaning of events in eliciting the stress response was highlighted. The main stress syndromes were also identified. A stress quiz was included to check your understanding of the stress concept and dispel some of the common misconceptions about stress. Finally, a stress checklist was included to allow you to determine the number and severity of stress related symptoms you are currently experiencing. Chapter 2 focuses more specifically on individual and environmental causal factors that contribute to the experience of occupational stress.

Chapter 2

Identifying the causes of your occupational stress

Introduction

The transactional model of stress introduced in Chapter 1 emphasized that stress is the result of an interaction between the individual and their environment. Stress is experienced when the individual appraises their coping resources to be insufficient to manage the demands of the situation that they are faced with. Occupational stress can be defined in a similar way. The United States National Institute for Occupational Health and Safety defines it as:

> The harmful physical and emotional responses that occur when the requirements of the job do not match the capabilities, resources, or needs of the worker.

Each employee brings with them a unique set of personal attributes and needs to the job and in turn the characteristics of the job itself and the working environment place demands on the employee. If the employee appraises that they have the capabilities and resources to meet the demands of the job, and the working environment also meets their needs, they experience job satisfaction. However, if the employee appraises that they do not have the required capabilities, personal attributes and coping resources to meet the demands of the job, or the job itself does not meet the needs of the individual, then occupational stress is likely to be experienced. This two way relationship and the central importance of the individual's appraisal in the experience of stress at work is illustrated in Figure 2.1.

The model proposes that the better the match between the employee and their work environment (i.e., a good person–environment fit), the lower the occupational stress experienced. Conversely, the poorer the fit, the greater the level of occupational stress experienced. The next section

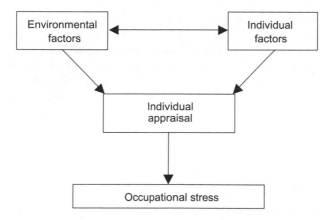

Figure 2.1 The transactional model of occupational stress

of this chapter provides an overview of the main individual and environmental factors that interact to cause occupational stress.

An overview of the causes of occupational stress

Occupational stress can be caused by individual factors, factors in the work environment and the home–work interface.

Individual factors

Individual causes of stress include a range of genetic/inherited, acquired/ learned and personality/trait factors.

Genetic/inherited factors

Genetic/inherited factors refer to those characteristics that we are born with. For example, some people are naturally physically stronger or intellectually more able than others. Someone who is physically strong is able to lift and carry greater weights than someone who is weaker, and this gives them an advantage in a manual job which requires a lot of lifting and carrying. Similarly, intellectually more capable individuals are going to be able to perform better than less intellectual individuals in jobs that require intellectual ability. People are also born with different temperaments and some individuals are by nature more timid, introverted, shy, less adventurous and risk taking than others. These natural inclinations manifest in such individuals in the way they cope with stressful situations. For example, they are likely to be less assertive and more avoidant than those who are outward going and adventurous risk takers. It has also been reported that there are sex differences in the way males and females deal with stress. However, it is debatable whether this sex difference should be considered as a genetic factor, or something which is learned through the stereotyping of male and female role models in society.

Acquired/learned factors

Acquired/learned characteristics are (as the name suggests) acquired and learned over time. For example, age is a factor which can influence how the individual deals with stress. Younger individuals tend to be more vulnerable to stress than older individuals, possibly because they have fewer coping strategies and less life experience to draw upon than older people. Life experience equips an individual with additional coping strategies which can inoculate them against stress. Level of educational attainment, knowledge and skills also determine how equipped an individual is to manage work related tasks. Those who are less well educated or trained to do a particular job are more likely to experience higher stress levels than those who are well trained and equipped with the knowledge and skills to do the job.

An individual's beliefs and assumptions are learned in childhood and adolescence and consolidated throughout life. These can play an important role in determining the meaning that we attach to life events and ultimately what we perceive as stressful. Cognitive therapists have been aware for many years now that in most situations it is not the situation itself that causes stress but the way that an individual interprets that situation. If these interpretations are faulty, the individual's reactions to that situation are also likely to be dysfunctional and result in stress. Beliefs also play a part in determining how the individual copes with stress.

A group of clinical psychologists led by Dr Jeff Young in the USA have called these faulty underlying beliefs 'early maladaptive schemas' (EMS). Young and his colleagues believe that these schemas are a product of the 'adverse early life experiences' (sometimes referred to as a 'toxic early environment'), which the individual was exposed to in childhood. Early maladaptive schemas have been defined as 'self-defeating patterns of thinking that are developed through childhood experiences and perpetuated in adult life'. The model proposes that these self-defeating patterns result in negative interactions with others in adult life. For example, as a result of their adverse early life experiences, an individual may develop a schema that results in them being particularly sensitive to rejection. As an adult the individual is extra sensitive to any situation that triggers the theme of rejection and is likely to experience powerful and sometimes overwhelming emotional reactions, such as anger, despair or anxiety, if their dysfunctional schema is activated. In the work context, this could cause significant problems if the person doing the rejecting is their line manager. It could be even worse if the individual with the unhelpful schema is the manager! Individuals with early maladaptive schemas are thus more vulnerable to experiencing stress as a result of relationship difficulties at work.

Personality/trait factors

Personality factors refer to those relatively enduring characteristics or traits of an individual which define who they are. For example, we say that someone is an 'extravert' to describe the characteristics of being sociable and outward going, or 'introverted' to describe the characteristics of being shy and withdrawn. Personality is thought to develop through the interaction of an individual's temperament (nature) with their early learning environment (nurture) and is consolidated by subsequent life experiences in adulthood. Both nature and nurture thus play a key role in determining an individual's personality.

There is a considerable amount of research on the influence of 'personality dispositions' on the level of stress experienced. In general these studies have found that there are certain personality traits which make individuals more resilient to stress than others. For example, individuals who are more hostile and competitive (Type A individuals) are more prone to stress than easy going and uncompetitive (Type B) individuals. Those with high trait anxiety are more prone to experiencing stress than those who are temperamentally more relaxed. Those who perceive themselves as having little or no control over their own destiny are more prone to experiencing stress than those who believe that they do have a degree of control over their own destiny. So, clearly there are some personality traits that are 'protective' and make an individual more resilient to experiencing stress and when these are absent, increase the likelihood of experiencing stress.

Factors in the work environment

Workplace factors include job demands, physical working conditions, control, supports, relationships, role, change, and pay and career prospects.

Job demands

There are a number of possible reasons why excessive job demands can result in increased stress levels at work. It may be a result of the actual volume of work itself, the pace of work, unrealistic time pressures, excessive responsibility, unachievable targets or deadlines, too many competing demands, difficulty of the tasks involved, inflexibility of working arrangements, lack of opportunities for sufficient rest breaks, shift working, or pressure to work long hours. Stress can also result from being given only partial tasks to complete and therefore never having the satisfaction of seeing a finished product. It can also result from having a lack of variety in one's work and (associated with this) feelings of boredom and monotony.

Physical working conditions

Working in an unsafe or uncomfortable physical environment can cause high levels of stress. Dirty, cramped, poorly lit, noisy, too hot or cold, stuffy conditions without facilities for taking breaks, can not only affect employees on a humanitarian level but also have a negative impact on their work rate and productivity. There are of course certain jobs which by their nature involve poor physical environments, such as sewage work, refuse collecting, and coalmining where miners work in cramped conditions without access to natural light. This can be made worse if shower and changing room facilities, the correct safety equipment and the right clothing are not made available to minimize the risk to employees.

Control

Employees need to feel that they have some discretion and control over the way in which they do their job and that they are able to influence the decision making processes in the organization in which they work. If they lack the autonomy and freedom to design and structure their work, this can lead to experiencing increased stress levels. For example, not having a say in the timing, sequence, pace and the way in which job tasks are done, not being allowed to manage one's own diary, having no say in work schedules, annual leave and shift rotas, or being unable to have any freedom to prioritize tasks are all ways in which an employee can experience increased stress in their job. Being excluded from the decision making process can also be a stressful experience. For example, working for an organization that does not allow its employees to participate in staff meetings with managers, or more formal involvement in trade union activities, can be a source of stress for some employees.

Supports

People work best if they feel supported in what they are doing. Supports at work can be both formal and informal. Some formal methods of support include the provision of regular managerial supervision, feedback on performance through personal development reviews, mentorship arrangements, identifying ongoing professional development needs through appraisals and the provision of training to meet these needs. Up-to-date technology, the right resources and equipment to do the job are also important in making the employee feel supported. When these formal support mechanisms are not in place, the employee is likely to feel unsupported in their work. However, even if an employee does have all of these formal supports at their disposal, they could still be feeling socially isolated if their work does not allow them to have frequent informal social contacts within their work setting.

Relationships

Good working relationships are crucial to the efficient and effective running of an organization. Many people spend more time at work than in the company of their domestic partners, so it is understandable that experiencing relationship problems at work can have a major negative impact on the psychological wellbeing of the individuals involved. While people should not necessarily expect to become best friends with those they work with, they should be able to expect to work in an environment of mutual respect and satisfactory working relationships. It is an unfortunate fact however that approximately one in six people report that they have been the victim of workplace bullying and harassment. Bullying not only is about being overtly aggressive towards another person but also can manifest itself in a wide range of more subtle forms of behaviour. These may include, for example, the use of put-downs, making others the butt of jokes, keeping them out of the information loop, pulling rank, showing favouritism, setting them up to fail and patronizing or prejudicial treatment. Bullies are emotionally immature individuals who can create havoc for those they work with by their dysfunctional, divisive and disruptive behaviours.

The work environment provides an ideal stage upon which dysfunctional re-enactments of power, control and status dynamics can take place, since the analogies between the work environment and the early family environment are numerous. For example, managers, supervisors and other authority figures can be seen as parent-like figures, and colleagues or peers as siblings in the family system. So, all the necessary actors are there to enable the toxic re-enactments to take place. Young's model of early maladaptive schemas, which was referred to earlier in this chapter (p. 26), is useful in terms of understanding the underlying psychology of such behaviours. For example, bullying can be seen as a re-enactment of the 'mistrust and abuse' EMS. However, it is not only bullying but also a wide range of other negative and disruptive behavioural patterns in the workplace that can be explained by the re-enactment of EMS. For example, the behaviour of the 'control freak' may be an over-compensation for experiences of having been dominated and controlled excessively in childhood. The maladaptive behaviour may be driven by a 'control or be controlled' dichotomy and the assumption that 'unless I maintain a tight control over others, they will control me'. Another example is the behaviour of the 'disciplinarian', who is driven by the 'punitiveness' EMS and the belief that 'all mistakes however small must be punished'.

These re-enactments can be particularly damaging if the dysfunctional individual is a manager, since there is the potential for them to misuse the authority inherent in their role. Dysfunctional re-enactments of EMS derived from toxic early environments can continue indefinitely in adult relationships if the individual is not made aware of them. Unfortunately, most people with personality issues do not have much insight into the impact that their behaviour has on others and are much more likely to blame others than themselves for interpersonal conflicts that arise. It is usually left to those around them to come up with creative strategies for managing their dysfunctional behaviour and tackling the trail of devastation that such individuals can leave in their wake.

Role

People need to be clear about what is expected of them at work and what the priorities, aims and objectives of the wider organization that they work in are. In order to ensure that employees are clear about their role, there needs to be a clearly identified management structure, clear lines of accountability and good channels of communication throughout the whole organization. It is important that managers and supervisors make sure that their employees have a well-defined sense of their job responsibilities. The terms and conditions of a job, an outline of organizational relationships, the lines of accountability, core functions, tasks and duties of a specific job should all be clearly written down in the individual employee's job description. Changes to the job description should be made only through negotiation and by mutual agreement between the manager and the employee concerned. If any of these requirements are missing, the employee is likely to experience a lack of clarity about their role and become confused by what the organization is wanting from them. Role ambiguity and role conflict are known to be significant causes of stress in the workplace.

Change

Organizations are not static things. They are continually evolving and changing in order to survive and remain competitive. The way in which this change is managed is crucial to the ongoing success of the organization and also in determining the levels of stress experienced by the workforce. Employees need to be consulted about change at work and how changes will impact on the job that they do. They should also have sufficient opportunities to question managers about proposed changes in their working practices. The culture of the organization is a key factor in determining how it manages change. If it is an enlightened one, the employer is likely to be open and transparent about the changes they need to make. They will involve the workforce in a consultation process, communicate clearly, explain how the changes are going to impact on the job that they do in practice and offer the employee support at each step along the way. The negative impact of change can thus be minimized as potential problems are recognized and resolved at each step. An enlightened organizational culture also acknowledges the impact that organizational changes can have on employees and is proactive in terms of putting positive strategies in place to manage it. Unfortunately, however, some organizations are not so enlightened. They manage change in a secretive way, withhold information and do not consult their employees about the changes. This can lead to high levels of distress among employees, which is driven by their fears and fantasies about the unknown.

Some organizations also have cynical and negative attitudes towards those who experience stress and perceive them as being weak. This attitude is captured by the cliché 'If you can't stand the heat then stay out of the kitchen', meaning that if you cannot take the pressure, you should not be in the job. The employee is blamed for creating their own stress and thus the organization conveniently lets itself off the hook by the failure to acknowledge the part played by the work environment in creating the stress experienced. This is analogous to pushing someone into a strong tidal current and then blaming them for not being able to swim out of it! Clearly the employer does have a responsibility for the welfare of the employees during times of organizational change and needs to take these responsibilities seriously.

Pay and career prospects

Employees are entitled to a fair wage for the job that they do. They are also entitled to expect that they are given equal opportunities in terms of career, promotion prospects and security of employment. In the UK employees are protected by equal opportunities, the minimum wage and anti-discrimination legislation. However, this does not always stop unscrupulous employers from trying to deny employees of their entitlements and this can be the cause of considerable stress for those individuals who are subjected to such discrimination.

The home–work interface

Employees have a range of responsibilities outside of work such as running a home, bringing up a family, caring for relatives, paying bills, to name but a few. Stress in life outside of work can impact on life at work and vice versa. This is known as the home–work interface. For example, a poor marriage and lack of social support outside of work can make an individual more susceptible to experiencing stress at work. Similarly, a couple both pursuing a career may experience strain in the marital relationship. For example, men are expected to move readily for job transfers and promotion if they want to progress in their careers and it is traditionally expected that their partner and family follow them. Dual careers can make this more complex. The traditional stereotype of the man as the breadwinner of the family may be challenged if the woman's income equals or exceeds that of their male partner and this can lead to marital tensions. It is not uncommon for successful women to reject promotion, or to avoid being more successful than their partner, in order to prevent such conflicts from arising. Also, the bulk of non-work domestic roles and responsibilities such as housework, cooking, shopping and childcare still tends to fall mainly on the woman of the household and this can cause stress if they are trying to do all this and hold down a job at the same time.

The employer's 'duty of care' to provide a healthy working environment

Case study: Schmidt

In 1947 W. F. Taylor, an industrialist and Tory radical, presented his prize case study of Schmidt, a pig iron handler, to an appreciative and admiring audience of employers. He began by describing Schmidt in what is now recognized as rather politically incorrect language, as a 'thick-skulled little Dutchman', who was by constitution something like a 'human ox' and was able to shovel twelve and a half tons of pig iron in a day. Taylor reported that through a process of scientific management he had successfully 'systematized' Schmidt to increase his output fourfold, up to fifty tons a day. For this increase in output, he rewarded Schmidt with a bonus of just over half his original pay. This was a pay rise that impressed Schmidt! Taylor claimed that he had achieved this by subtle manipulation of financial incentives.

This case study illustrates some of the prevalent management attitudes in the mid twentieth century. In particular it 'dehumanized' the worker and implied that employees are driven purely by financial incentives. Taylor rather arrogantly described them as 'greedy robots'. Unfortunately, it later emerged that Schmidt died at an early age of a heart attack, a fact that did not seem to disturb Taylor unduly, since at that time employee casualties were seen by many employers as an inevitable and acceptable sacrifice to make in order to make a profit.

The impact of employment legislation

Fortunately, the kind of management described by Taylor in the mid twentieth century has largely been eradicated. This has not been because unscrupulous employers have suddenly developed a social conscience but a result of the proliferation of employment laws aimed at protecting the individual employee from working in such harmful working environments.

In the UK employers now have a 'duty of care' enshrined in law towards their employees and are required to demonstrate that they are providing reasonable, safe and healthy working conditions and that failure to do so can lead to expensive litigation claims by employees. One example of this is the Health and Safety at Work Act 1974, which requires employers to take all reasonably practicable measures to protect the health, safety and welfare of employees at work.

Additionally, the Management of Health and Safety at Work Regulations (1999) legally require an employer who employs more than three workers to assess health and safety risks in the workplace and to introduce prevention and control measures based on those risk assessments. A statutory body known as the Health and Safety Executive (HSE) has been set up in the UK to ensure compliance with this legislation. One of its main functions with respect to work related stress risks has been to provide clear guidance to employers on how to manage them. In particular the HSE has published the *Management Standards for Tackling Work Related Stress*, which all employers have a responsibility to read and understand. Employers also have a legal duty under the health and safety legislation to do a risk assessment on their own workplace and make every effort they can to ensure that these standards are being met within the teams that they manage. Each standard spells out good management practice in one of *six* areas relating to demands, control, support, relationships, role and change.

Demands

Demands include issues like workload, work patterns and the work environment. The organization must make sure that tasks are achievable within the hours of the job, the employee has the skills and the job is designed to be within the capabilities of the employee. The management standard is that *'employees indicate that they are able to cope with the demands of their job and systems are in place locally to respond to any individual concerns'*.

Control

Control involves how much say an employee has in making decisions about the way they do their work, the pace of their work, work patterns and when breaks can be taken. The standard is that *'employees report that they do have a say about the way they do their work and systems are in place locally to respond to any individual concerns'*.

Support

Support includes the encouragement, sponsorship and resources provided by the organization, line management and colleagues. Employers need to ensure that they provide adequate information and support to do the job, systems are in place to support staff, employees know how to access this support, can access the right resources to do the job and receive regular and constructive feedback on their performance. The standard is that *'employees indicate that they receive adequate information and support from their colleagues and supervisors and that systems are in place to respond to any individual concerns'*.

Relationships

Relationships include promoting positive working to avoid conflict and dealing with unacceptable behaviour such as bullying and harassment. The standard is that *'employees have a positive environment to work in, are not subjected to unacceptable behaviours at work, that there are agreed policies, procedures and systems in place to respond to individual concerns'*.

Role

Role refers to whether employees understand their role within an organization and whether the organization ensures that the person does not have conflicting roles. The employer needs to ensure that employees are clear about their roles and responsibilities and that they are given sufficient information to enable them to do their job. The management standard is that *'employees indicate that they understand their role and responsibilities and there are systems in place locally to respond to any individual concerns'*.

Change

This refers to how change is managed and communicated within the organization. The employer needs to ensure that employees are given adequate notice, consultation, a timetable and support through any organizational changes. The management standard is that *'employees indicate that the organization engages them frequently when undergoing any organizational change and systems are in place locally to respond to any individual concerns'*.

Further developments in management standards

The management standards approach has generated a significant amount of interest not only in the UK but also internationally in Europe,

Australasia, Canada and the Indian subcontinent. Although each country tends to have its own way of regulating the safety in the workplace, the interest shown internationally would seem to indicate that the approach can, with some minor modifications, work within the regulatory systems present in these countries. It is flexible enough to be accommodated within a range of different regulatory systems and it has even been used in countries without regulatory systems in place.

The Health and Safety Executive has developed a risk assessment tool based on the six standards identified above, known as the Management Standards Indicator Tool. It is a questionnaire consisting of thirty-five items which investigate the presence or absence of known organizational risk factors for organizational stress and rates the employee's perceptions of the six key aspects from demands through to change. It is designed to be used as a screening tool for whole organizations but can also be used by individuals to provide information on their current working conditions. For example, it has been used in return to work interviews, individual risk assessments, job design and annual appraisals.

Identifying the main causes of stress in your own working environment

Before you can address the causes of stress in your own working environment, you need to identify what they are. The questionnaire in Table 2.1 is intended to help you identify the main causes of stress in your own working environment. Please read the questions and circle your answer. It is important that your responses relate to the *last six months*.

Interpreting the results of your questionnaire (Table 2.1)

Interpreting individual items

You will notice that on each of the subscales of the questionnaire there are shaded boxes, some are dark grey, others are a lighter shade of grey, or some are white. These shaded areas give you information about how your own rating compares to the HSE national benchmarks for each item derived from a 2004 survey of 5,800 workers. You can interpret your rating on each individual item by using the key in Table 2.2.

Interpretation of subscales

The key in Table 2.2 allows you to compare only individual items within each subscale using the HSE benchmark. In order to interpret your score

Table 2.1 Questionnaire to identify the main sources of stress in your work environment

1 Demands					
1 Different groups at work demand things from me that are hard to combine	Never 5	Seldom 4	Sometimes 3	Often 2	Always 1
2 I have unachievable deadlines	Never 5	Seldom 4	Sometimes 3	Often 2	Always 1
3 I have to work very intensively	Never 5	Seldom 4	Sometimes 3	Often 2	Always 1
4 I have to neglect some tasks because I have too much to do	Never 5	Seldom 4	Sometimes 3	Often 2	Always 1
5 I am unable to take sufficient breaks	Never 5	Seldom 4	Sometimes 3	Often 2	Always 1
6 I am pressured to work long hours	Never 5	Seldom 4	Sometimes 3	Often 2	Always 1
7 I have to work very fast	Never 5	Seldom 4	Sometimes 3	Often 2	Always 1
8 I have unrealistic time pressures	Never 5	Seldom 4	Sometimes 3	Often 2	Always 1

2 Control					
1 I can decide when to take a break	Never 1	Seldom 2	Sometimes 3	Often 4	Always 5
2 I have a say in my own work speed	Never 1	Seldom 2	Sometimes 3	Often 4	Always 5
3 I have a choice in deciding how I do my work	Never 1	Seldom 2	Sometimes 3	Often 4	Always 5
4 I have a choice in deciding what I do at work	Never 1	Seldom 2	Sometimes 3	Often 4	Always 5
5 I have some say over the way I work	Never 1	Seldom 2	Sometimes 3	Often 4	Always 5
6 My working time can be flexible	Never 1	Seldom 2	Sometimes 3	Often 4	Always 5

3a Managers' support					
1 I am given supportive feedback on the work I do	Never 1	Seldom 2	Sometimes 3	Often 4	Always 5
2 I can rely on my line manager to help me out with a work problem	Never 1	Seldom 2	Sometimes 3	Often 4	Always 5

(Continued)

Table 2.1 Questionnaire to identify the main sources of stress in your work environment *(Continued)*

3	I can talk to my manager about something that has upset or annoyed me about work	Never 1	Seldom 2	Sometimes 3	Often 4	Always 5
4	I am supported through emotionally demanding work	Never 1	Seldom 2	Sometimes 3	Often 4	Always 5
5	My line manager encourages me at work	Never 1	Seldom 2	Sometimes 3	Often 4	Always 5

3b Peer support

1	If work gets difficult, my colleagues will help me	Never 1	Seldom 2	Sometimes 3	Often 4	Always 5
2	I get help and support I need from colleagues	Never 1	Seldom 2	Sometimes 3	Often 4	Always 5
3	I receive the respect at work I deserve from my colleagues	Never 1	Seldom 2	Sometimes 3	Often 4	Always 5
4	My colleagues are willing to listen to my work related problems	Never 1	Seldom 2	Sometimes 3	Often 4	Always 5

4 Relationships

1	I am subject to personal harassment in the form of unkind words or behaviour	Never 5	Seldom 4	Sometimes 3	Often 2	Always 1
2	There is friction or anger between colleagues	Never 5	Seldom 4	Sometimes 3	Often 2	Always 1
3	I am subject to bullying at work	Never 5	Seldom 4	Sometimes 3	Often 2	Always 1
4	Relationships at work are strained	Never 5	Seldom 4	Sometimes 3	Often 2	Always 1

5 Role

1	I am clear what is expected of me at work	Never 1	Seldom 2	Sometimes 3	Often 4	Always 5
2	I know how to go about getting my job done	Never 1	Seldom 2	Sometimes 3	Often 4	Always 5
3	I am clear what my duties and responsibilities are	Never 1	Seldom 2	Sometimes 3	Often 4	Always 5

4	I am clear about the goals and objectives for my department	Never 1	Seldom 2	Sometimes 3	Often 4	Always 5
5	I understand how my work fits into the overall aim of the organization	Never 1	Seldom 2	Sometimes 3	Often 4	Always 5

6 Change						
1	I have sufficient opportunities to question managers about change at work	Never 1	Seldom 2	Sometimes 3	Often 4	Always 5
2	Staff are always consulted about change at work	Never 1	Seldom 2	Sometimes 3	Often 4	Always 5
3	When changes are made at work, I am clear how they will work out in practice	Never 1	Seldom 2	Sometimes 3	Often 4	Always 5

(Adapted from Health and Safety Executive Management Standards Indicator Tool with permission)
Note: This table is available to view and print from the following website: www.routledge mentalhealth.com/9780415671781

on each complete subscale, you will first need to work out your average score for each subscale of the questionnaire. The average score for each subscale can be calculated by adding up the total of all the items and then dividing by the number of items in the subscale (demands = 8 items; control = 6 items; managers' support = 5 items; peer support = 4 items;

Table 2.2 Key to questionnaire

	Indicates a score in the bottom 20% when compared to the benchmarked scores and it indicates that this item is likely to be a significant source of stress to you and requires your immediate attention.
	Indicates a score in the lower 50% when compared with the benchmarked scores and it indicates that this may be a source of stress to you, there is scope for some improvement on this item and that it needs addressing.
	Indicates a score in the top 50% when compared to the benchmarked score and it indicates a satisfactory/good response on this item at the time of completing the questionnaire.

(Source: data derived from the HSE survey *Psychosocial Working Conditions in Great Britain*, 2004)

Table 2.3 Mean ratings for each subscale

Management standard	In bottom 20 per cent compared to benchmark scores	In bottom 50 per cent compared to benchmark scores	In top 50 per cent compared to benchmark scores
Demands	Less than 2.9	2.9 to 3.1	More than 3.1
Control	Less than 3.2	3.2 to 3.5	More than 3.5
Managers' support	Less than 3.3	3.3 to 3.5	More than 3.5
Peer support	Less than 3.6	3.6 to 3.8	More than 3.8
Relationships	Less than 3.6	3.6 to 3.9	More than 3.9
Role	Less than 4.0	4.0 to 4.2	More than 4.2
Change	Less than 2.8	2.8 to 3.0	More than 3.0

relationships = 4 items; role = 5 items; change = 3 items). Once you have the average (mean) score you can make comparisons with the benchmark in Table 2.3.

The shaded areas in Table 2.3 are interpreted in exactly the same way as indicated in the key (Table 2.2) and allow you to identify where you stand in relation to the norms for each of the management standards. This information should be useful to you in terms of identifying which areas of your working environment are causing you stress. This information can then be used to help you identify which of the interventions outlined in Chapter 3 will be the most helpful to you.

Summary and main learning points from Part I

Part I of this book aimed to promote your understanding of the stress concept, its causes and consequences. In Chapter 1 the transactional model of stress was introduced, in which stress was conceptualized as being the result of an interaction between an individual and their environment. The central importance of the appraisal or meaning of an event or situation to the individual in the causation of stress was also emphasized. An overview of the sequence of physical and mental changes triggered in the stress reaction was also presented. You were then asked to complete a quiz to test your knowledge of stress. The subsequent list of answers provided was aimed at dispelling some commonly held myths and misconceptions about stress. The chapter concluded with a checklist which allowed you to identify the symptoms and assess the severity of your own current levels of stress. The key learning points from Chapter 1 are listed below:

*   Occupational stress is costing employers billions of pounds each year.
*   A certain amount of stress at work is normal and at optimal levels can actually be a motivator and enhance performance.
*   Prolonged high levels of chronic unmitigated stress are potentially harmful and can lead to more serious physical and mental health consequences.
*   The stress reaction consists of a sequence of physical, emotional, cognitive and behavioural changes known as the emergency response.
*   Stress is the consequence of an interaction between the individual and their environment.
*   The interpretation or meaning that an individual attaches to an event or situation is a key factor in determining whether or not they will experience it as being stressful.
*   Tackling stress in the workplace is worthwhile not only on humanitarian grounds but also because it make sound economic sense to do so.

   Chapter 2 of this book (the present chapter) focused on identifying the main causes of occupational stress. The transactional model of occupational stress was introduced, which conceptualized stress as being the consequence of a mismatch between the individual employee's capabilities, resources and needs and their work environment (i.e., a poor person–environment fit). An overview of the main individual and environmental causes of occupational stress was then presented. The chapter concluded with a questionnaire on the causes of work related stress, derived from the Health and Safety Executive's six management standards. Completion and scoring of the questionnaire allowed you to identify the main causes of stress in your own working environment. The key learning points from Chapter 2 are listed below:

*   Individual causes of stress include a range of genetic/inherited, acquired/learned and personality/trait factors.
*   Environmental causes of stress can be found in the demands of the job itself, the physical working conditions, amount of control and autonomy over the job, supports available, quality of working relationships, role clarity, the way change is managed, and pay and career prospects.

- The interface between work and home life is also a potential causal factor.
- Employers have a duty of care to ensure that they provide as healthy and stress free working environment as far as possible for their workforce.
- The British Health and Safety Executive has identified a number of management standards with respect to managing stress in the workplace, which employers are expected to comply with.
- Each management standard spells out good management practice in each of six areas relating to job demands, control, support, relationships, role and the way that organizational change is managed.
- Employers in the UK in any organization with three or more employees have a legal duty under health and safety legislation to do a risk assessment on their own workplace based on the six management standards.
- Employers in the UK are required to make every effort they can to ensure that these standards are being met within the teams that they manage.
- The management standards approach has generated a significant amount of interest in many countries around the world and is flexible enough to be accommodated within the range of different regulatory systems present in these countries.

About Part II of this book

Part II provides a range of interventions for tackling occupational stress. Researchers in the field have identified three levels of interventions for managing work related stress more effectively, known as primary, secondary and tertiary level interventions. Part II (Chapters 3 to 10) covers these three levels of intervention respectively.

Primary level interventions

Primary level interventions are aimed at changing the work environment itself to reduce or eliminate the cause of the stress at its source. These are covered in Chapter 3. However, sometimes it is not possible to change the work environment either because it is uneconomical for the employer to do this, or because there are aspects of the job itself that are inherently stressful. For example, if an individual is working in the emergency services or armed forces, there will clearly be stressful aspects of the job that cannot be removed. Where this is the case and the sources of stress cannot be readily removed, secondary level interventions are considered to be more appropriate.

Secondary level interventions

Secondary level interventions aim to teach the employee a range of coping skills or strategies to help buffer them against an inherently stressful environment and to assist them to develop the confidence to look after themselves more effectively in situations that would in actual fact be stressful to anyone. These are covered in Chapters 4 to 9.

Tertiary level interventions

Tertiary level interventions are appropriate when secondary level interventions are ineffective and the individual is experiencing one of the stress syndromes outlined in Chapter 1, which is impacting on their capacity to be productive in the work setting, or even to remain at work (p. 11). These aim to reduce and, it is hoped, eliminate the clinical level of distress they are experiencing by providing psychological therapy to assist them to return to their previous normal levels of productivity. Tertiary level interventions are covered in Chapter 10.

Interventions for occupational stress

Chapter 3

Primary level interventions aimed at improving your work environment

Introduction

This chapter focuses specifically on primary level interventions, which aim to reduce or eliminate the causes of stress in the work environment itself. Some jobs are inherently stressful, for example, working in the emergency services as a police officer, ambulance driver or firefighter, or as a soldier during wartime. The primary level interventions outlined in this chapter will not be appropriate in the context of these kinds of jobs because the stress experienced is an inherent part of the job. Where the working environment is largely free from such inherent stressors and the stress experienced is the result of badly organized work and/or poor management practices, the primary level interventions outlined in this chapter are the appropriate ones to use. However, it is recommended that you do a job analysis before deciding which primary level interventions to use. The reasons for this are outlined below.

Doing a job analysis

Doing a job analysis will allow you to establish whether or not you are already doing everything within your control to help yourself manage the demands of your job effectively. You can do a job analysis yourself. It involves standing back and looking rationally at the tasks you do in your job and to decide which tasks are essential, which are desirable and which are simply distractions. The case study of Tony illustrates the importance of doing a job analysis before engaging in primary level interventions to tackle stress.

Case study: Tony

Tony came into therapy suffering from stress at work. He described himself as a perfectionist with a strong need for approval. His job was to manage the food section at the local department of a national chain of stores. Whenever he was asked to do a job by his manager, he reported that he would always 'put himself out and go the extra mile' in order to show his boss how good he was at his job and get noticed for being the best. Tony came to therapy in a very angry and distressed state, since his boss had criticized him for being too slow and not getting work finished on time.

In therapy the possible reasons why Tony's boss had been critical of him were explored. Tony gave some examples of when he had been criticized and it soon became apparent what was happening. Whenever there was a shelf or freezer to restock, Tony would take it upon himself to also clean it thoroughly and in the process would look for out-of-date stock. Although it was not in his job description, Tony believed that cleaning the display cabinets would earn him greater respect from his manager. However, in reality all it was doing was making his manager irritated that he was taking so long with everything.

Tony was helped to realize that not sticking to the job asked of him was the cause of his boss's criticism. Tony agreed to do an experiment over a period of two weeks in which he stuck only to the jobs asked of him. It was a revelation to Tony because he found that sticking only to the tasks requested not only made him feel less stressed but also led to his manager praising him for completing tasks on time. It created a win-win situation for both of them. In fact there were already people employed to do the cleaning and check the dates on the stock, so Tony could have saved himself a lot of time and distress if he had stuck only to the tasks identified in his job description in the first place.

The benefits of doing a job analysis

Doing a job analysis is thus about developing a clear understanding of what you need to do to perform your job well and what are simply distractions. It can be seen from the case study of Tony that by getting a clearer understanding of his job he was able to identify the priorities and improve his performance at the same time as reducing the pressure on himself. By doing an analysis of your own job you may (like Tony) be able to identify some ways in which you can get your workload back under control, reduce the pressure on yourself and at the same time increase your efficiency in the eyes of your employer. In order to do this you need to be clear about what the important components of the job are. The roles and responsibilities outlined in your job description, positive feedback from performance reviews and the content of work incentive schemes can all be important sources of information in this respect. It can also be helpful to identify what the priorities of those identified as high achievers in your organization are. Once you are sure about what the important components of your job are, you can then prioritize those tasks which yield the greatest return in terms of recognition, reward and approval by your employer for the least effort on your part. In this way you can be sure that you are working as efficiently as you can. If, however, you are working as efficiently as you can but are still experiencing your working environment to be stressful, you need to consider employing one or more of the primary level interventions outlined below. These are based upon the six management standards that were introduced in Chapter 2.

Interventions aimed at reducing the demands of your job

Reducing the volume of work

There are usually aspects of the volume of work associated with your job that you can exert some direct control over, since they form part of your terms and conditions of employment. For example, you must ensure that you take all the daily rest breaks and annual leave that you are entitled to. You have a right to say no to more than your contracted hours and you do not need to agree to overtime against your wishes. Indeed, if you are feeling under stress it may be a good idea to reduce the amount of overtime you are doing, at least until you are feeling better in yourself. If your work has them, you may wish to make use of the flexible working arrangements on offer if you are experiencing high levels of stress. For example, you may be able to job share, work flexi-time, stop doing shift work, go part-time, work from home or even take unpaid leave where necessary. If the going gets too tough, it is legitimate to take a 'mental health' day off work every now and again in order to give you time to reflect on the situation and get some perspective back.

Your employer has no right to expect you to work any more hours than you are contracted to do. If you choose to help your manager out of a difficult situation because you want to, that is fine, but it should be your choice and you should never feel under pressure to do so. It is also the responsibility of your employer to agree clearly measurable, realistic and achievable targets with respect to the actual volume of work activity that you do, within the hours that you are contracted to work. The activity targets set should be comparable to those of your work colleagues who are doing a similar job to you and also to those doing similar work for other employers. Where this is not the case you need to draw this to the attention of your line manager for them to rectify the situation. You are entitled to equal pay for equal work and your employer could be liable for discriminatory practice if this is not the case. The fact that there may be too much work for the number of workers employed is your employer's problem and not an excuse to demand that you increase your output to an unmanageable level or work at an unsustainable pace.

Enlarging your job

Job enlargement is about giving the employee the opportunity to perform a greater range of different tasks in their job. It involves alternating one-sided excessively taxing or very boring tasks with different tasks within one job. Boring and monotonous jobs can be broken up and interspersed with more enjoyable tasks which provide some variety. Very sedentary and inactive jobs can be modified to include tasks which involve getting up and moving around regularly. High responsibility jobs can be interspersed with low level responsibility tasks. Socially isolated jobs can be modified to provide more social contact.

Examples of enlarging a job can include the following. An employee who spends a large amount of time sitting in front of a computer screen in an office can be given the opportunity of a change of scenery by spending more time out of the office. An employee who spends long periods of time travelling may be only too happy to spend a bit more time in the office. An employee who has to take a lot of responsibility much of the time may relish spending some time doing mundane tasks which require little responsibility. This form of job redesign does not need to cost the employer anything more, since all the jobs still get done but it can have a very positive effect in reducing stress resulting from poor job design.

Any changes to your work routine do of course need to be sanctioned by your line manager, since they may be a variation from your job description. However, you should not have too much difficulty convincing those of your work peers who are feeling bored or overtaxed in their work that a change of routine and responsibilities is a good idea. To implement these changes you will first need to find some work colleagues who would like to join you and then explain to your manager the reasons why you (and your work colleagues) would like to make changes to your work routine and what tasks you would like to exchange. It is important that you assure your manager that all the tasks will continue to be done to the required standard. If they remain unconvinced, you can suggest that the job rotation is done as a pilot project and evaluated after an agreed period of time. It is then up to you to demonstrate that it can work!

Enriching your job

Job enrichment is a specific form of job enlargement and is about allowing employees to deliver a more complete product and so to give their work more meaning and satisfaction. It means that employees do not stick to a very narrow range of partial tasks but get involved in a range of other partial tasks which allow them to be involved at a number of stages in the completion of a product. For example, an employee working on a car assembly line who is restricted to doing the same repetitive task may experience little satisfaction or meaning to their work, since they feel alienated from the finished product. However, if they are involved at a number of stages such as in the planning, preparation, construction, quality inspection and training new employees, they are likely to find their job much more rewarding. Again this form of job redesign does not need to cost the employer any extra but can help considerably in reducing stress due to the demands of a poorly designed job.

As for job enlargement, such changes to your work routine do need to be sanctioned by your line manager. Again, it should not be too difficult to convince your work peers who are dissatisfied or alienated from their work that such changes are a good idea. The main task here, however, is to convince your line manager of the benefits of job enrichment and to get them to support the proposed changes. If your manager remains unconvinced then (as for job enlargement) you can suggest that the changes are introduced as a pilot project and that they are properly evaluated after an agreed period of time.

Improving your physical working environment

If you have identified that your working environment is poor, there are a number of things you can do to try to improve it. For example, if you

spend long periods of time sitting at a desk but you are finding it uncomfortable, you should ask for a work station assessment to be carried out to
check that you have properly adjusted seating, and the computer and key-
board are correctly positioned and at the right height. This is particularly
important if you find you are experiencing backache or other aches and
pains. If you spend long periods of time at a computer, it is recommended
that you take a break from the monitor every 50 minutes. If you have a
physical disability, the employer is required to make reasonable adjust-
ments to your physical working environment to accommodate these, such
as providing you with the resources and equipment to allow you to do
your job effectively and providing disabled access and parking facilities.

If you work in an open plan office and are finding it too noisy and
distracting to be able to concentrate on your work, simple modifications
may be possible to give you more personal space and privacy. For
example, redesigning the office with partitions, screens or blinds is not
prohibitively expensive but can work wonders in this respect. Such
modifications would of course require the support of your manager.
Repositioning your desk so that you are not in the full glare of the office
or strategically placing a large pot plant is an even less costly way in
which to give yourself more privacy. Politely asking people to make less
noise or making use of any available separate meeting room or other
quiet area when concentration is needed are some ways of tackling noise
pollution, but if all else fails why not take in some ear plugs!

Check that your desk lamp has the right brightness of bulb in it and
make requests for any bulbs that have blown to be replaced. Check that
your office is at a comfortable working temperature and if it is not, then
request that the heating be turned up when it is cold and that there is air
conditioning when it is too warm, even if the only air conditioning is to
open a window. If windows do not open, ask for them to be fixed. Make
sure that you are well hydrated and have drinking water freely available.
Many offices provide water dispensers and it is reasonable to ask for one
in your own work area. If all else fails bring your own bottle of water in
from home. If you identify any safety hazards at work, inform your
manager immediately and request that they be contained or removed. If
the equipment or technology you are using is outdated, ask for the right
resources and equipment to do the job effectively. Finally, you can make
your work environment a more pleasant one to be in by bringing in
pictures of family and loved ones, desk plants and tea and coffee making
facilities for break times if they are not already provided.

Many of the suggestions made above to improve your physical work
environment do not cost much money and can be readily implemented.

Those which involve spending more money will of course depend on the goodwill of your employer to introduce. While there is no guarantee that your employer will agree to them, if you present a good case for introducing them a reasonable employer should consider them seriously, especially if you remind them that employees work more efficiently in a safe, supportive and comfortable physical working environment!

Interventions aimed at increasing the control you have over your job

The first step in taking more control over your work is to be clear about who you are accountable to and who has accountability for you. You do not have to take orders from those who have no authority over you. We sometimes assume that others have a level of authority over us that they do not actually have, just because they behave in an authoritative, bossy, over-confident or controlling way. If you are not sure, look at the 'lines of accountability' section in your job description to clarify this, or check it out with your line manager.

The second step is to be clear about exactly what freedom to act you do have ascribed to your role in the organization. Establish what you can do for yourself to change your work environment and what you cannot. If you are unsure about this, check the 'roles and responsibilities' section of your job description. If after having read your job description you are still in doubt about what authority you have, check these out with your line manager and ask for them to be made clearer in your job description. If you do not have a job description, you need to ask for one, in order to clarify these issues. Once you are clear about what freedoms you have, it is important that you exercise these to the full and take control of the things that are within your authority to change. After all, no employer can object if you are simply doing what is in your job description.

You may be pleasantly surprised about how much control you do actually have over your work, or how much autonomy a busy manager may be willing to delegate to you. Do not assume that others in the organization are going to sort this out for you. If you are waiting for someone else to come along and sort this out for you rather than trying to do it yourself, you could be waiting for ever! Also ask yourself if you are waiting for permission to do something when you do not need it. You may be imagining that there are restrictions or constraints upon you that are not in reality there.

Look for opportunities to influence the decision making processes in your organization either through formal channels such as trade union activity or by less formal ways such as greater involvement in staff meetings with managers. Many workplace organizations have a staff suggestion box and this provides a non-threatening means for more junior employees to have some input into the way their organization is run. If your organization does not have a suggestion box, you could make a suggestion that one is introduced! Also, explore ways in which you can have greater influence at a local level on some of the decisions made that directly affect you. Active involvement in lower level staff meetings can allow you to influence how work assignments and resources are allocated within your area or department. For example, increasing your involvement in the preparation of staff duty, overtime and annual leave rotas can give you more influence and control over these aspects of your work.

Simply managing your own diary could enable you to have greater control over the timing and sequence of your work. For example, it can allow you to intersperse difficult and stressful appointments with less stressful ones. You are the best judge of these and it is something that others are not necessarily best placed to decide for you. It can also let you have more control over the pace of your work and give you the opportunity to build 'breathing spaces' into your daily timetable rather than filling it with back-to-back appointments and meetings. You can ensure that you incorporate rest breaks, lunch breaks and 'quality time' into your daily or weekly schedule. Quality time is free space booked into your diary each week which allows you to deal with those unexpected tasks or situations which need dealing with as a matter of urgency. By definition you do not know what these are going to be until they happen but in many lines of work they do happen with amazing regularity and so it makes sense to plan for these in advance by making space for them before they happen. Of course, if an urgent situation does not arise, this time is not wasted since it can be used for catching up on more routine tasks.

Interventions aimed at increasing the supports you have at work

Supports at work may be formal or informal. Informal supports consist of those which the employee makes use of in the course of their everyday work but which are not enshrined in the formal policies and procedures of the organization. An example of informal support is that provided by having social contact with one's colleagues during the course of the daily work routine. Feeling isolated at work can be a source of stress. If you are feeling isolated in your work, you need to consider ways in which you can increase your social contact with other people at work. For example, this might involve actually going to see a colleague in a neighbouring office rather than sending them an email or telephoning them. It could be calling into the reception office to collect your mail each morning, or taking the opportunity to stop and chat to a colleague in the corridor. If there is a place where people meet up for morning break, or a staff canteen for lunch, you can make sure that you frequent these places on a regular basis. Make sure you accept any invitations to attend staff social gatherings where you can meet your colleagues on an informal basis. You could consider joining one of the staff clubs such as the social club, quiz team or darts team if they exist.

If the less formal options are not available, you may need to share the problem of your feeling isolated with your line manager and see if there are ways in which your job can be redesigned to provide you with more social contact. For example, you could ask if you can be moved into a more centrally located or shared office space or take on more tasks which involve increased face-to-face contact with people. You may also consider altering your duty rota or changing your shift patterns if it means that you will have more contact with your work colleagues. Also, make sure you attend all the meetings you are supposed to since, as well as having a formal purpose, meetings can provide an opportunity for some less formal social contact. Try to be as creative as possible in finding solutions to this problem.

Alternatively, if social isolation is a problem shared by a number of employees working in an organization, setting up a staff support group could allow all these people to meet up and share their experiences. This would be possible only if the idea had the support of your manager and there was a mutually acceptable time and place where you could all meet up. If, however, you reach a point where you have exhausted all the options, or the job by its nature restricts the opportunities for social contact, you may need to consider ways of improving your social life outside of work to compensate for this.

In addition to the informal and less formal interventions described above, it is the responsibility of your employer to make sure that formal mechanisms and support structures such as regular supervision, performance reviews, mentorship arrangements and continuing professional development appraisals are in place. The employer is also responsible for ensuring that the employee is properly trained to do the job which they have been employed to do. Where a shortfall in the employee's knowledge, skills or experience to do the job effectively is identified, the employer should support the employee to do the necessary training in order to do their job effectively. If you identify that there is an absence of these formal support mechanisms in your own workplace, you need to draw this to the attention of your line manager and/or your human resources department if you have one.

Alternatively, it may be the case that formal support mechanisms are in there but are not being implemented on a regular enough basis, or being given sufficient priority. If this is the situation, you may need to give your line manager a prompt by requesting an appraisal, or requesting the time and funding you require for a training event which is already identified as one of your continuing professional development needs. It may help to cite when you last had an appraisal or when you last attended a training event. Let us hope your manager will react positively to your reminder; they should support you if your requests are reasonable. Remember, these formal support mechanisms are in place for the benefit of the organization as well as the employee. While they may make the employee feel valued and supported, they are also there for sound economic motives to ensure that employees are working as efficiently and effectively as possible. It is also worth remembering that if professional development needs are ignored, your supervision needs not addressed, or your performance not appraised, your employer has no case to argue if your work performance is subsequently identified as being substandard.

Interventions aimed at improving working relationships

Employees are entitled to a positive environment to work in and not to be subjected to unacceptable behaviours at work. They are also entitled to expect that there are agreed policies, procedures and systems in place at work to respond to their individual concerns. The interventions outlined in this section are aimed at promoting positive working relationships, assisting the individual to avoid conflict and helping them deal with unacceptable behaviour in a rational and systematic way. This section focuses on one of the most extreme forms of unacceptable behaviour, that of bullying, but the strategies outlined are equally applicable to other forms of unacceptable behaviours in the workplace. It is a well-known fact that bullies prefer easy targets and will steer away from any battle that they believe they could just possibly lose. When confronted by a bully, it is therefore important that you try to disguise any feelings of vulnerability that you may have by exuding an air of firmness, authority and confidence. Try to remain calm and develop a rational plan of action through which you can disarm the bully rather than reacting emotionally as the bully expects. Five steps to developing an action plan for tackling bullying are suggested below.

Gather evidence

Keep a diary of every incident that happens. Record the date and time, where it took place, what was said by whom and make a note of any witnesses present. You should also collect any old appraisals, job references and correspondence relating to your good character and/or highlighting your strengths and ability to cope. Copies of any incriminating emails from the perpetrator should also be saved. You should make sure that you are very familiar with your job description, since a good knowledge of your job description will be necessary in arguing your case. Arm yourself with as much evidence as you can. You can also check to see if your organization has an anti-bullying policy and a grievance procedure and if so familiarize yourself with it.

Find allies to support you

Don't allow yourself to become isolated. Make use of available supports both at home and in the workplace. If you have witnesses, ascertain their perceptions of what took place and if possible get them to support your case. Try to identify others who are going through a similar experience to you and will join you in this evidence gathering exercise. This will prevent the perpetrator from dismissing your experiences as a personality clash. You can also informally and confidentially make contact with someone from the human resources department, your union representative, or someone in the occupational health department and get their point of view about the situation. You can keep them informed of any developments and it will then be easier to involve them at a later date if necessary.

Stand up to the bully

Assertiveness is the key to standing up to a bully. You need to communicate to them both verbally and non-verbally that you are not afraid of them. Start off by being polite and diplomatic and ask them, in a calm and relaxed manner and with a smile on your face, for a few minutes of their time to discuss the problem. Don't approach them in a public situation since they may feel that they are losing credibility by agreeing to a meeting in front of other people. Choose a place and time when they are on their own and not too busy. Look them in the eyes and adopt an upright posture with your shoulders back and head held up straight. Make sure that what you say is clear and precise, at a normal volume and in a normal tone of voice. If necessary you may want to rehearse what you are going to say to the person in advance, for example by practising in front of the mirror, or doing a role-play exercise with someone who is supporting you. You may also want to rehearse your responses to any reactions that you anticipate the perpetrator may present you with. Do not respond to any taunts, since to do so will only give the bully encouragement from knowing that they have upset you.

Present the bully with the evidence

Presenting factual evidence is the best way of confronting the bully. Point out their behaviour and the impact that it is having on you. Inform them that you don't intend to put up with it any more and what you expect to change about their behaviour. If their response is not a positive one, it may be necessary to spell out what the consequences will be if they do not change. Do not be afraid to mention your trade union, human resources or a senior manager, since this will let them know that you mean business.

Be prepared for the backlash

The bully may initially respond by being aggressive and attempt to intimidate you into a more submissive position. However, if you are prepared for this and have a strategy for managing it, you can weather this without giving in. For example, the bully may react by trying to blame you for the situation. However, stay calm and simply repeat your request that you expect them to change their unreasonable behaviour. Give them a cooling off period and continue to monitor and record their behaviours.

Take things further if necessary

If the bully does not change, you may not be left with any other option than to take things further. This may involve taking out a grievance, or getting your trade union involved. If the bully is your manager, you will need to bypass them and go directly to a higher authority. It is important that you are willing to take things further, otherwise you will lose your credibility with the perpetrator, who may interpret your unwillingness to take things further as a sign of weakness and believe they can go on persecuting you without any consequences. They could even increase the behaviour as a way of punishing you for standing up to them.

Interventions aimed at clarifying your role at work

One of the main ways in which an employee's roles and responsibilities are made clear at work is through their job description. If you do not have a formal job description, it is important that you obtain one. This will give you a clear idea of the functions of your job and what is expected of you. Going through the tasks and duties outlined in a job description provides both the employee and the line manager with an opportunity to sort out and reach agreement on any discrepancies in expectations before they become problems. The employee also needs to be made aware of the organization's mission statement (i.e., the main purposes and aims of the organization) and have access to all of the policies and procedures of the organization. If you do not have this information, it is reasonable to ask for it to be made available to you.

Managers should also ensure that employees are given regular job appraisals, since these are an important way of communicating to an employee whether or not they are meeting the objectives of the organization. If the employee is not achieving the targets set for them, the appraisal process should provide a clear and unambiguous way of informing them of this and what they need to do in order to ensure that they are achieved in the future. If you are not having regular job appraisals (sometimes called individual performance or personal development reviews), it is important that you ask for them to be arranged, for example on a quarterly basis. These can be supplemented with monthly management supervision meetings which allow you to obtain more frequent feedback on your performance and the opportunity for any discrepancies or disagreements.

Interventions aimed at improving the way that change is managed in your workplace

If you work in an unenlightened organization where change is managed in a secretive way, information is withheld, employees are not consulted about changes, where there are negative attitudes and/or a 'macho' culture about stress, you will clearly have problems in terms of trying to change it. The first step is to try to make use of any formal mechanisms through which you can bring these issues onto the agenda, such as staff and management meetings. However, it is highly unlikely that you are going to have much influence on your own. Group pressure is required and in order to have an impact, you need to recruit others to support the campaign and work collaboratively to bring about a change in management attitudes. Do not assume that everyone is automatically going to reject what you say, since once you start to bring this into the open, you may be surprised how many people feel the same way as you do about it. Even if not everyone feels the same way as you do, this is not a reason to do nothing.

Changing the culture of an organization requires changing attitudes from the most senior level downwards. To achieve this, strong and persuasive evidence needs to be presented that emphasizes change is required. For example, factual evidence of the negative impact that the stress due to the poor management of organizational change is having upon employees within your own organization would be very persuasive. Persuasive evidence may include higher than average sickness absence, high staff turnover, higher than average retirement due to ill health, increased accidents at work, or litigation and compensation claims. Even if this factual information is not readily available, it may be possible to gather more descriptive evidence through the verbal and written reports of past and present employees, through your own experiences and observations, or through the grapevine to support the case.

The research on how costly work related stress is to the individual, organizations and the country (see pp. 6–8) should be publicized and disseminated as widely as possible to all levels of the organization in order to persuade others that a change in organizational culture is necessary. For example, your employer needs to be aware that addressing the social and welfare needs of employees, rather than costing an employer, can actually increase productivity and profits. It thus makes sense not only on humanitarian grounds but also for sound economic reasons. After all, a happy workforce is a productive one.

Interventions aimed at improving the home–work interface

The following are some tips aimed at improving the home–work interface:

• Do not take work home or make yourself available all the time.
• Switch off your work mobile and give your home telephone number to as few people as possible. It is easy to convince yourself that you are indispensable but this is a dangerous assumption to make. No

one is indispensable. Also no one ever got to the end of their life wishing that they had spent more time working and less leisure time!

- Switch off both mentally and physically from work when you are at home. Leave work behind you when you set off for home and leave home behind you when you set off for work.
- If you find commuting to work stressful, try leaving a bit earlier or at different times to beat the rush. You could also try to find an alternative less stressful route or means of transport to get to work.
- Make use of strategies to help you relax if you are on public transport such as reading a non-work related book or listening to calming music. If these are not successful, you can try using more formal relaxation techniques such as listening to a relaxation CD on your journey (as long as you are not driving) or practising positive thinking techniques. See Chapters 8 and 9 for further information on relaxation and positive thinking techniques.
- If the stress persists, in the longer term you might consider moving home to a more convenient location nearer work, or alternatively moving your job to a more convenient location.
- If you experience a lack of social supports in work, you can compensate for this by finding alternative social supports outside of work. Similarly, you may feel the need to find alternative sources of self-esteem outside of work. Both of these strategies can act as a buffer against stress at work.
- If you feel that you are doing too much at home in terms of the household chores, try to negotiate a better deal for yourself by sharing and delegating some tasks and responsibilities to others in your household. This might be with your partner or your teenage children. Traditionally the bulk of housework still tends to fall on the woman of the household, so this may need addressing especially if the woman is working full-time. If there is a lack of support or cooperation from the rest of the family, it may even be necessary to consider going on strike! They will soon get the message if the tea is not ready or their clothes are not washed and ironed!
- Ensure that you make proper childcare arrangements that fit in with work, either using a paid childminder, or deciding on who in the family is going to take on this role. After all, it is difficult to relax at work if you are constantly worrying about where your children are and whether or not they have been picked up at the right time from school. When deciding the childcare arrangements, it is important to acknowledge who is the main breadwinner in the family. Although this has traditionally been the man, it might not make sense if the

woman is earning more money. It does not make sense for the woman to give up work or reduce hours to look after children if she earns more than her partner, simply because she is female!

- Dual careers (i.e., where both partners have a career) can also cause stress and problems between partners. One may feel that their career advancement is suffering because they are always following their partner's career moves. If you are in this situation it is important to negotiate a fairer deal for yourself. This might for example involve agreeing to take turns when promotion or other career advancement opportunities come around. This can of course be frustrating when it is your turn to forgo an opportunity but it is at least fairer and in the long run will prevent the build-up of frustration and resentment between a couple.

Some tips for negotiating with your employer

Successful negotiation requires that the employee feels sufficiently empowered to address the presenting problems in an assertive and confident manner. Below are a number of tips aimed at helping to negotiate effectively with your line manager:

- Plan what you are going to say and do in advance of meeting your line manager. If necessary write the key points down on a sheet of paper. It is likely that your manager is going to be busy and you will only have a limited amount of time to communicate your needs, so the clearer and more concisely you do so the better.
- Make sure that you clearly articulate the problem and the impact that it is having on you in terms of your mental and physical wellbeing. Assuming that your manager is a reasonable person and receptive to your problems, this should lead on to a discussion of ways in which the problems you have identified might be resolved. Informing your manager of the difficulties that you are having also allows you to share the problem with them rather than having to struggle with it on your own. If your manager is sympathetic to your plight and has the means at their disposal to resolve the problem, an immediate solution may be possible. For example, if the problem is workload, this might be resolved quickly by a manager agreeing to hire extra staff on a temporary basis, redeploying staff from other areas that are working under capacity, delegating some of your tasks to others, updating equipment so that certain parts of the work can be automated or allowing overtime payments for those who wish to do it.

- Do not be too idealistic in your negotiations. Work is in some respects like a marriage and the key to a good marital relationship is compromise. Make sure that the changes you are requesting are realistic and achievable within the context of the organization in which you work.
- Do not be overly critical or negative. Try to adopt a balanced perspective when negotiating with your employer by acknowledging the positives as well as the negatives in your working environment, such as the comfortable physical working environment, the pleasant view from the window, some of the perks of the job such as the good pension scheme, the generous leave entitlement, the amount of in-service training and study leave, the company car, being allowed to leave early sometimes, the annual bonus, the fact that tea and coffee are provided free of charge, or even having the job is better than no job! Of course if the work environment is a particularly poor one, it is going to be more difficult to identify the positives about it, but it is also easy to take some of the positives for granted when feeling stressed.
- Do not assume that your boss automatically has all the answers to your problems. Your boss may well be struggling with the same issues as you are. Try to work collaboratively by helping with possible solutions, rather than just presenting problems.
- Do not assume that your boss is going to be deliberately obstructive or dismissive, since this will lead to a negative atmosphere from the outset. Believe it or not, most people are actually fair and surely the bottom line is that both your manager and you want what is best for the organization. Whatever you do, do not threaten to take further action before you have given your line manager the opportunity to respond to your concerns.

What to do if your line manager is not receptive to your plight

If you find that your line manager is unhelpful or unreceptive to your plight, there is usually a range of further options available to an employee. These are usually outlined in the policies and procedures of the employing organization. They may involve bypassing the direct line manager and going to a more senior manager, seeking advice from the human resources service, or from the workplace occupational health service. Other alternatives include seeking advice from a workplace trade union, or health and safety representative who will have some expertise in this area. Also, remember that in the UK it is mandatory for your organization to carry out a stress risk assessment and there are strong expectations that they then act on the findings. If your employer has not done this, you may need to point this out to them that they are in breach of their duty of care to their employees. Get to know your rights and make use of existing policies and procedures for complaints for discrimination, bullying and harassment and pursue them through the appropriate channels. In the UK workplace, health and safety representatives have been identified who have the power to conduct periodic inspections of the workplace to ensure that environmental stressors are properly controlled and the Health and Safety Committee has a key role in ensuring that policies and procedures are implemented. The committee looks at sickness absence, referrals to occupational health services and may conduct surveys and focus groups. Employers may ignore their health and safety obligations at their peril!

What to do if you do not get the problem resolved within your workplace organization

If you feel that you have a good case and have not had any satisfactory solution to your grievance, it is possible to seek support outside of the organization. For example, in the UK there is an independent government body known as ACAS (the Advisory, Conciliation and Arbitration Service), which offers a mediation service for employers and employees. ACAS has specialists who can help you and your employer sort out a problem informally and hopefully avoid the need for more formal legal action. The contact details for ACAS can be found in the Appendix. If a problem cannot be resolved at this level, you can seek legal advice from specialist employment lawyers but this can be an expensive option. Before doing so check with your union representative since the union may be willing to fight the case on your behalf if they think you have a good one.

It may be possible to get a new manager who is more sympathetic, or to be redeployed to a new job in a different part of the organization where you do not have to continue to put up with difficult individuals or working practices. While this will remove the source of stress for you, it does not tackle the source of the problem in the work environment or remove the person causing the problem from the workplace. Also, you may feel that it is unfair that you have had to make changes for reasons that are not your fault. However, for the sake of your mental health this may be a preferable option.

If there is no opportunity for redeployment, as a last resort you may decide to vote with your feet and leave the job. You can still pursue legal action even after you have left a job if you can prove that your reasons for leaving amount to constructive dismissal. If you do decide to resign, make sure that your employers know the reasons for your leaving and put this in writing. While this may not help you immediately, it could help you when making a compensation claim later on. It may also provide valuable evidence to help others who experience similar treatment to you fight the case in the future if the situation persists. Also, make sure you take all the evidence with you when you leave, so that you can use it if you decide to seek compensation. A specialist employment lawyer will be able to advise you on whether you have a case to pursue and some even work on a no-win, no-fee basis.

Chapter 4

Living a healthy lifestyle

Introduction

Whereas the primary level interventions outlined in Chapter 3 directly addressed the working environment itself, secondary level interventions focus on teaching the individual a range of strategies to help them cope more effectively in a working environment that is by its nature inherently stressful. The remainder of Part II (Chapters 4 to 10) provides an outline of the most effective secondary level interventions that can be used to combat stress. These include 'living a healthy lifestyle' (the present chapter), 'developing effective time management skills' (Chapter 5), 'developing assertiveness skills' (Chapter 6), 'developing effective interpersonal skills' (Chapter 7), 'developing relaxation skills' (Chapter 8) and 'changing the way you relate to your work' (Chapter 9). The rest of this chapter focuses on the first of these, namely the importance of living a healthy lifestyle.

Living a healthy lifestyle

Living a healthy lifestyle means getting regular exercise, eating a healthy diet, restricting the use of medication and other drugs, such as alcohol and caffeine, stopping smoking, and getting enough rest and sleep. Recommendations are made in all these areas based upon the latest evidence of what constitutes a healthy lifestyle.

Regular exercise

Exercise not only keeps one physically fit, helps control weight, lowers blood pressure and is good for your heart but also is a great 'stress buster'. For those who have not done much exercise for a while, the starting point for becoming more active may simply mean walking to the shops rather than using the car, doing some gardening or household tasks that you may have been putting off for a while, or playing a gentle game of football with your children in the local park. It is very easy to talk yourself out of doing exercise by making excuses such as you are simply 'too busy', 'do not have the right equipment', 'can't afford it', or it's 'too hot', 'too cold' or 'it's raining'. Begin by being honest with yourself and acknowledge the excuses that you are making not to exercise. There are many activities that you can do which need not take much time, do not cost anything and do not require specialist equipment. Even if there are genuine obstacles, try to be creative in thinking of ways to free up some time to do exercise. You may be more likely to enjoy and sustain an exercise programme if you do it socially or competitively with friends. If you are not sure about what activities are available, try to find out through your local leisure centre, gym, library, newspaper or on the internet.

Any kind of exercise can carry with it certain dangers if you try to do too much too soon. So, it is important if you have not been doing much exercise for a while, that you build up gradually. A graded exercise programme should be followed, not doing too much too soon. If you have any physical health problems that you think could restrict the kind or level of activity that you can do, it is recommended that you seek the advice of your doctor before starting a planned programme of activity. Do not push yourself too much too soon. Set yourself targets that are achievable and build up gradually. For example, a target for someone who has done very little exercise for a long time may be simply to have a brisk short walk. Also you do not have to do all the exercise in one go. You could for example do 10 minutes of exercise in the morning and repeat it again in the afternoon. Also, take notice of what your body is telling you. You do want your heart rate and breathing to be faster than when you are inactive, but you do not want to reach the point where you are feeling so breathless that you are unable to talk, or are feeling physically unwell.

Some tips for doing more exercise

Start with modest targets and build up steadily. Ideally you want to build up to approximately 30 minutes of moderate intensity exercise every day. As stated earlier it can be difficult to find this time in a busy schedule, so think of ways in which you can build at least some of this exercise into your daily routine. For example, take the stairs rather than the lift, go for a walk during your lunch break, walk the children to school, walk to the local shops, play a physical game with your children, do the gardening, take the dog for a walk, or wash the car. Ideally, the exercise programme should be a combination of 80 per cent 'stamina' and 20 per cent 'flexibility' exercises. Ideal stamina exercises include activities such as jogging, rowing and cycling. The aim of flexibility exercise is to flex or rotate all the joints in the body. For example, swimming and yoga are good flexibility exercises. Many of these activities can be carried out indoors when the weather is bad, for example by using a running, rowing or cycling machine. If you cannot afford an exercise machine, you could buy a skipping rope. You can even watch your favourite television programme while doing such exercise! Even if you are unable to exercise daily, try to do about half an hour of exercise around three times a week. This will help you sleep better, feel more relaxed and have a better appetite. The important thing is that you try to stick to the programme. A word of caution, however: if at any time you experience chest pains or other kinds of physical distress, it is important that you stop immediately and get a check-up with your doctor before you continue.

Some employers encourage their employees to keep physically fit by offering them the opportunity to join a gymnasium at reduced corporate membership rates or offering such facilities within the workplace itself. If these benefits are available to you within your own workplace, ensure that you do make use of them. Some employers have cycle to work schemes which offer the opportunity to purchase a cycle at a reduced rate. This has the joint benefits of reducing the pressure on car parking places at work and also giving the employee the opportunity of becoming physically fitter.

A healthy diet

Sticking to a healthy and balanced diet helps avoid obesity, coronary heart disease, high blood pressure, bowel cancer and late onset diabetes. A healthy diet essentially involves moderation with most foods which, combined with exercise and other lifestyle changes, leads to better health. Most of us are aware that if we eat too many fatty foods, biscuits, sweets or cakes, we are likely to put on weight. It is a simple equation as can be seen in Figure 4.1. If the input of energy (calories) exceeds the amount of energy expended, the excess unused energy is stored in the body as fat.

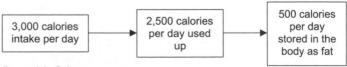

Figure 4.1 Calorie equation

Fat is stored in our bodies with considerable ease and yet requires lots of effort (physical exertion) to get rid of. The recommended calorie intake for an adult woman of average build is approximately 2,000 a day and for men it is approximately 2,500 calories a day. This is a rough estimate since daily calorie requirements can vary considerably depending on lifestyle and other factors such as age, height, weight, level of activity and body composition. In order to lose one pound in weight you need to have a negative calorie intake of 500 calories a day. Given that it can take up to an hour of quite vigorous exercise to burn off around 500 calories, it is preferable not to allow the excess calories to build up in the first place.

The traditional wisdom is that cutting down on fat, especially foods containing high cholesterol (no more than 70 grams a day), is a healthy way to lose weight. Fat in polyunsaturated form such as that found in vegetable and fish oils is thought to be healthier than saturated fats found in red meat, hard cheese and cream products, which contain high cholesterol. A maximum of 20 grams of saturated fat per day is recommended. A maximum of 90 grams of sugar and 6 grams of salt per day are also recommended. A diet rich in dietary fibre in the form of wholemeal bread, fibre-rich cereals, fruits and vegetables is also advised. High carbohydrate foods such as pasta, bread, potatoes and rice can help keep your energy levels up at times of stress, rather than foods containing refined sugars such as cakes, chocolate and biscuits, which may give you an initial burst of energy but it is short lived. If your diet is a healthy one it will usually give you all the daily vitamins that you need and so expensive dietary supplements are not necessary. Most supermarkets now provide helpful dietary advice on the food packaging, identifying the amount of calories, fat, sugar, carbohydrates and salt in the product, so take some time to look at this information before buying the food.

Some tips for eating more healthily

Do not go shopping when you are hungry, since you will be more likely to buy and fill up your cupboards with foods of a higher calorific content than when you are not hungry. Make sure that you have a proper high carbohydrate breakfast, since carbohydrates will give you the energy that you need to carry you through the morning until lunchtime and will stop you from snacking. Carbohydrates are found in breakfast cereals and are the ideal way to start the day. Make sure that you also stop for something to eat at lunchtime. It is healthier where possible to eat grilled, steamed or boiled rather than fried food and to prepare your own food freshly rather than buying pre-prepared meals that often contain a variety of additives such as salt, sugar and preservatives. However, when at work it is often not possible to prepare your own food, because of lack of facilities or lack of time. So, you may have to rely upon others to do this on your behalf. Many larger employers provide a staff canteen, in which employees can eat on a daily basis and should offer a range of healthy dietary options for employees to choose from. If healthy options are not available, this needs to be drawn to the attention of the employer, so that they have the opportunity of introducing them onto the menu. If you do not have a staff canteen offering healthy options, or buy sandwiches, it is important you make sure that what you are eating is healthy. For example, make sure that the food is not too fatty or dripping in mayonnaise. Fried foods such as fish and chips should not be included as a routine part of a daily diet and should be reserved for a special treat.

Some other tips include trying where possible to eat with other people rather than on your own, since evidence suggests that you are less likely to overeat in company than when you are alone. If you feel tempted to snack between meals, try to distract yourself by thinking about something which is not food related, or engage in an activity that is incompatible with gaining access to food or eating. If this proves particularly difficult, limit the amount of money that you bring with you to work, by bringing just enough for your lunch and a drink. If visiting the staff canteen with its wide array of options proves too much of a temptation to you, bring a packed lunch and go for a walk at lunchtime instead.

Monitoring food intake

If reducing your food intake is proving to be a bigger problem than you anticipated, you may need to do some more formal monitoring of your food intake using a food diary. This entails monitoring what you eat each day and when you eat it. Table 4.1 is an example taken from a food diary.

Keeping an accurate food diary entails recording everything you have eaten each day. This will allow you to identify your total intake and also the high risk times in terms of the time of day, situational triggers and mood states when you are most likely to overeat. Once you have identified these, you can plan a timetable of alternative activities at these high risk times which are incompatible with eating. For example, you might plan a social activity such as meeting friends, do some exercise or go and take a bath. Try to avoid periods of boredom or prolonged inactivity, since these are also high risk times for overeating. Also, avoid areas where stocks of food are kept and try to keep out of the kitchen between meals.

Table 4.1 A sample taken from a food diary

Date/time	Situation	Thoughts and feelings at the time	Food intake
Sunday 7pm	Sitting watching TV	Feeling bored and thinking of going back to work on Monday	Two slices of cheese on toast Bag of crisps
Sunday 9pm	Watching TV advertisement about food	Feeling worried about all the work I have to do the next day	Pork pie and brown sauce
Sunday 11pm	Getting ready for bed	Feeling sad and thinking about how I have wasted my weekend and eaten too much	Piece of cake Two chocolate biscuits Cup of hot chocolate

Restricting your food stocks at home by not buying lots of snack foods (such as biscuits, chocolate, crisps and sweets) will reduce the temptation to overeat, since the food will not be there to snack on. You can use a calorie conversion chart to help you monitor your food intake in terms of calories and weighing scales to monitor your weight on a regular basis. Another strategy is to plan your meals days ahead, so that you know what you will be eating and when, and try to stick to it.

Some bigger employers provide employees with access to dietary advice and support from a dietician through their occupational health service, so make sure that you use this facility if it is available and you feel that you require some more expert dietary advice. Similarly, you should be able to get advice from your family doctor if you feel that you are unable to tackle the problem on your own.

Fluids

The body is made up of 90 per cent water and one of the physical effects of stress is dehydration. Experts recommend that when under stress an individual should drink around four pints of suitable liquid every day, in addition to the liquid obtained from food and from milk on cereals and in beverages. Basically this equates to eight large glasses of water a day. The provision of conveniently located water dispensers in the workplace can help prevent this from happening. If these are not provided, you should ask for them to be made available. Otherwise, make sure that you bring in a water bottle that you can refill throughout the day to prevent yourself from becoming dehydrated.

Medication and other drugs

People under stress are more likely to take drugs to help them combat the stress. When we talk about drugs, most people think about prescription drugs such as tranquillizers. However, much more commonly used and often more damaging are the drugs which we self-prescribe, such as alcohol, nicotine and caffeine. While we tend to think of drug addicts as people hooked on heroine, we do not usually think of drinking excessive amounts of alcohol, tea, coffee and cola drinks as an addiction. Yet they are all addictive and can result in physical damage if we use them to excess. Ideally, one should try to do without drugs of any kind for stress related problems and instead try to tackle the root causes of the stress itself. However, in reality some prescribed medication may be helpful and necessary in alleviating symptoms in the short term.

Alcohol

Drinking alcohol is not all bad and there are lots of positive reasons why people drink. For example, it can be a refreshing, relaxing, social activity and they may enjoy the taste of it. People also drink to celebrate or 'loosen up' at a party. Alcohol is a good stress reducing drug, which when used in moderation can have beneficial physical and psychological effects. The recommended safe limits for alcohol intake for men is 21 units a week and no more than 4 units per day. For women it is 14 units a week and no more than 3 units a day. A unit is a standard (75 ml) glass of wine, a single pub measure of spirit or half a pint of an average strength beer, lager or cider. Super strength drinks of course have more units of alcohol in them. Also, it is important to remember that if you are drinking at home, you are more likely to be pouring yourself larger than pub measures.

Drinking more than the recommended safe limit of alcohol on a regular basis can result in potentially harmful physical, psychological and social consequences. Even if you are drinking within safe limits but drink all your weekly units in one go (i.e., binge drinking) it could still be causing you problems in terms of your physical and psychological wellbeing. It can also affect your relationships and behaviour both at work and in your personal life. It is estimated that about 25 per cent of men and 14 per cent of females drink more than the recommended safe limits and it is a growing problem among teenagers. However, many people who have a drink problem either deny it or attempt to minimize the impact that it is having on them. If you find that you are unable to relax, feel confident or mix socially without first having a drink, or use alcohol as a temporary escape from negative mood states, you are likely to be using alcohol as an inappropriate coping strategy. If you find yourself drinking to excess on a regular basis, have neglected your duties or responsibilities, suffered frequent hangovers, been unable to remember what happened the night before, or harmed someone either physically or emotionally after drinking, it is very likely that you have a drink problem. Family, friends or work colleagues may already have commented on this but you may have chosen to ignore what they have said. You may also be having more conflict and arguments with people, or having frequent low moods, which are having a damaging impact on your relationships.

If any of the above applies to you, or you simply feel that you may be drinking too much, this needs tackling. The first task is to establish how much you are actually drinking. You can do this by keeping a 'drinks diary', which involves recording the number of units of alcohol you are drinking every day. People are often surprised or even shocked at how much they actually do drink in a week. For example, an individual might say to themselves 'I only have one or two cans a night at home, so I certainly do not have a drink problem'. However, even drinking two cans of average strength lager each evening adds up to 28 units per week, which is above the safe recommended limit of alcohol intake for a man. If after doing some self-monitoring using a drinks diary you recognize that you need to reduce your alcohol intake, make some rules for yourself around limiting your intake. Below are some tips for controlling your intake of alcohol.

Some tips for reducing your alcohol intake

1   Stick to within the recommended number of units of alcohol per day or per week.
2   Start drinking alcohol later on in the day and never drink alcohol in the mornings.
3   Drink alcohol only when in company.
4   Have at least three or four alcohol free days a week.
5   Spread your alcohol intake out over the week and do not drink all your units in one go.
6   Go out later in the evening and come home earlier.
7   Do not go out for a drink straight from work.
8   Do not drink on an empty stomach. Go home, get changed and have a meal before going out.
9   Do not drink alcohol at lunchtimes. Apart from anything else this is not advisable if you have to go back to work in the afternoon.
10 Drink lower strength alcohol or non-alcoholic drinks.

11 Drink more slowly. Take sips rather than gulps and have a conversation between sips. Alternatively, get up and do something active such as dancing or a game of pool or darts.

12 Set yourself a limit on the number of drinks that you are going to have before you go out.

13 Do not take more money out with you than you need and leave the cash card at home. This will ensure that you do not buy more drinks than you intend to and are unable to get extra cash to go on to a late night drinking venue.

14 Eat with a drink since this slows down the rate of alcohol absorption into your bloodstream. This can be a meal or something less substantial such as a bag of crisps or peanuts.

15 Keep a very limited stock of alcohol in the house or none at all. This will reduce or eliminate the temptation to drink more alcohol when you get home after a night out.

16 If drinking at home, use bar measures rather than simply pouring it into a tumbler. This will also help you monitor your intake more accurately.

17 Do not give in to social pressure to drink more than you intend to. Learn to say 'No' to any coercion to drink more than you want to.

18 Miss a round or have a non-alcohol drink even if others are drinking alcohol.

19 Keep out of buying drinks in rounds. Buying in rounds tends to lead to everyone drinking at the rate of the fastest.

20 Go a different way home from work if you feel tempted to call in at the pub. By doing this you can avoid the temptation created by the sound of clinking glasses and the smell of alcohol as you walk past.

21 Identify the high risk times for drinking excess alcohol and engage in activities that are incompatible with having a drink such as offering to be the driver for the evening, exercising, or arranging to do something with your family instead of going to the pub.

22 Identify high risk mood states such as when feeling under stress, angry or depressed and find alternative ways of coping with these other than drinking, such as by seeing a counsellor.

23 If they do not already know, let people close to you know that you are having a problem with restricting your intake of alcohol and allow them to help you.

24 If necessary change your social circle to one that is not centred round drinking alcohol. This might sound a drastic step but may be necessary if you are unable to control your drinking any other way. It is more likely that your 'friends' are simply 'drinking partners' than true friends if the only thing that you do together is drink.

If you find that you cannot practise controlled drinking by using any of the strategies listed above, total abstinence may be the only alternative. After all, if you find yourself unable to say 'No' to the first drink, it is unlikely that you are going to have the will power to say 'No' to subsequent drinks. In conclusion, there are basically two rules to adopt when using alcohol. The first is to use it in strict moderation. The second is that you should stop using it altogether if you realize that you are unable to practise controlled drinking or you are becoming dependent on it. If you are unable to stick to these rules, you may require more help, in which case you should ask your doctor to refer you to an alcohol advisory service for additional help and support. See also the organizations listed in the Appendix.

Caffeine

Caffeine has benefits in that it helps you stay alert and concentrate when you are feeling tired. However, it is also a stimulant drug which affects your brain and central nervous system, and if taken late at night can have a negative impact on the amount and quality of sleep. It is found in tea, coffee, soft drinks (such as cola), chocolate, painkillers and high energy drinks. It is estimated as a rough guide that having more than 600 milligrams of caffeine a day may cause problems but people who are prone to anxiety can react to much smaller doses. The average can of a soft cola drink contains 36 milligrams of caffeine but a mug of tea can contain around 100 milligrams and fresh coffee 200 milligrams (depending on the size of the mug of course). Symptoms of caffeine overdose include restlessness, agitation, increased desire to go to the toilet, headache, stomach ache and increased heart rate and breathing. Some experts consider that there is a link between even mild coffee intake and heart disease. So, the message here is to make sure that your intake of caffeine is within the safe recommended limit of 600 milligrams per day. This amounts to three or four cups of coffee per day depending if it is fresh or instant coffee, or five cups of tea a day. Drink more water or pure fruit juices, avoid high energy drinks and limit the use of painkillers. There is a range of caffeine-free products on the market, which can help you manage your intake more effectively.

Nicotine

People who smoke tend to do so more when under stress and many people report that it does reduce their stress levels temporarily. However, the negative effects of smoking far outweigh the positive ones. The link between smoking, cancer and a range of other fatal diseases is well established. Even passive smoking is not considered safe. Rates of heart disease are higher even among non-smokers if they are exposed consistently to a smoky atmosphere. Smoking in public buildings is now illegal in a number of countries and this has gone some way to reducing the problem of passive smoking. It has also made it a little bit easier to give up the habit for those who wish to. Because smoking is addictive, people who try to stop often find it very difficult and suffer withdrawal symptoms. These include craving for nicotine, restlessness, irritability, sleep problems and a tendency to overeat. It can take considerable will power to stop and the individual has to really want to stop smoking. However, there are some tips that can help you stop.

Some tips for stopping smoking

1   Educate yourself about the longer-term dangers of continuing smoking and also what to expect in terms of withdrawal symptoms when you try to stop.
2   List the pros and cons of continuing to smoke, including the effects that it could have on your family and loved ones if you do not stop.
3   Reduce gradually. Start by monitoring how many cigarettes a day you smoke and then reduce by one or two per day. Expect the early stages to be difficult.
4   Set a date to stop smoking and plan a gradual reduction programme leading up to that date.
5   Take only the number of cigarettes that you intend to smoke out with you and plan the number you intend to smoke in advance.
6   Do not accept cigarettes from others. Inform them that you are trying to stop and ask them not to offer you one again. Also, do not give cigarettes to others since they are more likely to offer you one back if you do.
7   Have your first cigarette later in the day and do not light up as soon as you wake up in the morning. Gradually try to make the time when you light up your first cigarette later each day.
8   Identify the high risk times for smoking and try to plan activities which are incompatible with smoking.
9   Buy cigarettes with lower nicotine content.
10   Take fewer puffs on your cigarette and leave more of a stub.
11   Limit the amount of money that you take out with you, since if you do not have money on you, you cannot be tempted to buy more cigarettes.
12   Make use of nicotine patches, gum or inhalers to help you cope with the nicotine withdrawal symptoms.

13 Do not buy duty free cigarettes on holiday and do not keep stocks of them in the house.
14 Try to quit with someone else. It can be easier if you are doing this with someone.
15 Tell people you are stopping. They can encourage you and it will make you feel more motivated to stick to what you have said.
16 Do not give in to pressure to smoke by others. Learn to say 'No' to any coercion to smoke.
17 Keep a money jar in which to put all the money that you have saved from reducing or stopping smoking. This can amount to quite a substantial amount. Use the money to treat yourself for your successes by buying something that you have been wanting for a while. You could even use it to save for a long overdue holiday. At today's prices stopping smoking twenty cigarettes a day will save you thousands of pounds a year!

Sleep and rest

Sleep problems are very common and most of us have at some time or other experienced them to some degree. Have you ever gone to bed feeling very tired but as soon as the light goes out, your mind starts working overtime? Have you ever got off to sleep but woken after a few hours in the middle of the night, tossing and turning in your bed unable to get back to sleep? Have you ever woken up a few hours earlier in the morning and lay there clock watching, knowing that you have a busy day ahead of you and that you are going to feel exhausted all day? If your answer to any of the above questions is 'Yes', it is likely that you have suffered from one of the three types of sleep disturbance known respectively as initial, middle and late insomnia. Sometimes, even if you have slept right through, you may still feel as if you have not had a proper night's sleep and lack energy through the day.

Stress is a major cause of insomnia. When under stress the individual may feel better when they are busy and distracted but when they go to bed a whole host of worries crowds in on them. Sleep problems are also commonly found in depression, low mood and bereavement reactions. Poor bedtime routine such as eating or drinking a lot just before you go to bed, or not giving yourself enough time to wind down from work, can cause sleep problems. Age is another factor in that as you get older you require less sleep but may still be trying to get a similar number of hours as you needed when you were younger. Often linked to age is the need to go to the toilet during the night and this can disrupt one's sleep pattern. However, this can also happen during pregnancy or if you drink too much fluid just before going to bed. Environmental factors such as noise, too much light, unfamiliar surroundings, physical discomfort, excessive heat or cold can be causal factors, as can the discomfort caused by a bed that is too hard or soft, physical pain and illness, or the effects of medication. Shift work can also seriously affect your sleep pattern, especially if the shift patterns change frequently and can prevent you from getting into a good sleep routine.

There is a common misconception that we need a minimum of eight hours sleep per night and if we do not get it, we will become ill. It is true that many people aim to have this much sleep and are in the habit of getting their eight hours a night. However, this is not the same as needing this much sleep. People differ in how much sleep they require and this can range from four to ten hours a night depending on the individual. Thus, the amount of sleep required is very much an individual thing and some people simply do not need as much sleep as others. On average, newborn babies sleep up to seventeen hours a day, children about eleven hours, teenagers and young adults about eight or nine hours per day. The average requirement for adults is six to eight hours per night and older people tend to need less sleep. The need for sleep also varies depending on how much physical activity a person does. For example, if a person is retired and physically not very active, they may need less sleep. However, if they are in a very physically demanding job and running around trying to bring up a young family at the same time, they may require a lot more sleep. People often worry that if they do not get enough sleep, they will become seriously ill. However, research has shown that even with quite severe sleep deprivation, the individual is unlikely to experience severe physical or mental symptoms. It can make the individual feel mildly depressed, but this lifts once the individual catches up with the lost sleep. However, it can also make you feel more irritable, less vigilant and can lead to making more mistakes, and poorer concentration and memory. It also feels unpleasant, can impact on your ability to do your work effectively and can lead to accidents. Thus, sleep deprivation needs to be taken very seriously.

There are five different levels of sleep, ranging from the lightest level (stage one), to deep sleep (level four) and 'rapid eye movement' (REM) sleep at level five. REM sleep is the level at which most of our dreaming occurs. There are various views about what the function of dream sleep is. One view is that it serves to process and organize all the information that we have taken in throughout the day, while others believe that it has something to do with unconscious processing of drives and motivations and can be interpreted (Freudian theories), and others that it has no meaning at all. Whatever the reason, the body goes through the sleep cycle from level one to five and back again about five times each night. As with the amount of sleep we require, the sort of sleep we require also varies with age. Older people tend to spend less time in REM sleep and wake more during the night but do not seem to suffer any ill effects.

The first step to overcoming a sleep problem is to identify what the causes are. You need to establish whether or not the sleep problem is the primary or secondary problem. For example, if the sleep problem is a secondary consequence of another problem such as stress at work, the primary problem (i.e., work related stress) may need to be tackled before the sleep problem can be resolved. Similarly, if there are medical causes, you will need to seek the appropriate medical treatment such as pain relief medication to help you overcome the associated sleep problem. You may need to seek help from a counsellor or psychologist to help you through problems of depression, bereavement or relationship difficulties in order for your sleep pattern to return to normal. However, where sleep is the primary problem there are a number of helpful tips that you can make use of to get your sleep pattern back to normal. These are listed below.

Some tips to help you sleep better

1   Doing some physical exercise during the day will help you sleep better.
2   Start winding down at least an hour before you go to bed. Put your work away and do something relaxing, which will slow you down both mentally and physically. This might be reading a book or listening to some relaxing music.
3   Do not eat too much for two hours before going to bed. As soon as you eat your body starts to work on digesting the food and this can make it difficult to get off to sleep. A very light snack is all right before bed but do not eat during the night if you wake up.
4   Do not drink too much during the evening since this will make you want to get up during the night to go to toilet. Also, go to the toilet just before you get into bed. This will make it less likely that you will want to get up in the night.
5   Do not use alcohol to help you sleep. While it may help you get off to sleep, it creates an 'arousal spring' as the effects of the alcohol wear off during the night, leading to you waking up. It can make you want to go to the toilet during the night. It can affect the quality of sleep that you have by reducing the amount of REM and deep sleep that you have.

6 Limit your intake of caffeine. It is a stimulant and is likely to keep you awake. Try to cut out drinks containing caffeine from the early evening onwards. Have a warm milky drink which does not have caffeine instead.

7 Do not smoke for at least a few hours before you go to bed. Nicotine, like caffeine, is a stimulant and will keep you awake.

8 Try not to use medication to help you sleep unless it is absolutely necessary. It is not a long-term solution, can change the quality of sleep that you experience and can lead to you becoming dependent on the drugs prescribed. Also, if you are on medication for other conditions, check that the sleep problems that you are experiencing are not a side effect of the medication.

9 Do not work in the same place that you sleep. Keep them separate. You will then learn to associate the bedroom with relaxation and rest, rather than work.

10 Try to develop a bedtime routine. This will help train your body to know when it is time for sleep. This may include washing or having a relaxing bath, cleaning your teeth, getting your pyjamas on, setting the alarm clock, checking the place is locked up and switching off all the lights. All of these things will inform your body it is time for sleep. Go to bed at a regular time but do not go to bed until you feel sleepy.

11 Make sure that your bedroom is well aired. Fresh air will help you sleep better.

12 Make sure the bedroom is not too hot or too cold. A temperature of about 18 degrees Celsius (64 °F) is the ideal.

13 Check that your mattress is comfortable, well sprung and not too old, hard or soft. If necessary replace it.

14 Make sure that your sheets and pillows are clean and comfortable.

15 Essential oils such as lavender or rosemary on your pillow may help you relax and get off to sleep.

16 Ensure that your bedroom is dark. If necessary get curtain liners or wear an eye mask.

17 Make sure that there is not too much noise. If necessary ask those creating the noise to turn it down. Alternatively, use ear plugs or a radio or iPod with earphones to mask other noise until you get to sleep.

18 If you are worrying about things, set aside some worry time well before you go to bed. If necessary, get a pen and paper and write a 'to do' list and then put it aside until the morning. Remind yourself that there is nothing you can do about it now and give yourself permission to relax.

19 Try not to go to bed on an unresolved argument. Try to make it up before you go to the bedroom if possible.
20 If you are unable to get to sleep, do not just lie there. Get up after 20 minutes or so and go out of the bedroom and do something relaxing until you start to feel sleepy. Return to the bedroom only when you feel sleepy.
21 Never 'clock watch'. It will only make you feel worse. Turn the clock round so you cannot see the time.
22 Comfort yourself in bed. Use a hot water bottle, cushion or bed socks.
23 Do not lie in. Get up at your normal time in the morning even if you are feeling very tired. It is better to struggle through the day tired and then catch up with your sleep the next night. This will ensure that your sleep cycle does not become disrupted.
24 Do not catnap during the day or evening as this will have a negative impact on your sleep pattern at night.
25 Try not to worry about not getting enough sleep. Tell yourself that 'at least I am resting'. Remind yourself that you may be one of those people who does not need so much sleep and that you may be trying to have more than you need.
26 If necessary, use relaxation, breathing and imagery exercises to help you get in the right state for sleep. These are covered in Chapter 8.

Summary

This chapter emphasized the importance of living a healthy lifestyle. This includes getting regular exercise, eating a healthy diet, ensuring a moderate use of alcohol and other drugs such as caffeine, stopping smoking, restricting the use of prescribed medication as far as possible and getting enough rest and sleep. These recommendations are based upon the latest evidence of what constitutes a healthy lifestyle. Health promotion programmes run by many workplace organizations and health care organizations aim to educate individuals about the importance and benefits of adopting a healthy lifestyle. This is particularly important when one is working in a stressful occupation. Many larger workplace organizations now offer a range of staff benefits. Examples of these include reduced cost gym membership, stress management advice and workshops, life coaching, access to dietary advice, healthy options at the staff canteen, educational campaigns aimed at offering advice to employees about safe limits for consumption of alcohol and smoking cessation clinics. Are you aware of the range of staff benefits on offer in the organization in which you work? If not then you are encouraged to find out what they are and to make use of them where possible.

An exercise

Some of the main learning points with respect to lifestyle habits covered in this chapter are summarized in Table 4.2. Please read through the checklist and circle a 'Yes' response for those which you feel you are already achieving and a 'No' response for those which you identify that

Table 4.2 Checklist of lifestyle habits

Exercise		
Are you doing at least 30 minutes of exercise two or three times a week?	Yes	No
Do you follow the recommended combination of 80 per cent stamina and 20 per cent flexibility exercises?	Yes	No
Diet		
Is your daily intake of calories within the recommended limit of 2,000 for a female or 2,500 for a male?	Yes	No
Is your daily intake of fat within the recommended maximum of 70 milligrams per day?	Yes	No
Is your daily intake of saturated fats within the recommended maximum of 20 milligrams per day?	Yes	No
Is your daily intake of sugar within the maximum recommended daily limit of 90 milligrams?	Yes	No
Is your daily intake of salt within the maximum recommended daily limit of 6 milligrams?	Yes	No
Do you have enough fibre in your diet?	Yes	No
Do you always have breakfast?	Yes	No
Do you choose healthy options for lunch?	Yes	No
Do you drink 2 litres (8 glasses) of water a day?	Yes	No
Drug use		
If you drink alcohol are you sticking to within the recommended safe weekly number of units of 21 for men or 14 for women?	Yes	No
Are you sticking to within the recommended safe daily number of 4 units of alcohol?	Yes	No
Are you sticking to within the recommended maximum of 600 milligrams of caffeine a day?	Yes	No
Have you stopped smoking? (No safe limit)	Yes	No
Sleep		
Are you getting a sufficient amount of sleep? (around 6 to 8 hours for the average adult)	Yes	No
Are you getting enough good quality sleep?	Yes	No

Note: This table is available to view and print from the following website: www.routledge mentalhealth.com/9780415671781 you need to do more work on. This will allow you to identify those unhealthy habits that you need to change.

Developing your own 'Healthy Lifestyle Plan'

If you have answered 'Yes' to every question in Table 4.2, either you are already living a very healthy lifestyle or you are not being honest to yourself. However, for most of us there are likely to be at least a few questions to which we have answered 'No'. Where you have answered 'No' to a question, this indicates that there is some work that needs to be done in that area if you are going to be able to claim that you are living a healthy lifestyle. The first step therefore is to make a list of the changes that you need to make in order to achieve this and these will form your goals. Once you have identified the goals, go back to the appropriate sections in this chapter and identify the interventions that you need to implement. The next step is to start implementing the interventions that you have identified in the plan. Set yourself a timescale for achieving each of your goals and review your progress towards achieving them on a regular basis. If you are determined, focused and disciplined enough you will be successful.

Chapter 5

Developing effective time management skills

Introduction

Time is a precious, limited and non-renewable resource. It passes quickly, so it is important that we make the most of every moment given to us. If we use our time wisely, it can have long-term benefits on psychological wellbeing later on in life. Knowing that we have made the best of our time and not wasted it leads to greater self-acceptance, fulfilment and feelings of achievement in later life. On the contrary, if we have wasted time, it can result in feelings of dissatisfaction, a longing to turn back the clock and a desire to live our time again. However, making the most of our time is not just about being busy. It is possible to be extremely busy without being very productive at all. The key to achieving is being selective about the tasks that we take on rather than simply being busy in an unfocused way. Two case studies in this chapter aim to illustrate the differences between being busy and being productive. The first case study is of John, who works as a middle manager for a firm of accountants. He prides himself on working hard under pressure but often feels that there are simply not enough hours in the day to do his job and frequently feels angry and resentful about the demands being placed on him. The second case study is of Peter, who has a very similar job to John but rarely reports feeling stressed. The case studies describe a typical day in the life of each person.

Case study: John

John wakes up late for work having forgotten to set his alarm clock the night before. He attributes this to the fact that he was working late on a report due in today so he did not get to bed until the early hours of the morning. He is unable to find a clean and ironed shirt, so puts yesterday's one on. He has just enough time to 'splash his face' and grab a slice of toast on his way out of the door before getting into his car. On his way to work John notices that the car fuel gauge is on empty and has to take a detour to the nearest petrol station. In doing so he gets stuck in a queue of traffic and ends up being even later getting into work. John has to present the report that he was working on last night to the board meeting at 10am but it is not yet completed. So, he decides to use the hour before the meeting to complete it. However, as soon as he starts to work on it, a member of his staff knocks on his door wanting some advice on an issue. John prides himself on always being accessible to his staff and so spends the next 20 minutes helping him. As soon as he has completed giving the advice, the telephone rings and it is one of John's clients, wanting to discuss a contract with him. This leaves John with no time to prepare and he has to rush to the board meeting without having completed the report. He just about manages to muddle his way through the presentation but realizes that he is going to have to miss his lunch break in order to get the report finished and on his boss's desk by the deadline. During his lunchtime John's boss calls in to his office to enquire how he is progressing with the project he had agreed to do for him two weeks ago. John cannot recall having agreed do this but manages to bluff his way through the conversation by making out that it was almost completed. His boss appears happy with his response because it means that he can give him a further project to work on. John feels unable to say 'No' to the extra work partly because he finds it difficult to say 'No' to people and also partly because he has made out to his boss that the first project is completed. When his boss leaves it begins to dawn on John that he is going to have to work on the project that evening in order to catch up. This means that he is going to have to miss his son's school open evening and the trip to the theatre that he had promised his wife. He feels anxious about telling his wife he is unable to go to the theatre, guilty that he is missing yet another of his son's school open evenings and angry that he is going to have to work yet another evening.

Case study: Peter

Peter wakes up to the sound of his alarm clock at 7am feeling well rested having had a good night's sleep. He takes a refreshing shower and puts on the clean clothes that he had laid out the night before. He watches the morning news and chats with his family while having breakfast. He then takes the packed lunch that he had prepared the night before out of the refrigerator. Peter has prepared a packed lunch because he realizes that he is going to be very busy today and may not have time to go out and get lunch. He sets off for work at 8am promptly in order to avoid the worst of the rush hour traffic and unlike John has an almost full tank of petrol because he always checks the fuel gauge the night before. He makes good time and arrives for work 20 minutes early. Peter also has a report to present at a board meeting that morning but because he has prepared it well in advance, he decides to use the extra 20 minutes he has to rehearse what he is going to say at the meeting and to clarify in his own mind what he wants to get out of it. He now has an hour before the board meeting so decides to check his emails and mail. He redirects his telephone, switches off his mobile and asks the secretary to take any calls. He keeps his replies to emails brief and to the point and wherever possible uses ready made templates for his letters. Once he has completed this task, Peter gets a knock on the door from one of his staff who wants some advice. Peter is sure that his colleague Mike is the best person to give this advice and so redirects the member of staff to Mike. He has half an hour before the board meeting and decides to use this time to catch up with a number of telephone calls that he has saved up. He goes to his office and puts the 'Do not disturb' sign on the door and deals with them all in one go. While being sociable, he also keeps his conversations short and deals with the issues presented in a focused way. He then goes to the board meeting and presents his paper, which seems to go down well with the boss. Once he has presented it, however, he realizes that the rest of the agenda is not relevant to him and excuses himself from the meeting at 10.30am. This frees up some extra time before lunch for him to catch up with his in-tray. Since it is a warm and sunny day Peter decides to go to the local park to eat his packed lunch. He comes back from lunch feeling refreshed and ready for the afternoon's onslaught. Peter has pencilled in some time that afternoon to work on a project that his boss had set for him but on arrival back at the office at 1pm, he finds that another unexpected meeting has come up. Since the meeting is not a particularly high level one, he decides to delegate attending it to a junior colleague. This frees him up to focus on the project he has been asked to do. That afternoon he gets a telephone call from his boss, who is looking for someone to attend a meeting on his behalf. Peter explains that while he could go to the meeting, he already has a project that his boss has set him to complete and will not be able to meet the deadline if he has to go. His boss tells him to keep working on the project because it is more important and he will find someone else to go to the meeting. Peter spends the rest of the afternoon working on the project and manages to complete it. He leaves work at 5pm and arrives home at 5.30pm. At home he has tea and spends the evening with his family. Before going to bed at a reasonable time, he gets all his things ready for the next day and sets his alarm clock.

What can we learn from the case studies of John and Peter?

The case studies of John and Peter illustrate how two people working in very similar jobs can manage their time very differently. John is constantly running around trying to catch up with himself, believing that it is his job that is causing him to feel under stress. Peter, however, despite having a very similar job, appears to lead a relatively relaxed and well-organized existence which allows him time to balance both work and home responsibilities to good effect. Which one is most like you? Also, can you identify in terms of time management, what it is that Peter is doing successfully that John is not doing? Let's explore this in a bit more detail.

Perhaps one of the most noticeable differences between John and Peter is that Peter appears to think and plan ahead. He puts his clean and ironed clothes out the night before and prepares a packed lunch for the next day, so that he can be sure that he does not miss lunch if things are busy at work. He ensures that he has filled his car up with fuel and has prepared his work for the next day in advance. He has a well-organized routine in which he gets up for work at 7am, leaves for work at 8am to avoid the rush hour, gets home on time and goes to bed at a reasonable hour. As a result of thinking and planning well ahead and being well organized, Peter is able to use the time he has available to the best effect and ensures that the demands of his work do not encroach upon his personal life. By contrast, John has done very little if any planning ahead and he leads a comparatively chaotic lifestyle. As a consequence of being so disorganized, he allows the demands of his job to frequently spill over into his personal time and experiences higher stress levels than Peter.

Peter also makes the best use of his time by prioritizing well and staying focused on the task in hand. At work he identifies the priority tasks that he needs to do and does not allow himself to be sidetracked. He uses a range of simple but effective practical techniques to stop himself from being distracted. These include redirecting his phone, switching off his mobile, asking a secretary to take his calls and putting up a 'Do not disturb' sign on his office door. Many hours can be wasted sitting in meetings that may be of little or no practical value to one's immediate job. However, Peter is also good at managing the amount of time he spends sitting in meetings and excusing himself from those which are not the best use of his time. On the contrary, John appears to struggle with prioritizing and is easily distracted by low priority tasks when he should be addressing the more important and urgent ones. He also struggles to assert himself with his boss at work, whereas Peter has no problems in this respect. Peter also appears to be more accomplished at the art of delegation as illustrated by his ability to delegate the attendance at a meeting to one of his junior colleagues and also redirect a member of his staff to one of his colleagues for advice. John is either unable or unwilling to delegate tasks in the same way.

Of course it could be argued that some of the differences between John and Peter are not just a consequence of how effectively they manage their time but are a result of having quite different personalities. Peter may by nature be more easygoing and well organized than John. However, even if John's more chaotic and disorganized behaviour is a result of his personality, this is not a reason to do nothing about it. In fact it could be argued that people with personalities like John have a greater need to learn some effective time management strategies than those who do not. Also, some causes of time being wasted are organizational in origin and as such are beyond the control of the individual. These may, for example, be due to inadequate workforce supervision, poor management planning, poor communication, lack of the right resources and equipment, IT problems, low staff morale and a mismatch of skills to the tasks being given. However, there is nothing to suggest that organizational factors contributed to the different experiences and ultimately the different stress levels experienced by John and Peter.

In conclusion, learning effective time management skills allows the individual to create more time and use it more efficiently. As illustrated by the case studies of John and Peter, these skills include being able to prioritize between urgent, important and routine tasks, planning ahead, being organized, staying focused and being able to delegate effectively. Research has shown that developing effective time management skills in the work setting has a number of benefits not only for the individual employee but also for the organization. These include greater efficiency and effectiveness at work, higher productivity, enhanced job satisfaction, reduced stress, increased leisure time and more room for forward planning. The rest of this chapter focuses on some of the main strategies that you can learn to help you manage your time more effectively.

Developing effective time management skills

Plan ahead

One of the keys to successful time management is planning your goals ahead and then ring-fencing the required amount of time to achieve them. Some people report that spending time planning simply creates an additional pressure on their already precious time and that they are simply too busy to do this. However, it is estimated that 1 per cent of working time spent planning produces an average saving of one hour a day. This sounds like a pretty good return on your time. However, time spent planning does conform to the law of diminishing returns and it is possible to waste time by 'overplanning'. The world is not entirely predictable and it is estimated that you can accurately plan only about 40 per cent of your time. So your plans need some flexibility built in to them in order to accommodate the unexpected. The level of planning required at work depends upon the time frame that you are working to. There will be certain goals which require long-term planning such as identifying the strategic objectives of a business over the next five years. Some may focus on the next financial year and others may be much more short term, focusing on the week or month ahead. The level of planning that you get involved in will depend on your role in the organization. There are a number of interventions that can help you plan ahead more effectively both in the longer and the short term.

Be clear about what your goals are

The first step in goal planning is to identify what your priorities over a period of time actually are. In the work setting these should consist of a combination of your own personal goals and the corporate goals of your employer. Many employers carry out annual 'personal development reviews' with their employees and these can be very helpful in terms of identifying their work related goals over an extended time period, usually over a year. Once you have identified and agreed these goals with your employer, you should experience a clearer sense of direction and purpose in your job. It will also allow you to plan ahead in order to achieve the identified goals. These longer-term goals can then be broken down into more manageable chunks or shorter-term objectives on the way to achieving the longer-term goals. You can then set a time frame for achieving each of these objectives and review your progress towards achieving them on a regular basis. If your own workplace does not already operate a personal development review system, it would be well worth asking your employer to introduce one.

Manage your diary effectively

It may sound obvious but the use of a diary can be invaluable in the task of planning ahead because it allows you to do so much more than record appointments. It allows you to get an overall impression of the demands being placed upon you both on a daily basis and also over the longer term. It can help you identify busy periods, prioritize, delegate, reschedule, identify deadlines, avoid appointment clashes, spread out stressful and less stressful tasks, balance your workload, avoid back-to-back meetings, build in travel time, start and finish on time, build in some prime time and also time to deal with the unexpected. Also, using a page a day diary will allow you to plan a visual representation of each day in some detail and thus reduce any inefficient management of your time.

Create some 'prime time' for yourself

It is easy if you are not careful to end up fragmenting your timetable with meetings and low priority tasks that squeeze out any time for achieving your longer-term goals. To avoid this happening ring-fence some blocks of time, for example a couple of hours a few times a week, which you can dedicate to working on your longer-term objectives. Resist the temptation to cancel your prime time unless you are absolutely forced to. Make sure that you use the time you have allocated to best effect by having a clear plan of what you want to do and minimizing distractions.

Prepare for meetings

A successful meeting is time and money well spent but a poor meeting is a waste of time and money. A lot of time can be wasted at meetings by people being inadequately prepared for them and not having a clear idea about exactly what it is they want to get from the meeting. It is estimated that as much as three-quarters of a manager's time can be spent in meetings but it is uncertain how much of this is wasted time. Even if a meeting is relevant, much time can still be lost through people arriving for it late, allowing meetings to run over, getting sidetracked, poorly chaired meetings and not prioritizing the agenda properly. Make sure that you are not one of these people by ensuring that you do adequately prepare for meetings, are clear about the purpose of the meeting, who is going to be attending and what you want to get from it in advance. Read over the minutes of the previous meeting and the agenda for the next one and make notes about the key points you wish to address. Plan what you are going to say and how you are going to say it in the most succinct way. Give yourself sufficient time to get to the meeting on time and from the meeting to your next appointment. Excuse yourself from meetings or parts of meetings where your attendance is not required. Make use of teleconference facilities if your organization has them. They can save you a lot of travel time and are often more businesslike than face-to-face meetings. Do not be a slave to attending meetings which you perceive to be of questionable value to you simply because they have been handed down to you. Ask yourself whether it is a good use of your time.

Choose the best time to tackle difficult tasks

It is a well-known fact that people differ in terms of the time of day at which they function most effectively. Some people describe themselves as a morning person, whereas others describe themselves as an afternoon or an evening person. These variations are the result of what are known in the scientific world as circadian rhythms. There are certain times of the day when each of us is at our best physically and psychologically and this can differ from individual to individual. If we are aware of them, we can plan ahead and fit our schedule around them by taking on more difficult tasks when we are at our best and save other tasks for the times when we are not.

Overcome procrastination

Procrastination is illustrated in the following case study.

Case study: Jenny

Jenny hated doing the job of ironing clothes. She knew that it had to be done but she found it boring and there were so many other things in life that were much more enjoyable and interesting. Her typical response when faced with a pile of clothes to iron was 'I'll do it later' and usually she did catch up with it at some point later on. However, when Jenny got married and started a family, not only did she have less time but also she had more clothes to iron. Her partner worked long hours and there was no one else to help her, so she continued to put the task of ironing off until 'later'. The pile of ironing began to accumulate, so she put it out of sight in the utility room. When the utility room was full, she began to hide it in the airing cupboard. Her family started to wonder where all their clothes had gone. Eventually it all became overwhelming for Jenny and she did not know where or how to begin tackling the massive pile of ironing.

What can we learn from the case study of Jenny?

The case of Jenny illustrates the behaviour of procrastination. It is putting things off until later what we could or should be doing right now. In order to break the pattern of procrastination, you must first be able to recognize when you are doing it. This is not always as easy as one might think because there are numerous subtle avoidance behaviours that people can use. In the work setting, for example, they may focus on non-essential and unimportant tasks on their 'to do' list, rather than those which really need dealing with. They may sit down to start a high priority task but then decide to have a quick cup of coffee, check their emails, or sort out a filing cabinet before getting started. Alternatively, they may decide to go for a wander around the office and end up engaged in conversation with someone. So, be honest to yourself and admit it when you are doing this, and then ask yourself why.

Feeling overwhelmed by a task is probably the most common cause of procrastination but there are other reasons why people display this behaviour. Sometimes they are perfectionists and will not begin a task until they are certain that they have the time, all the right equipment or full information to be able to complete the whole task in one go, to the high standards dictated by their perfectionism. Others may have a fear of failure and procrastination is a 'failure avoidance' strategy, in that if they do not start the task they cannot fail at it. Others may actually lack the organizational or decision making skills to manage the task, or simply dislike doing it. However, while it may be helpful to understand why a person might be putting a task off, the most important thing is to identify and break this maladaptive pattern of behaviour and replace it with a healthier one. Whatever the reason, if you are unable to delegate the task to anyone else, you need to find a way of motivating yourself to tackle the task. The following interventions are a few ways of doing this.

1   If a big task seems overwhelming, it can be broken down into several smaller more manageable chunks and each one tackled in turn.
2   Build in a reward to motivate yourself, such as giving yourself a treat when you have completed a piece of work. This could, for example, be giving yourself a treat at lunchtime if you have been successful. This will give you something to look forward to.
3   Ask one of your peers to check up on you intermittently and encourage you to continue to complete the task.
4   Identify the negative consequences of not completing the task. This may be particularly relevant in the work setting where you are expected to complete tasks as a matter of routine.
5   If at all possible 'do it now' rather than putting it off. Set yourself a start time rather than focusing on the completion time.
6   If you cannot do it immediately, operate a 'bring forward' system in your diary to ensure that you pick it up again at a later time and complete it by the deadline.
7   Challenge unhelpful attitudes leading to procrastination such as perfectionism and failure avoidance. Experiment with being average rather than always trying to be perfect and learn to accept that everyone makes mistakes from time to time.
8   If you identify that you lack organizational or decision making skills, explore the opportunities for pursuing a training course to learn these skills.

In the case study of Jenny, she was encouraged to break the task of catching up with the backlog of ironing into manageable chunks. She allocated half an hour each day to doing ironing and over a period of a few weeks was able to catch up with it. She did not criticize herself and gave herself a small treat each day after she had successfully completed the task. Although this was a domestic non-work related task, the same principles can equally be applied to the workplace.

Learn to delegate

Delegation is one of the most important time management skills we have at our disposal. It is not just a matter of telling someone else what to do or passing something that you do not want to do on to a colleague. If handled effectively, not only can it have benefits for the individual who does the delegation in terms of freeing up their time but also it can create a valuable personal development experience for the individual to whom a task has been delegated. There are a number of tips for delegating successfully. First, the task identified must be suitable for delegation. Second, the individual to whom the task is being delegated needs to be capable of doing it and clearly understand what needs to be done. Third, the required outcomes need to be measurable and achievable within a given timescale. Finally, the individual doing the delegated task may need some supervision and support, particularly if it is new to them. They may worry that if they delegate a task, it may not be done correctly, or they do not like the feeling of not being directly in control, they fear that they may get the blame if things go wrong, or that others may think that they are being lazy. It can take time to overcome these concerns and train the person, but the ultimate pay-off at a later date means that it is a good investment of your time. The acronym 'SMART' is a useful one to remember in the context of delegating.

S = Specific
M = Measurable
A = Achievable
R = Relevant
T = Time bound

There are other reasons why some people find it difficult to delegate. For example, they may lack the confidence to ask another person, they may feel anxious about the reaction that they might get if they do ask, they may feel unable to trust others enough to delegate or they may simply be unaware that they have the authority to do this. If you are one of these people, you need to identify the reasons why this might be and attempt to overcome these obstacles. It is also important to remember that if you do manage people, it is highly likely that the authority to delegate to others is already invested in your managerial role and job description. If you are unsure about this, have a look in your job description. The important thing is practice. Even if you feel uncomfortable about delegating initially, the more you practise this technique, the more skilled and confident you will become at doing it. Remember that the way in which you ask the other person is an important factor in determining the success of this technique. Ask in a polite but authoritative way which communicates an air of confidence, even if inside you are not feeling this way. It may feel at first as if you are acting, but after some practice it will begin to feel more natural. It is also helpful to remember that although it is mostly managers who delegate, you do not have to be a manager to do this. However, you do need to be able to ask politely.

Stay focused

In time management terms, success is about selecting the minimum number of tasks required to produce a desired outcome with the least possible effort. It is about learning to identify and focus on 'high pay-off' behaviours rather than those which waste our time. There is a principle used in decision making known as the Pareto Principle, which states that it is possible by doing only 20 per cent of the work to generate 80 per cent of the advantage of doing the entire job. The reasoning behind this '80:20' rule is that a large majority of problems are caused by relatively few key causes. The economy of effort reported can thus be achieved by identifying and focusing on the key causes, resulting in the maximum overall effect. This sounds like a very attractive proposition, which could have significant implications in terms of time management. It suggests that it is possible to select a small subset of core tasks related to any given job that will produce the maximum overall effect with comparatively little effort or time expenditure. Thus, simply being 'busy' is not the same as managing our time effectively. It is particularly important to acknowledge this in the work context, in terms of achieving organizational objectives of effectiveness and efficiency.

It is also a curious observation that the time taken to do a task tends to expand to fill the time available for its completion. That is, the more time we have at our disposal, the more time we tend to take. Retired people often say that they do not know how they ever managed to find the time to go to work because they are so busy in retirement. If, for example, you have a whole morning available to do the weekly shopping, it is likely that you will spend that time doing the task, but if you work full time, it is quite possible that you will get through the same shopping list in half the time. So how do people with little free time achieve this economy of time? They do it by being focused on the task in hand. For example, they might go straight to the shopping aisles required, do not stop to browse, do everything at a faster pace and avoid stopping for to chat on the way. Even though it may be enjoyable, social chatter can be a massive time waster. Similarly in the work setting, limiting social chatter in the corridor can free up a considerable block of time throughout a week. Coffee and lunch breaks can inadvertently extend considerably due to social chit chat in the staff room or canteen and while this can seem like fun at the time, it ends up making the individual feel rushed once they get back to work. It is important to make sure that you take only your allocated allowance of time for breaks if you do not want to get behind in your work. Also at work, face-to-face and telephone conversations should be polite but whenever possible kept brief. Manage interruptions by making use of a secretary to take calls (if available) or the use of an answer phone. This will help you stay focused and reduce the distractions created by all the other demands impinging on you in the workplace. If you are unable to stop interruptions when you need quiet time and space for planned concentration time slots, find somewhere else in the building to work and if necessary work from home or another site.

Prioritize tasks

Prioritizing is about identifying what is important to you. In the work setting it refers not only to what is important to you personally but also to your employer. A common technique used to categorize tasks in order of importance is called 'ABCD analysis'. Tasks are categorized into groups on the following criteria:

A = Urgent and important tasks
B = Important but not urgent tasks
C = Urgent but not important tasks
D = Neither urgent nor important tasks

Start off by making a 'to do' list of all the tasks that you have to do and then categorize each task into one of the groups A, B, C or D, according to how urgent and important it is. Once the tasks have been grouped the order of priority within each group can be further refined by ranking the tasks in each of the groups. This is done by giving each task a score from 1 to 10 (1 = urgent/important; 10 = not urgent/important at all). These are then ranked into a hierarchy and the top priority items (i.e., the A1 tasks) can be tackled first and the others lower down the hierarchy (i.e., A2, A3 … A10) tackled later on. Once the A category tasks have been done, you can move on to the B category and C category tasks. D category tasks are those which are neither urgent nor important and unless you have the luxury of some free time to do them, they can be dropped. Do not be a slave to tradition. Challenge anything that you think could be wasting your time and do not simply do it just because it has always been done that way. It is also important to remind yourself that other people's priorities are often not the same as your own. They may flag tasks up as being urgent and requiring immediate action in terms of their priorities but these tasks may be quite low on your own list. Where this is the case you may need to negotiate a mutually acceptable compromise. Also, some people are simply impatient and want something done immediately when next week will really do. Recondition the expectations that other people may have about your time and availability. Give them the message that your time is precious also. The grid shown in Table 5.1 may be helpful to you when prioritizing tasks into a 'to do' list.

Be organized

You may have all the other time management strategies in place but these can be sabotaged if you are not well organized. It is often said that the state of a person's desk reflects the state of their mind. The more paper that is on your desk, the more likely you are to be inefficient. Office workers can waste a lot of time simply looking for papers in a badly organized office. See your desk as basically a place to work and not a place to store your work on. Of course, busy people do make a mess from time to time but it is important that the mess does not lead to disorganization. If you do not have a good filing system, then make one. Try to deal with each piece of paper as it comes in, rather than allowing papers to accumulate in a pending tray. File things that you are going to deal with

Table 5.1 Grid for prioritizing tasks

Category A Urgent and important – 'Firefighting'	Category B Important but not urgent – 'Quality time'
Category C Urgent but not important – 'Distraction'	Category D Neither urgent nor important – 'Time wasting'

later and make use of a 'bring forward' system in your diary to ensure that you do not forget them. Shred or bin out-of-date or irrelevant papers. If you do not have someone to help you, make some time in your weekly or monthly routine for filing and getting rid of rubbish, so that it does not get a chance to accumulate. Also try to be organized in your work. Do not start lots of jobs at the same time. Manage your emails and telephone calls rather than letting them manage you. Dealing with your calls and emails all in one go can be a more efficient way of managing your time. Ring-fence time slots in your daily routine when you make calls and reply to emails and when you will be available to receive calls. During these time periods, make arrangements not to be disturbed by other activities and stick to the allocated time slots.

Developing an action plan to manage your time more effectively

This chapter began by outlining the two case studies of John and Peter. John was constantly running around trying to catch up with himself but Peter was a well-organized individual who managed his time effectively. A number of strategies that can be employed to help you manage your time more effectively were outlined. If you identified that you are more like John than Peter, you definitely need to learn some time management strategies. It is more likely that you are not like the two extremes of Peter and John but somewhere in between the two. If this is the case, there is still room for you to learn to manage your time effectively. However, even if you are aware that you are not managing your time effectively, you may not be clear about what changes you need to make. The starting point is to do a time log of everything that you do over a given period of time such as a typical day or week. You will need to break the whole of your working day down into blocks of time as small as 5 or 10 minute periods and record exactly what you were doing at this time. This might seem like a very laborious and time consuming activity in itself for someone who is already busy. However, the pay-off in terms of the valuable information it gives you about the way in which you use your time is well worth it in the longer term. Once you have this baseline of activity, you can identify the things you do well and things you do not do so well in terms of managing your time. The questions below will assist you in identifying those areas which need addressing. Ask yourself:

1   Am I wasting some time?
2   Do I have difficulties planning ahead?
3   Am I a procrastinator?
4   Am I finding it difficult to delegate tasks?

5 Do I find it difficult to stay focused on tasks?
6 Do I have problems prioritizing effectively?
7 Am I untidy and disorganized in my work?

If the answer to any of the questions above is yes, you need to identify the specific unhelpful behaviours or attitudes that need to be changed and

Table 5.2 John's action plan for managing his time more effectively

Action required	Start date
1 **Establish a more regular routine** – do not work after 7pm at night, go to bed at 10.30pm and set alarm clock, get up at 7am and have a proper breakfast.	Today. Go to bed at 10.30pm and set alarm clock for 7am.
2 **Be more organized** – make sure that I have clean and ironed work clothes ready the night before, prepare packed lunch the night before.	Today. Prepare packed lunch every evening. Check I have sufficient clothes ready for the week every Sunday.
3 **Plan ahead** – fill up with fuel before the gauge gets to empty, leave for work at 8am to avoid rush hour traffic, do not leave reports until the last minute and prepare for meetings in advance.	Fill up car with fuel every Saturday afternoon. Leave for work 8am tomorrow morning.
4 **Prioritize more effectively** – identify the most urgent and important tasks that need doing and allocate time accordingly.	Tomorrow morning at work.
5 **Stay focused** – stick to the task in hand and do not allow self to be distracted by other less urgent and less important tasks.	Tomorrow morning at work.
6 **Delegate more** – identify those tasks that can be delegated to junior colleagues and delegate accordingly.	Ask junior colleague to attend low level board meetings every Tuesday and Thursday.
7 **Be more assertive with boss** – say no to extra work, be honest with boss about the difficulties experienced with current workload.	Next management supervision meeting on Friday.
8 **Establish a better balance between personal and work life** – clearer separation of work and home life, do not take work home, prioritize home life over work on some occasions.	Plan theatre trip with wife on Wednesday evening at 7pm. Ensure that I attend son's open evening next term.

make a list of them in order of priority (1 = top priority). Select a date when you are going to start implementing these changes and stick to it. Review your progress on a regular basis, for example on a weekly basis. The example in Table 5.2 refers to the changes that John in the case study at the beginning of this chapter included in his own action plan.

If like John you have identified that unassertiveness is one of the causes of your taking on too much work, you are encouraged to pay particular attention to Chapter 6 on developing assertiveness skills. Before you finish the present chapter, however, have a go at making your own action plan to identify the range of interventions that can help you manage your time more effectively.

Chapter 6

Developing assertiveness skills

What is assertiveness?

Unassertive people have difficulty in standing up for their rights and can be an easy target for bullies, or alternatively they can come across as being overly forceful and aggressive. Submissive individuals readily relinquish responsibility and tend to assume the role of victim in social interactions with others. Aggressive people get what they want from situations at the expense of others by being intimidating and punishing towards them. On the contrary, assertive individuals are able to get what they want from interactions with others by expressing their needs and preferences in a forthright and confident way without violating the rights of others. Assertiveness lies in the middle ground on the continuum of behaviour between submissiveness and aggressiveness, as illustrated in Figure 6.1.

It is about expressing one's needs, wants, opinions, feelings and beliefs in direct, honest and appropriate ways and preferably to create a win-win situation for all those involved.

Why are some people unassertive?

There are various reasons why a person may be unassertive. Submissive individuals may be anxious about upsetting others, lack confidence, fear conflict, or worry that others will disapprove of them. In the work

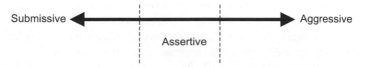

Figure 6.1 The submissiveness–aggressiveness continuum

situation they may worry about losing their job if they do not go along with what others want, especially if it is someone in authority. Alternatively, it might be a way of avoiding taking responsibility and thus not being blamed if things go wrong. It can also be a way of gaining protection and being looked after by someone they perceive to be stronger than they are. Unassertive people often feel guilty if they refuse a request, do not realize that they have rights too and have irrational negative thoughts about themselves. They may also confuse assertiveness with aggression and equate non-assertiveness with politeness. Alternatively, they may confuse being manipulative with being assertive and attempt to get what they want out of situations by indirect or underhanded means. Similarly, aggressive individuals may confuse assertiveness with submissiveness or weakness.

What are the consequences of being unassertive?

In the short term, being submissive may lead to a temporary reduction in anxiety due to the sense of relief the individual experiences from having avoided a potential conflict, or escaped from a situation which would have made them feel guilty. The experience of reduced anxiety can serve to reinforce the unassertive behaviour. Similarly, the aggressive individual may temporarily rejoice in hollow victories, but subsequently suffer the disapproval and condemnation of others around them. However, in the longer term, unassertive behaviour can lead to further erosion of what is already a fragile or low self-esteem in the individual concerned. It can lead to strong negative emotional reactions such as feelings of irritability, anger, guilt, frustration, resentment or self-pity. It can also lead to physical symptoms associated with chronic tension such as muscular aches and pains, neck ache, backache and headaches.

Being unassertive can also have negative effects on others, who at first may feel sorry for the unassertive individual but ultimately it can lead to a lack of respect for them, because they do not know what that person stands for. They may begin to doubt that person's integrity, believing they say one thing and go away and do another. They may become irritated that the unassertive individual is not open about their needs and does not say what they really want. With respect to aggressive individuals they may feel resentment and a desire to get even with them. In addition, unassertive individuals can have detrimental effects on the workplace organization because they do not handle conflicts satisfactorily. They may tend to avoid making difficult decisions and this creates problems because things are simply left to get worse, or they behave in an overly forceful and domineering way which exacerbates conflict situations. If the unassertive person happens to be in a managerial position, those they manage can start to lose respect for them.

Two case studies will illustrate the differences between being unassertive and assertive. The first case study is of Caroline, who works as a staff nurse on a busy neurosurgical unit in a National Health Service hospital in the North of England. She dislikes conflict and tends to go out of her way for approval from others. She likes to think of herself as being helpful and finds it difficult to say no to people, in case she hurts or offends them. This has led to Caroline getting into difficult situations on numerous occasions. The second case study is of Rosie, who is a confident individual and is able to assert herself effectively. Rosie works as a secretary providing temporary cover when required for companies that are short staffed. This requires her to work in a range of different work environments for short periods of time. Rosie does not find it difficult to say no or deal with confrontation and she is prepared to stand up for her rights when required to do so.

Case study: Caroline

Caroline had just started her first job after qualifying as a staff nurse. A few weeks after she had begun working on the neurosurgical unit, one of the male medical consultants came into the office and ordered her to put the kettle on and make him a cup of tea. Caroline knew that this did not sound right but decided that it was better not to 'cause a fuss', so did what was asked of her. A few days later the same medical consultant came into the office and told her to get the medical case notes ready for the ward round. Again she realized that it was not her job but did not feel able to say no to him. The next week he ordered her to get the case notes ready again. When she had done this, he clicked his fingers and ordered her to follow him down to the ward and bring the notes with her. The next thing Caroline knew was that she was trying to balance a heavy pile of case notes, while rushing down a long corridor following the consultant, who was empty handed. This made Caroline feel angry and resentful but yet again she said nothing. The consultant who was by this time in the distance then turned round and shouted down the corridor at her, in front of patients and visitors, to 'hurry up'. Due to her vision being obstructed by the height of the case notes she did not see a trolley and bumped into it. She then stumbled and the case notes went flying all over the floor. Needless to say the consultant did not come to help her pick them up but in a loud and booming voice shouted 'You bloody idiot'. At this point Caroline ran off crying and locked herself in the staff toilet. She was not crying because she was sorry for dropping the case notes but because she was feeling so angry about the way she had been treated by the medical consultant. She was determined not to allow this to continue happening and after discussing the situation with her supervisor, they agreed that she needed to develop her assertiveness skills.

Case study: Rosie

In her work as a secretary Rosie was asked to provide temporary cover for a finance company in the City of London. When she arrived, Rosie noticed that it was a largely male dominated environment but thought no more of it at the time. A few days after starting in the job she noticed that her 'boss' was paying quite lot of attention to her. On one occasion he sat on her desk to dictate a letter. It made Rosie feel uncomfortable that he was sitting so close to her, so she asked him if he would mind moving, because him sitting so close was making her feel uncomfortable. Her boss's response was to say, 'Oh, touchy aren't we'. Rosie's reply to this comment was, 'No, I am not touchy, I just don't like people invading my personal space'. Undaunted, her boss invited her out for lunch the next day, which Rosie turned down. When he asked her why, Rosie explained that she did not have to give a reason and suggested that they focus on the job more. Her boss was quite a persistent individual who did not take rejection very well and continued to invite her out for lunch for the next three days running. Rosie's response was always the same, to look him in the eye and in a steady, polite, firm and clear voice say, 'No thank you'. By the fourth day her boss announced that she was 'playing hard to get'. On hearing this comment Rosie became more assertive in her response. She informed her boss that she found his comment offensive and that he had no right to treat her in this way. She informed him that if his behaviour persisted, she would inform her employing agency of his conduct. At this point her boss approached her, put his arm around her shoulder and said, 'You wouldn't do that, would you?' Rosie immediately moved away from him and in a loud voice that the rest of the office could hear, said, 'How dare you ... you are not allowed to touch people in that way ... it is harassment and there are laws against that sort of behaviour. The days when a boss could abuse a member of staff in this way are long gone and if you ever do anything like that again, I will take out a grievance against you for sexual harassment'. Her boss went pale and looked visibly shaken. At this point she demanded an apology, which he readily gave. Rosie could hear muffled laughter in the office and afterwards another female member of staff came up to her and said, 'Well done, he had that coming for a long time now and it is about time someone put him in his place'. Needless to say, Rosie did not have any more problems with her boss for the rest of the time she was there.

These two case studies illustrate very different ways of reacting to difficult interpersonal situations. Although the case study of Caroline is intended to illustrate an example of unassertiveness, it also highlights some broader issues. At an organizational level, it illustrates the inequities that can still exist between men and women in the workplace. In this case it illustrates the stereotypical role of nurses (usually female) as handmaidens to the medical profession. It also highlights the unequal roles of men and women and sexist attitudes that are often found in our society. However, the case of Rosie also demonstrates that women do not have to put up with such treatment. Rosie could have put in a complaint about her boss there and then but decided when she saw his reaction that he had well and truly got the message, so it was unnecessary to take it further. You may feel that she should have reported him anyway but Rosie felt she had achieved what she wanted to without taking it further. However, it is important to acknowledge that unassertiveness is not just a gender issue and many men also have significant problems in being assertive.

How can you become more assertive?

Assertiveness skills can be learned through training in four main areas. The first of these is education, which involves learning to recognize the differences between aggressive, submissive, manipulative and assertive behaviours. The second area is about knowing your rights. The third and fourth areas are developing assertive attitudes and developing assertive behaviours, which you can then put into practice.

Education

Education involves learning to recognize the differences between aggressive, submissive, manipulative and assertive behaviours in their verbal and non-verbal expressions. The distinctions between these behaviours are illustrated in Figures 6.2, 6.3, 6.4 and 6.5.

Aggressive behaviour

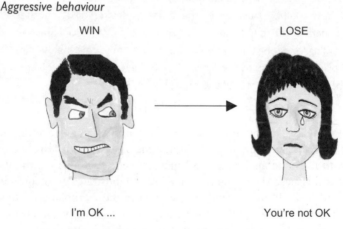

WIN   LOSE

I'm OK ...   You're not OK

Figure 6.2 An aggressive interaction (drawings reproduced with the permission of Peter Binns)

Figure 6.2 sums up an aggressive interaction. Aggressive behaviours include being pushy, trying to force people into things, attacking, intimidating, blaming, putting others down, humiliating, not listening, deciding for others and ordering people around inappropriately. Non-verbally the aggressive person communicates through facial expressions such as raised eyebrows, a firmly set jaw, scowling, a fixed eye gaze to try to stare you out and gestures such as finger pointing, fist thumping and adopting an upright posture to make themselves appear taller. The aggressive individual is also likely to invade your personal space by standing too close in an attempt to intimidate you. Verbally they may speak in an abrupt way with a raised voice and in a hard and sharp tone. They make extensive use of verbal statements which are either boastful and sarcastic, or contain putdowns and threats, and emphasize blaming words. They are dismissive of the rights of others and in terms of the power dynamic they try to put others in an inferior position to themselves. This creates a win-lose situation in which the unassertive person is the loser.

Submissive behaviour

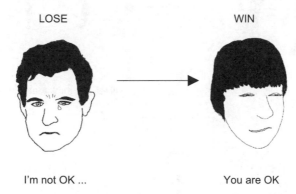

Figure 6.3 A submissive interaction (drawings reproduced with the permission of Peter Binns)

Figure 6.3 illustrates a submissive interaction. Submissiveness is about always putting the needs of others before your own. It involves not feeling able to express your needs or say what you want, going along with things to avoid conflict, to gain the approval of others, or to avoid rejection. In the short term agreeing to things that you do not really want to do and letting others make decisions for you can reduce anxiety, but in the longer term it can result in the build-up of frustration and resentment. The submissive individual does not complain to another person's face but may complain to others behind the scenes about the way they are being treated. Submissive behaviours include avoiding eye contact with others, nervous and hesitant movements, hunched posture and adopting a false looking smile. Verbally a submissive individual speaks in a quiet, uncertain, shaking monotonous voice filled with hesitancy, pauses and frequent throat clearing. The content of the speech includes long and rambling statements in which they take ages to get to the point, repeated permission seeking, self put-downs and excessive apologies. In terms of the power dynamic, submissive people allow themselves to be manoeuvred into a powerless position by more dominant and forceful individuals. This creates a lose-win situation, in which the submissive person is always the loser.

Manipulative behaviour

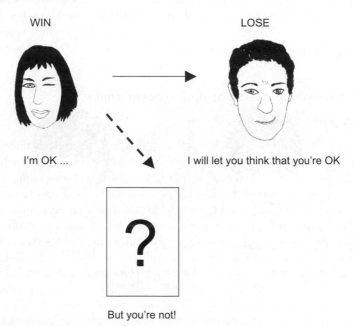

Figure 6.4 A manipulative interaction (drawings reproduced with the permission of Peter Binns)

Figure 6.4 illustrates a manipulative interaction. Manipulative individuals make others believe that they are getting treated fairly when in reality they are not. They are good at persuading others that they are being truthful when they are not being totally straight and honest with them. They are able to con them into doing things by being two faced and appearing to support them when really they are putting them down. They say one thing to the person's face but another behind their back. Manipulative people often confuse their behaviour with being assertive. They behave 'as if' they are being assertive but in reality their motives are more aligned to those of the aggressive individual. For example, they may smile and adopt the verbal and non-verbal behaviours of an assertive person but are dismissive of the rights of others. This creates a win-lose situation, in which the manipulative person is the winner in the short term. However, it does not usually take very long before other people become wise to a manipulative person's unacceptable behaviour and begin to mistrust them and their motives, and they begin to get a reputation for such behaviour.

Assertive behaviour

WIN   WIN

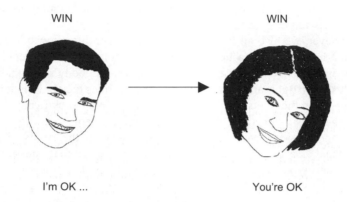

I'm OK ...   You're OK

Figure 6.5 An assertive interaction (drawings reproduced with the permission of Peter Binns)

Figure 6.5 illustrates an assertive interaction. Being assertive is knowing your rights, asking for what you want clearly, gently and firmly, standing up for yourself, making your own decisions and allowing others to make theirs, listening to what others have to say without necessarily going along with them, respecting yourself and recognizing that you also have a responsibility to be respectful towards others. This creates a win-win situation, in which both parties in the interaction are winners. This is of course the best outcome for all concerned.

Knowing your rights

Most employers recognize that employees have a number of rights in the workplace and these are usually written into their contracts of employment, such as annual leave entitlement, terms of employment, sickness pay, study leave entitlement and maternity or paternity leave. Most of these are statutory rights covered by government legislation. At work these rights may extend to non-statutory rights such as the right to a job appraisal, time off in lieu, in-service training and continuing professional development without loss of pay. Also, this extends to having a right to know what is expected, to be consulted about decisions made affecting you, to refuse certain requests, to make mistakes occasionally without fear of being sacked and so on. Employers have rights also. They have the right to expect that their employees turn up to work on time, adhere to a certain dress code, use their time productively, put any mistakes they make right, learn from their mistakes and try not to repeat them. They also have a right to expect that employees abide by the terms and conditions of their employment. It can be seen therefore that employers and employees have both rights and responsibilities towards each other.

However, we also all have rights and responsibilities towards each other as human beings, which are deemed necessary to live a decent life. In order to behave assertively, one needs to have a good understanding of what these rights are and also what responsibilities they have in terms of respecting the rights of others. Unassertive people either do not know what their basic rights are, or if they do, they feel unable to ask for them to be met. Assertiveness training thus focuses on the rights of the individual as a human being since it is in these areas that unassertive individuals typically experience the most problems. The aim is to learn what their rights are and how to ensure that they get them met. Aggressive and manipulative people are dismissive of the rights of others, so the task for them is to learn that they have a responsibility to respect others' rights and the right of others to be assertive.

A 'Bill of Rights'

So what are these basic human rights? The Bill of Rights below outlines some of these rights:

- I have a right to be treated with respect.
- I have a right to be treated as an equal.
- I have a right not to be bullied or harassed.
- I have a right to be listened to.
- I have a right to make mistakes from time to time.
- I have a right to celebrate my successes.
- I have a right to ask for my basic needs to be met.
- I have a right to change my mind.
- I have a right to say no to an unreasonable request.
- I have a right to express my own opinions.
- I have a right to express a preference.
- I have a right to disagree.
- I have a right to have feelings and to express them assertively.

The list above is by no means an exhaustive list and can be added to as and when you identify any others. Remember also that you have a responsibility to respect these rights in others.

What can we learn from the case study of Caroline?

Going back to the case study of Caroline earlier in this chapter, it can be seen that she was not asserting her rights. She either did not know what her rights were, or she felt unable to ask for them to be met. The medical consultant was a bully who by his aggressive and domineering stance was able to intimidate Caroline into a submissive position. Because she was new to the service and was not completely clear about the roles and responsibilities of her job, the consultant was able to take advantage of her. The situation was made worse by her desire not to get into a conflict situation or say no to his requests. This led Caroline to feel powerful feelings of anger and resentment and eventually the recognition that she needed to develop her assertiveness skills. She certainly would have benefited from having some of the assertiveness skills outlined in the rest of this chapter.

Developing assertive attitudes

This aspect of assertiveness training focuses on changing the way that you think. In most cases it is not the situation itself that is problematic but the way in which the individual thinks about it. For example, if an individual believes that they are inferior to others, they are more likely to feel anxious and behave submissively in a conflict situation than someone who is confident and self-assured. Similarly, if an individual believes that others are out to take advantage of them and cannot be trusted, the person is more likely to behave in a hostile and defensive manner. Therefore becoming assertive requires an individual to identify their unhelpful and dysfunctional beliefs and replace them with more rational and healthy ones. These attitudes are formed as a result of previous life experiences, often originating from childhood and being consolidated in adulthood. They form part of the way in which the individual sees the world and relates to others. Some examples of such dysfunctional attitudes which can lead to unassertive behaviour are briefly discussed below.

Aggressive people suffer from what some psychologists have termed 'aggressogenic' thinking. That is they are hypersensitive to any perceived injustices or unfairness and tend to mistrust others whom they believe are out to hurt, abuse or humiliate them. Examples of aggressive attitudes include 'It's a dog eat dog world out there', 'Get others before they get you', 'Attack is the best form of defence', 'Others can't be trusted' and 'Aggression gets results'.

Examples of unassertive attitudes include 'My opinions don't count', 'I am not as important as others' and 'It is safer not to challenge people'. They are driven by fear, uncertainty and feelings of underlying inferiority.

Manipulative attitudes are based upon a weak or absent code of ethical and moral conduct or rules for living. Examples of manipulative attitudes include 'Others are there for the taking', 'The feelings of others are irrelevant' and 'I am entitled to get what I want, regardless of the consequences for others'.

Examples of assertive attitudes include 'I have a right to be treated with respect', 'I am equal to others', 'I am as good as anyone else' and 'My views are as important as anyone else's'.

In order for an individual to successfully alter their unhelpful attitudes, they first of all need to become aware of what these actually are. They then need to challenge them with more healthy and rational alternative ways of thinking. The tools and techniques used for changing unhelpful attitudes are discussed in more detail in Chapter 9, so will not be duplicated here.

Developing assertive behaviours

Assertive behaviours include both non-verbal and verbal aspects. The non-verbal communication of assertive individuals involves maintaining good eye contact but not staring at others, making open gestures and movements, adopting a relaxed posture, respecting the personal space of others and displaying sincere and non-threatening facial expressions. Verbally the assertive individual communicates in a firm and steady tone of voice, which sounds warm and sincere. They make clear statements which are concise and to the point. They give constructive advice and criticism and suggestions rather than blaming others unfairly, or attempting to put them down in any way.

If you are an unassertive individual, you need to practise behaving in a more assertive way towards others. In the first instance this might involve rehearsing in your imagination how you would deal with a range of situations that you currently find difficult. Role-playing scenarios with others can also be a particularly helpful way of practising assertive behaviours. The individual may make a hierarchy of behaviours which they wish to change and start off by practising small changes, such as making a request, refusing a request, disagreeing with someone, giving an opinion, giving praise, receiving praise and so on. Once you feel sufficiently confident through rehearsal and role-play to practise these skills in a real life situation, you can start to engage in what are called 'behavioural experiments'.

A behavioural experiment involves practising a new way of behaving and observing the outcome of behaving differently. For example, it might involve practising any one of the non-verbal aspects of behaviour mentioned above, such as maintaining good eye contact, adopting open gestures and movements, or developing a more relaxed posture. Alternatively, it could involve practising your verbal skills by adopting a different tone of voice or sounding warmer and more sincere. Through observing the outcomes of these behavioural experiments, the individual begins to disconfirm their negative assumptions and builds up valuable evidence to support the positive effects of their new more assertive behaviours. As the individual gains confidence they gradually move up through a hierarchy of increasingly more difficult scenarios.

Other useful assertiveness techniques to help you

In addition to developing the assertive attitudes and behaviours discussed above, there are a number of other practical tools and techniques that you can add to your assertiveness tool kit. These are outlined below.

Use the 'broken record' technique

The broken record technique allows you to stay focused on your request or statement without falling prey to manipulative comments, irrelevant logic or argumentative baiting from others, who may be trying to cloud the issue, or create a smokescreen to throw you off course. It involves calm repetition of a statement or a request over and over again. In the second case study in this chapter, Rosie used the broken record technique to respond to her boss's repeated request for her to go to lunch with him. She repeatedly said 'No' and was not thrown off course or sidetracked by any of his comments or behaviours. Parents often use this technique when telling their children that it is bedtime. The child may protest vehemently and come up with numerous reasons why they cannot possibly go to bed right now (clouding the issue) or they may throw a tantrum in the hope that the original request may be forgotten (creating a smokescreen). However, it is not only children who behave in this way and once you start to become more assertive, you will become more aware of just how many adults try to manipulate you in this way.

Use fogging

Fogging or 'fielding the response' involves indicating that you have heard what the other person has said without getting hooked onto what they say. This skill allows you to acknowledge what the other person has said but to still continue with your statement or request without feeling angry or defensive about it. For example, one of your work colleagues has asked you to swap a shift and work a Sunday for them. However, you have got something planned and anyway it is not in your contract to work on Sundays, so you say 'No'. Your colleague then accuses you of being unhelpful and selfish. Instead of ignoring what your colleague has said, you can respond by saying, 'I realize that you think that I am being unhelpful and selfish but the answer is still no'. You do not become defensive or angry or get hooked on the accusation but continue to assert yourself by saying 'No'. While they are entitled to express their opinion, you clearly indicate by your response that you do not agree with them.

Be concise

Being concise allows you to say exactly what it is you want to say by avoiding unnecessary padding and keeping your statement simple and to the point. In order to do this you need to decide what it is you want to say and say it specifically and directly. This keeps misunderstandings to a minimum. For example, you need a report completed by one of the staff that you line manage by the end of the week and if it is not completed, you will be held responsible. You do not need to be apologetic or hesitant about asking, or justify yourself by giving long-winded explanations. Nor do you do need to play on people's friendship or good nature, or sell the request by flattery. Keep your request, direct, short and to the point by asking the question, 'Can you get that report to me by Friday?'

Be specific

In many assertive statements, it is better to be specific. If you have to make a criticism of another person for any reason, it is important to identify the specific behaviour that you are objecting to rather than making vague assertions or condemning them as a whole person. Be prepared to pinpoint the things that are bothering you. For example, rather than simply labelling someone as a 'bad driver', it is more helpful to be specific about what aspect of their behaviour you are unhappy with by making a clear statement such as 'You are driving too fast in a 30 mile an hour limit – would you slow down please?' Similarly, when setting limits on others, you need to be specific about the things that you are not prepared to do. For example, if you are giving someone a lift to work each day and they are usually not ready to leave when you arrive, you may have to set a limit on their behaviour by making a statement such as, 'I am happy to pick you up on my way to work as long as you are ready to leave at 8.30am'. If they continued to not be ready on time, you may need to set firmer limits by making a statement such as 'If you are not ready when I arrive, I shall have to leave without you'.

Clarify

If you think that you may have misunderstood something that the other person has said to you, you need to ask for clarification from them. This will enable you to check your assumptions and clear up any misunderstandings before you respond to a situation. Misunderstandings are often at the root of conflict, so it is important that these are ironed out at the earliest opportunity.

Use 'I' statements

It is a fundamental skill of assertiveness to own your own thoughts, feelings and behaviours. If you use 'I' statements you communicate to others that you are speaking for yourself and not blaming them unfairly. This in turn helps reduce defensiveness in others who are more likely to give 'I' messages back to you. For example, it sounds less blaming to say 'I feel so angry' than to say 'You are making me angry'. Another example would be to say 'I think that there may be a better way to do this', than to say 'You are doing it all wrong'. This may sound like playing with semantics but in reality it can have a significant impact upon how others react to you.

Active listening

The active listening technique is an excellent way of managing angry, anxious or otherwise emotional people. Demonstrating that you are listening and trying to understand someone is in fact one of the most effective ways of calming them down. You can check out how much you understand them by a technique called 'paraphrasing'. This essentially involves summarizing what you think they have been thinking, feeling and saying to you at various points along the way. For example, if you are listening to someone who is telling you about a recent incident at work, you can check out whether you have correctly identified their emotion by saying to them 'So it sounds to me as if you are feeling very angry about what happened?' and their thoughts by saying 'It seems like you think that you have been treated unfairly'. This communicates understanding and acceptance of the other person's feelings and thoughts without being judgemental or giving advice to them.

Aim for a workable compromise

Aiming for a workable compromise is a useful skill to use when there is clearly a conflict between your needs and wishes and those of someone else. Remember that assertiveness is about creating a win-win scenario rather than a win-lose one. The aim is to negotiate a true compromise or the middle ground that sufficiently accommodates the needs of both parties. To continue the example above in the section on being concise, your boss has asked you to have a report ready by Friday but you know that given all the other tasks you have to do, you are not going to be able to meet the deadline. So, rather than simply avoiding dealing with the situation, you inform your manager that it is not going to be possible to complete the report by Friday. Through negotiation with your boss you agree a workable compromise whereby you are given a slightly extended deadline for the completion report on the understanding that some of your other routine duties are taken off you and delegated to one of your colleagues in the office. This creates a scenario in which by compromising, both you and your boss create a win-win situation.

Negative assertion

The skill of negative assertion allows you to handle hostile or constructive criticism from others more assertively without feeling crushed by it. It allows you to react to appropriate criticism in a less defensive and more accepting way. For example, you have arranged to meet your work colleague for lunch at midday but it has totally slipped your mind. Later on that afternoon your colleague rings you and is very angry with you, accusing you of letting them down, stating that they had waited for you for half an hour. Instead of becoming angry and defensive and rejecting what is essentially appropriate criticism, this technique allows you to accept your faults without beating yourself up about them. You thus respond by saying that it is fair criticism and apologizing for letting them down. You also acknowledge that you can sometimes be forgetful especially when you are busy and that you will try not to let it happen again. This will de-escalate the situation, whereas if you were to become defensive and aggressive, it would be more likely to make the situation worse.

Empathic confrontation

You can use the technique of empathic confrontation when someone is clearly ignoring your rights and being aggressive towards you. The empathic part is about acknowledging that the other person is upset with you. The confrontation part is about explaining to them that you are finding their behaviour towards you unacceptable and an obstacle to reaching a solution to the problem. An example of empathic confrontation would be: 'I can see that you are feeling very angry towards me at the present time but when you are behaving in this way (e.g., aggressive, threatening, critical) towards me, I do not think that we are going to be able to resolve this issue.' This technique allows you to get your point across to someone who is being aggressive towards you in a way which does not inflame an already volatile situation.

Self-disclosure

The self-disclosure technique involves voluntarily admitting to feelings that you would normally hide. For example, you could disclose to an audience that you are 'feeling anxious' about doing a presentation. Alternatively, you might disclose to your colleague that you are 'feeling guilty about being off work yesterday when there was so much to do', or you disclose to your boss that you are feeling 'angry about the way they treated you in front of everyone at the meeting'. The immediate effect of this is to reduce the level of your emotional distress, enabling you to relax sufficiently to get back in control of your feelings, rather than allowing your feelings to control you. It also lets others know what impact they are having on you and gives them the opportunity to alter their own behaviours. It is important of course that the extent of your self-exposure is proportional to the situation that you are confronted with and you need to be able to gauge this correctly. An 'inappropriate' level of self-disclosure (i.e., too much) could actually lead to unintended and detrimental consequences in terms of eliciting negative reactions from others.

How assertive are you?

In order to become more assertive, the first thing you need to do is identify those areas in your life in which you are experiencing difficulties in being assertive. The questionnaire in Table 6.1 can be used to help you do this and it can be utilized in one of two ways. The first way is to identify those specific areas in which you are unassertive (i.e., those individual items which you have scored 3 or 4). The second way to use this questionnaire is to give yourself a total score for how assertive you are (by adding up the scores of all the individual items). A total score between 25 and 100 can be obtained by adding up the scores for all the individual items. A scoring and interpretation key is provided at the end of the questionnaire to allow you to do this calculation and interpret your own total score. Now please spend some time going through each item on the questionnaire and indicate by ticking against each one which statement applies to you (i.e., hardly ever/sometimes/often/most of the time).

Table 6.1 scores and interpretation

Scoring of individual items

- Each item rated 'hardly ever' scores 1.
- Each item rated 'sometimes' scores 2.
- Each item rated 'often' scores 3.
- Each item rated 'most of the time' scores 4.

Interpreting the total scores for the questionnaire

- A total score of 25 = highly assertive. You are able to assert yourself successfully in nearly all the situations you are presented with and hardly ever experience difficulties asserting yourself.
- A total score between 26 and 50 = moderately assertive. You are able to successfully assert yourself most of the time but do occasionally experience difficulties in some situations.
- A total score between 51 and 75 = unassertive. You frequently experience significant difficulties asserting yourself in a range of situations.
- A total score between 76 and 100 = very unassertive. You are experiencing major problems being assertive in most situations and for most of the time.

Table 6.1 An assertiveness questionnaire

How often do you find it difficult to:	Hardly ever 1	Sometimes 2	Often 3	Most of the time 4
1 Stand up for your rights				
2 Say 'no' to a request				
3 Give an opinion				
4 Disagree with someone				
5 Confront others				
6 Make a request				
7 Ask others for help				
8 Accept criticism about yourself				
9 Make a complaint				
10 Criticize someone else				
11 Admit it when you do not know something				
12 Admit to making a mistake				
13 Share your feelings				
14 Speak up at meetings				
15 Deal with someone who is assertive				
16 Deal with someone who is aggressive				
17 Feel and act in a self-confident way				
18 Give negative feedback to someone				
19 Apologize when you are at fault				
20 Put yourself forward for things that get you noticed				
21 Take responsibility for making decisions				
22 Stand up to someone who is pushing you around				
23 Accept praise or a compliment from someone				
24 Deal with authority figures				
25 Stand up to persistent people				

Note: This table is available to view and print from the following website: www.routledge mentalhealth.com/9780415671781

Developing an action plan to become more assertive

The questionnaire you have just completed will have helped you identify some of those specific areas in your life in which you are experiencing difficulties with assertiveness. In order to become more assertive, you need to put what you have learned in this chapter into practice. This can be achieved by developing an action plan tailored to your own areas of need. It consists of systematically going through the following steps:

1 Check that you understand the assertiveness concept and the differences between assertive, aggressive, submissive and manipulative behaviours.
2 Ensure that you understand your basic assertive rights. Draw up a 'Bill of Rights' to assist you with this.
3 Identify those areas of your life in which you are having difficulties in being assertive.
4 Write down a list of all the situations and people that give rise to problems at work, at home and more generally. The questionnaire in Table 6.1 will also help you with this task.
5 Identify those aspects of your beliefs, attitudes and behaviours that need to be addressed.
6 Challenge the unhelpful beliefs and attitudes you have identified using the cognitive techniques outlined in Chapter 9.
7 Teach yourself the necessary verbal and non-verbal assertiveness skills through techniques such as rehearsal and role-play. Make use of assertiveness training groups run by your organization if they are available to you.
8 Practise your assertiveness skills in real life situations through the use of behavioural experiments and graded (gradual) exposure to a range of scenarios.
9 Persevere with the goals you have set yourself and use setbacks as an opportunity for further learning rather than self-criticism.
10 Be patient, because changing long-established patterns of thinking and behaviour can take time.
11 Reward yourself for your successes.
12 Ask for help and support from family and friends.

Chapter 7

Developing effective interpersonal skills

Introduction

People working together can achieve so much more than when they work in isolation. Indeed society would grind to a halt if each of us did not play our own specific part within it in an atmosphere of mutual cooperation. However, the need to get on socially with others goes much deeper than this. Humans are by nature social beings and have a psychological need to belong to a group and to be accepted by others. In today's modern society where most of us already have our basic physical needs for food, shelter, warmth and safety met, the reasons for this may not appear to be very obvious. However, from an evolutionary perspective, belonging to a group and being socially accepted has important survival value. For our ancestors, being an accepted part of the tribe was crucial in terms of giving the individual much needed protection against the many hostile forces in their environment. It is not an overstatement to say that for our ancestors, being an outcast from the tribe was in many cases tantamount to receiving a death sentence! It was also necessary to ensure that their basic physical needs could be met in a consistent way. While in today's modern society it does not necessarily have the same survival value, the evolutionary importance of the need to be accepted and part of a group continues to drive our social behaviour. It also plays an important part in determining our identity, roles and status within the particular society or culture in which we live. Effective interpersonal skills are thus a crucial prerequisite to achieving social acceptance, a sense of identity and status within the society in which we live.

What are interpersonal communication skills?

Interpersonal communication skills are a set of 'competencies' that we make use of in our interactions with others. People who lack these skills are unable to communicate with others effectively and tend to experience problems in social situations. Poor social skills can manifest in a number of ways both verbally and non-verbally. Verbally they can manifest in ways such as monopolizing conversations, talking too loudly, interrupting others, being a poor listener and failing to recognize the signals which tell the individual that they are boring people. Non-verbally individuals with poor social skills may display annoying mannerisms, have poor eye contact, or adopt body postures and facial expressions which are inappropriate to the situation. They may demonstrate judgemental attitudes, or come across to others as unsupportive and disrespectful. They may show a lack of interest in what others have to say and may also have a poor grasp of the rules guiding what is considered to be appropriate physical contact within the cultural context in which they live. They may be poor at accepting criticism, handling confrontation, negotiating with others and prone to making inappropriate levels of self-disclosure. They also tend to be poor at making poor social judgements, lack self-awareness and have little or no insight into the impact that their behaviour is having on others.

On the contrary, people who are socially skilled are able to maximize the chances of getting the best out of other people and produce the desired effects on others in social situations. They are usually good at making a positive first impression on others and come across as being supportive and encouraging to others. They are able to make appropriate self-disclosures, give and receive constructive criticism in a way which is respectful towards others and possess good conversational skills, which include being able to listen to others without talking over them or interrupting them. They are able to give their opinions confidently in conversations and are competent at handling difficult people and conflict. They demonstrate consistency, loyalty, warmth, honesty, openness and empathy in their interactions with others. Skilled interpersonal communicators are also able to demonstrate 'higher order' social skills such as showing awareness of the impact that they have on others, recognizing emotional states in others, attributing motives, showing empathy and negotiating with others. In the work context, interpersonal skills are all about how we work with others successfully with the aim of maximizing productivity. We do not have to actually like those we work with but we do need to have a satisfactory working relationship with them. Research has shown that we consistently underestimate the amount of time we spend in face-to-face contact and the impact that our own behaviours have on others in the course of our daily work. In conclusion, socially competent people are those who are aware of the impact that they have on others and demonstrate the skills necessary to get the best out of others. For example, many successful business leaders and leading politicians, despite their other shortcomings, are clearly highly skilled interpersonal communicators, who are able to bring people together with a common aim and get the best out of them.

Why are some people interpersonally less skilled than others?

We know through observation that some individuals appear to be naturally outward going, while others are by nature more shy and withdrawn. However, learning and environmental influences, especially in our early developmental years, also play a crucial role in determining how we ultimately interact with others as adults. Like a flower that fails to bloom, some individuals fail to develop to their full potential socially. This can occur as a result of poor early learning experiences such as inadequate parenting or the absence of a positive role model which the child can learn from. Also, negative social experiences in early life may lead to the child avoiding social situations. However, a healthy, supportive, stable, secure and encouraging early environment tends to give the child the right start in life, which enables them to practise their social skills and eventually go out and face the outside world with confidence. Through exposure to a wide range of social interactions, the child learns how to behave socially and get the best out of people and situations. They learn an awareness of their own and others' motives and are able to pick up subtle cues about the behaviour of others and act on them promptly. For example, they learn to recognize the early non-verbal signs of aggression in another person, such the fixed staring eye contact, the adoption of a threatening posture and the invasion of their personal space, and they can then take immediate remedial action to diffuse the situation. Alternatively, they learn to recognize the verbal and non-verbal signals that someone is attracted to them by the tone of the other person's voice, the content of their speech, the length of their eye contact and dilation of their pupils, their posture and facial expressions. People with poor interpersonal skills are not good at doing this.

What are the consequences of being interpersonally unskilled?

As a result of their poor performance in social situations, interpersonally unskilled people often become isolated. They do not get invited out socially very much and others tend to avoid being in their company if possible. Since they lack awareness and insight into the impact that their behaviour has on others, they are unable to appreciate the link between cause and effect or modify their behaviours accordingly. Consequently, they can experience chronic feelings of loneliness, abandonment and rejection. They feel that they do not belong to any group, or that they are an outsider looking in on others and this can lead to considerable distress. They may feel angry and frustrated because they feel that they have been unfairly treated or misunderstood by others. Alternatively, they may experience strong negative emotional reactions and physical symptoms associated with chronic tension or depression, such as muscular aches and pains, neck ache, backache and headaches. In the longer term this can lead to further erosion of what is already a fragile or low self-esteem in the individual concerned. They may also lack awareness of some of the more subtle rules around dress sense and etiquette, and thus dress and behave inappropriately for the occasion. They often lack a sense of fashion or style and choose to wear clothing, colours or a hairstyle that makes them stand out and alienates them from others even more. The impact of the behaviour and presentation of the socially unskilled person on others is invariably a negative one in that others do not want to be seen with them or spend time in their company. It is likely that they have alienated those around them by their inappropriate behaviours and comments.

Developing your own interpersonal skills

Even if you are someone who is by nature rather shy, it does not mean that you are incapable of learning the skills to overcome your shyness and behave in a more outward going and sociable way. It is also possible to rectify the effects of faulty social learning experienced by individuals in their earlier life by teaching them more effective and healthy interpersonal skills later on in life. There is a wide range of non-verbal and verbal interpersonal skills that can be learned and an overview of these is presented below.

Non-verbal skills

Non-verbal skills refer to body language such as posture, gestures, facial expressions, eye contact and non-verbal aspects of voice projection which provide us with important cues about the attitude or state of mind of a person. They also include having an understanding of the need to respect the personal space of others, what constitutes appropriate touching and physical contact and how one communicates through one's appearance and dress. Some researchers estimate that about 80 per cent of our communication is non-verbal. If this estimate is an accurate one, understanding non-verbal communication can provide us with a wealth of information about others and help us to communicate more effectively. An outline of some of the main non-verbal communication skills is presented below.

Body posture and gestures

Body posture can indicate whether the person is interested, attracted to the other person, or being defensive, or is angry or bored. The basic posture which indicates interest is the trunk of the body leaning slightly forward in a relaxed way. Boredom can be indicated by a slouching posture with the head tilted to one side. Body posture is usually accompanied by gestures. A gesture is a non-verbal bodily movement such as moving the arms or waving the hands, nodding of the head, winking or rolling of the eyes, that expresses a particular meaning. For example, folding one's arms in a conversation is a gesture that can indicate a person is being defensive by putting a barrier between themselves and others. Other examples include waving goodbye, making a peace sign or an offensive gesture towards someone to indicate your dislike for them. Also, certain gestures communicate that someone is attracted to another person, for example, leg crossing, knee pointing, hair tossing, extended eye contact, adjustment of clothing, touching and moving closer to the other person. Physical posture and gestures can thus provide a lot of valuable information about the person using them. Another example of this is mirroring, which involves imitating the body language of others. It has been demonstrated to help build empathy and rapport in a social interaction, as well as putting the other person at ease. It creates a connection between two individuals that communicates that they understand each other and gives the message 'I am like you'. Once there is a rapport present, the extent of mirroring becomes much more noticeable and finely tuned.

Facial expressions

Facial expressions are an important form of non-verbal communication because they communicate the emotional state of the individual. Facial expressions can be voluntary, for example, smiling at someone we know when we see them at work. However, they are more often involuntary and as such can convey information that the individual may be trying to hide. Certain facial expressions correspond to certain emotions regardless of the individual's race or culture, such as smiling when we are happy, or frowning when we are sad. For example, it is possible to identify when someone is looking happy or sad by their facial expression, whether they are British, Chinese, Indian or any other race. Being able to correctly identify what people are feeling by observing their facial expression is an important social skill, in terms of being able to demonstrate empathy with others. For example, asking someone 'Are you all right?' if they are looking sad communicates to them that you are a sensitive person, who cares about the welfare of others. It is also important to acknowledge the importance that our own facial expressions can have on others. For example, greeting a stranger with a smile can be a very good way of putting them at their ease and can go a long way in terms of making a good first impression on others when we first meet them. It gives the message that 'I am a friendly person and I want to get to know you'.

Eye contact

If you do not look at someone when you are talking to them, they are likely to get the idea that you are ignoring them, you are untrustworthy, or you do not like the look of them. People who suffer from social anxiety often avoid eye contact but far from being seen as anxious by others, their behaviour is often interpreted by others as being aloof or antisocial, rather than due to anxiety. Maintaining eye contact for too long can also be interpreted negatively and staring at someone can give them the feeling that you are angry with them. Also by breaking eye contact at the wrong point, you may give the other person the impression you are not paying attention to them. So, with respect to eye contact, the length of time you make contact and the timing of breaks in eye contact, are both important communication skills. It is helpful to conceptualize breaks in eye contact as being similar to taking breaths between sentences. There are points in a verbal interaction where breaks seem to occur naturally and these are analogous to full stops and commas in written communications. Eye contact is no different in this respect in that there are points in an interaction where breaks in eye contact should occur naturally. There are no fixed rules and there do seem to be cultural variations with respect to what is appropriate eye contact. However, if you find social situations difficult, practising appropriate eye contact will improve your social skills. In summary, you need to use varied eye contact to communicate effectively. It is also useful to know that eyebrow movements and the rate at which a person blinks can also provide useful supplementary information about a person's emotional state. For example, excessive blinking is thought to be an indication that someone is lying and raised eyebrows communicate surprise.

Voice projection

We communicate with our voices even when we are not using words. It is possible to convey a considerable amount of valuable information through one's tone of voice, pitch, volume and speed. For example, if someone's voice, is shaky, high pitched and fast, they may be communicating that they are anxious. Alternatively, if a person is talking in a slow, quiet and monotonous voice, it may be indicating that they are sad or depressed, or a loud and booming voice may indicate anger. These non-verbal speech sounds provide valuable information about the person's underlying feelings. If you are attending well, you will be able to pick up information about the other person through their voice as well as their eye contact, posture, gestures and facial expressions. Also, the tone, pitch, volume and speed of your own voice is important. Speaking in a slow, calm, soft, warm and empathic voice can help a lot to get the other person to relax and open up to you.

Personal space

Personal space refers to an invisible boundary that individuals draw around themselves. If someone stands too close to us, it can feel uncomfortable and is referred to as invading our personal space. Research has shown that there are four different zones of interpersonal space that we draw around ourselves. The closest zone ranges from touching to about 18 inches (46 cm) apart. Only people who we are very close to are allowed to invade this space, which is reserved for lovers, our children, close family members and friends. The next zone ranges from 18 inches to approximately 4 feet (122 cm) and is reserved for friends and work colleagues who we know reasonably well. The third zone ranges from 4 to 8 feet away and is reserved for strangers and new acquaintances. The final zone starts at 8 feet (244 cm) away and is termed public distance. It is the distance reserved for public performances such as at the theatre, giving a lecture or speech to a larger audience. It is an important social skill to be aware of the rules relating to personal space and to stand at the appropriate distance when interacting with someone. Being too close to the other person can make them feel uncomfortable or intimidated, but too great a distance may communicate being detached and coldness.

Touch

Related to personal space is touch. We communicate a lot through touch. Examples of the everyday use of touch include giving someone a pat on the back when they have done something well, giving a firm hand shake as a welcome gesture, giving someone a hug when you meet them, or placing a hand on someone's shoulder to comfort them. In terms of deciding what level of physical contact is appropriate, it depends on how well you know the person and how intimate with them you are. For example, you would not walk along holding hands with someone who you were not fairly intimate with, but you may hold their hand to look at their engagement ring. There are also certain areas of the body that are considered out of bounds if the relationship is not an intimate one and if invaded could result in someone being grossly offended and even constitute a criminal act. An example of this would be to touch a female who you did not know intimately on her chest or bottom. There is also a risk of some kinds of 'innocent' forms of touch being misinterpreted. For example, a demonstrative person may put their hand on another person's knee or wrist when talking to them. They may mean nothing by it, but there is a risk that it could be misinterpreted as a gesture indicating that they are attracted to the other person. It is thus important to be aware of the rules relating to appropriate physical contact in a given culture. There are also cultural differences which should be taken into account when interacting with people from other cultures.

Personal appearance and presentation

Apart from the practical value of wearing clothes to protect us from the elements, one's appearance and dress sense are an important part of non-verbal communication. The clothes someone wears, the fashions they follow, the hairstyle and make-up they choose can tell us a lot about the individual concerned and serves an important social and cultural function. For example, a uniform can provide information about a person's occupation such as the uniform of a nurse or police officer. Wearing a particular colour of shirt can provide information about the football team that someone supports. In younger people, wearing certain clothes and having a particular hairstyle indicate an affiliation to a particular youth culture or group. For example, men having long hair and wearing a leather jacket usually give a message about that person's tastes and values. In our society, women wearing sheer clothes and displaying a lot of skin when out socially can be an indication that they are looking for a partner. Clothing can also reflect religious beliefs, for example, Muslim women are required to wear modest clothing and cover most parts of their bodies. In certain cultures, what one can wear is even regulated by law. It can also reflect social class and status, for wearing an expensive watch, jewellery, expensive perfume or aftershave and designer clothing communicates that an individual is wealthy. Thus, the way a person dresses, the clothes they wear, the hairstyle they choose, their make-up, jewellery and the fashions that they follow, all communicate potentially valuable information about the person they are, or would like to be. It is important therefore that the choices you make in terms of your own appearance and presentation give the right message to others and maximize your chances of social success.

Verbal skills

In addition to having well-developed non-verbal skills, an individual also needs to have good verbal skills in order to be an effective communicator. Being a good listener is the key to this and involves not doing too much of the talking and giving others the space and time to respond to you. Making effective use of listening skills in this context gives one more influence on the direction that a conversation takes by allowing them to selectively attend to certain utterances while neglecting others. There are a number of selective listening skills which can be learned to enable you to get the best possible response from the person you are interacting with. These are outlined below.

Paraphrasing

Paraphrasing is a type of attending to another person which demonstrates the ability to give back in one's own words pieces of information that the other person has been communicating to you. A paraphrase is basically a 'translation' of the essence of what the other person has been saying to you. It communicates to the other person that you have been listening to them. It also allows you as the listener to check that you have understood what they have been saying to you correctly. For example, if a work colleague has just spent 5 minutes giving you numerous examples of how the boss has let them down in the past, you might paraphrase what they have been saying by the statement 'So your boss is pretty unreliable then'. This communicates that you have been listening to them and that your understanding of what they have been saying is correct. However, an inaccurate paraphrase can confuse the other person and it can give them the idea that you have not been listening to them, so it is important that you get it right.

Reflecting feelings

Whereas paraphrasing emphasizes the content of what the other person has been saying, reflecting feelings focuses on the emotional aspects of the communication. Feelings can be communicated verbally, non-verbally, or through a combination of both. Non-verbal cues include observing the speed of speech, loudness of voice, the tone of the words, bodily posture, facial blushing and the individual turning their eyes away from you. Verbally they may be using affective words such as scared, happy, bored, disappointed or angry to indicate how they are feeling. By attending to all these aspects you can identify and label what the other person is feeling as well as the intensity of their feelings. As with paraphrasing it is important when you reflect back feelings, to correctly identify not only the emotion but also the right intensity of feeling. If you are not entirely sure, it is best to do this in a tentative way. Returning to the example given above of the work colleague who has just spent 5 minutes telling you how unreliable their boss has been, you may through observation of a number of verbal and non-verbal cues conclude that they are feeling very angry. You would then reflect this back using a tentative statement such as 'It sounds to me as if you are feeling pretty angry about the way you have been treated?' If your colleague then replies 'You bet I am!' then you can be certain you have accurately reflected their feelings. An accurate reflection of feeling demonstrates that you understand the other person on an emotional level and can give them the confidence to confide in you and disclose more of their feelings to you.

Summarizing

Summarizing is an attempt to condense or crystallize the essence of what has been said. The key purpose of summarization is to help another individual pull their thinking together. A secondary purpose is to check whether or not you as a listener have understood things correctly. When summarizing the listener selects out key statements and behaviours from the interaction and restates them as accurately as possible, thus helping the other person to see the situation more clearly. Summarizing is different from paraphrasing in that it covers a longer time period and involves a broad range of issues. Again, it is important to state your summary in a tentative way, so that the person you have been listening to has the opportunity to correct you if necessary. Summaries are particularly useful when trying to clarify a long and complex story or sequence of events.

Minimal encouragers

Minimal encouragers give the person you are communicating with the message that you are listening to them and so make them want to tell you more. Encouragers may be non-verbal such as a nod of the head, leaning forward with interest or engaging in more intensive eye contact. They can also take the form of verbal encouragement such as 'uh-huh', 'tell me more', or 'of course'. Sometimes it may involve a simple restatement of the other person's last four words, for example, 'so it made you feel pretty bad then?', or even an appropriately timed silence, giving the other person time to reflect, form their thoughts or regain their composure.

Asking open questions

Asking closed questions does not provide the opportunity for the person you are interacting with to elaborate upon a conversation. They also provide very little information because they can usually be answered with a simple 'Yes' or 'No' answer. The following dialogue between an interviewer and an interviewee illustrates the restrictive nature of the closed question:

Interviewer: Do you think that you have developed the necessary level of skills, knowledge, experience and confidence to be able to deal with a range of different client groups in various settings at both local and national level?
Interviewee: Yes.

It can be seen from this example that although the interviewee has clearly answered the question asked, it has not allowed them to say anything about the knowledge, skills and experience they do have relevant to the job. So let's rephrase the question into an open one:

Interviewer: Tell me about what skills, knowledge and experience you have gained over the years and how you think this can be

applied to working effectively with the range of different client groups in this company.

Interviewee: Well I think I will start by telling you a bit about my work experience since leaving university and then I will go on to say what skills I feel that I have developed over this time period as a result of these experiences ... [then moves on to qualifications and how the work experience, skills and training relates to being able to do the present job effectively...].

Another example would be to ask someone 'Did you have a happy childhood?' (a closed question to which the answer is simply 'Yes' or 'No') as opposed to saying 'Tell me about your childhood' (open-ended question which allows for a lengthy response). The open-ended question makes the other person in the interaction give more information. In general the rule is that if you want to give someone room to talk, ask open questions. However, if you want some specific information or simply want to check something out with the other person, ask closed questions. Closed questions are not taboo, but they are not the best way of eliciting information from someone.

Immediacy

Sometimes in the course of a conversation things crop up which, if not addressed immediately, can interrupt the subsequent flow and quality of further interaction. Take, for example, the situation where a manager has called a meeting with an employee to discuss a particular project that they want them to take on. When the individual arrives, the manager begins to outline the project to them but notices that the individual is looking sad and tearful. The manager chooses to ignore this and continues with the task in hand but notices the individual is now crying. The manager then asks why the person is crying and is informed that they have just experienced bereavement. It is no good the manager then ignoring this information. Some time must be taken to address the immediacy of the situation before any meaningful work related tasks can be addressed. Another example would be where a workplace counsellor is doing an assessment on a client who is an employee but each question they ask is met with an abrupt response. The counsellor is unable to elicit the information that they need and so must address the immediacy of the situation before the interview can progress. As a result the counsellor is able to establish that the employee is behaving this way because they are worried about the issue of confidentiality. The counsellor thus needs to reassure the employee that the session is confidential before any meaningful communication can continue. Having an awareness of the technique of immediacy and when to use it is important in such circumstances, and major communication difficulties can arise if it is not addressed.

Concreteness

When we listen critically to a story that someone is telling us, the description can sometimes appear to be rather vague. Concreteness means getting the other person to communicate as specifically and clearly as possible to you. In turn you should also attempt to be as concrete in your responses to others. Concreteness is a compound skill which also includes making use of the other skills already mentioned, such as listening, encouraging, asking open questions, paraphrasing and reflecting feelings. All of these things can add up to a more concrete conversation. Concreteness involves interpreting long, vague accounts with clarifying questions, or splitting up a complex sequence of events into manageable chunks. It involves the use of concrete open questions such as 'What happened exactly?', 'What did she say?', 'How did you react to that?', 'What went wrong?' or 'Can you give me an example?' in order to elicit the information that you require to make sense of a communication. The following is an example of a dialogue between an employee and their line manager which illustrates the combination of a range of listening skills used in concreteness.

Employee: Nothing seems to be going right for me in my work, at home, or with friends – I'm ready to throw in the towel.
Line manager: A number of different things appear to be going wrong for you at the present time. (paraphrase)
                 Shall we talk about each of those things one by one? (immediacy)
                 What would you like to discuss first? (open question)

Appropriate self-disclosure

Talking about yourself too much and too soon can be a major turn-off for the other person. Appropriate self-disclosure is about knowing when and how much to talk about yourself. For example, if a complete stranger sitting next to you on the bus started without invitation to tell you their whole life history and intimate details about their sex life, it is likely that this would make you feel highly uncomfortable. However, if your best friend confided in you some personal details about their sex life, you would probably consider this to be acceptable. What is appropriate to disclose is dependent on how well and intimately you know the person you are talking to. The skill with self-disclosure is to have an awareness of what level is appropriate to any given situation. Getting this right can enhance a relationship whereas getting it wrong can do considerable damage to it.

The use of small talk

There are different levels of conversation. At the most superficial level the content of the conversation may be about trivial and inconsequential issues such as, for example, the weather or the price of apples. These superficial topics are often used to break the ice and then lead to the next level of conversation which is a little more in-depth and personal. Conversation at this intermediate level may, for example, include asking someone about the job that they do or where they live and so on. Once we have got to know someone better at the intermediate level, we tend to then move on to deeper and more meaningful topics which are more personal in nature. It is important when first meeting a person that we do not judge or dismiss them as being superficial on the basis of our first conversation with them. While some people feel comfortable skipping the first two stages and talking at a personal level from the outset, others do not and it is important to respect this. A superficial conversation about the price of apples may in reality be that person's way of saying that 'I would like to get to know you better' and it is often worthwhile going through this initial stage on the way to getting to know someone who ultimately could become a lifelong friend!

In conclusion, effective communication requires being competent in a range of non-verbal and verbal skills. Non-verbally an individual needs to be able to recognize non-verbal cues, such as eye contact, body posture, movement and facial expressions such as nods, frowns and laughter. It also involves knowing what constitutes appropriate physical contact. The rules of contact vary in different socio-cultural contexts and with the closeness of the relationship. The closeness of appropriate contact thus varies and the individual needs to be aware of these rules. For example, in the work setting placing an arm on the shoulder of a distressed work colleague may be appropriate in that context but may not be so in the context of a meeting with a non-distressed work colleague. Individuals also communicate non-verbally through aspects of appearance such as the way an individual dresses. Effective verbal communication involves skills such as the ability for not monopolizing conversations, showing interest, having an ability to listen and being able to recognize the signals which tell us we are boring people. Verbally skilled individuals display effective listening skills and attending behaviours such as communicating warmth and empathy, talking in a soft voice, adopting a non-judgemental attitude, good eye contact, use of friendly facial expressions and adopting an interested posture by leaning forward with arms uncrossed. It also includes the use of listening skills such as summarizing, paraphrasing and reflecting back, which all demonstrate attending and listening. It is important to identify the style of communicating that you feel most comfortable with. For example, some more extravert and outward going people like being in the spotlight and displaying a more gregarious and loud persona, whereas others who are more introverted and quieter prefer to present themselves in a less outward going manner. There is no right and wrong in this respect but the important thing is that you come across as warm, genuine and sincere in your interactions with others. It also involves being sensitive and aware of others people's styles and preferences and respecting these.

Higher level interpersonal skills

Up to this point in the chapter we have been outlining the basic interpersonal skills required to communicate successfully in a social interaction. However, there are higher level skills that may be required by a particular occupational group, because they are intrinsic to the work that they do. For example, health professionals working on the front line with patients may frequently have to break bad news to patients or their relatives about death and dying. Where this is the case and there is an identified need to develop these higher level interpersonal skills, it may be appropriate for the workplace organization to offer workshops on 'breaking bad news' to those health professionals. Similarly, general managers may have to discipline people, make them redundant, or have to deal regularly with complaints and conflict. Another example would be police officers being able to identify inconsistencies between the verbal and non-verbal aspects of communication associated with lying when interrogating suspects. In these examples, training them to do their work more effectively by developing such high level skills should be provided by the employers. This training could be incorporated into their continuing professional development needs, or delivered in a series of specialist workshops. Other work related examples of higher level interpersonal skills include developing one's presentation skills, managing people's reactions to organizational change, advanced negotiation skills and the appropriate use of power in working relationships. More generally, higher level interpersonal skills also include the ability to give and receive emotional support, predicting the behaviours of others, making social judgements and developing self-awareness. Workshops which include not only education about the specific skills involved, but also a range of exercises of a more practical nature, which includes the use of role-play and/or audio-video feedback, can be particularly helpful in learning these social skills. The content of the workshops will vary according the needs of specific occupational groups or the stage in one's career.

Developing cognitive skills

As mentioned in earlier chapters, cognitive approaches focus on what is going on in the person's head. What someone is thinking impacts on their subsequent feelings and behaviours. Underlying the behaviour of socially unskilled people is the feeling that there is something about them that is 'not good enough' or 'inferior', or others are out to 'hurt', 'humiliate', 'lie' to them or 'cheat' and 'cannot be trusted'. In turn this may lead to beliefs that they have been 'unfairly treated' or 'misunderstood' by others. These negative beliefs in turn create a vicious cycle in that they lead to more defensive, suspicious and hostile behaviours towards others, which court rejection. An integral part of becoming more confident and competent in social interactions is to help the individual to identify the unhelpful and dysfunctional beliefs that are preventing them from functioning more effectively. They then need to learn how to replace their dysfunctional beliefs with more rational and healthy ones. The tools and techniques used for identifying, challenging and changing unhelpful attitudes are covered in depth in Chapter 9 so will not be replicated in this chapter.

How interpersonally skilled are you?

Interpersonal skills can be understood as a set of competencies which combine together to create effective communication with others. Disaggregating the specific skills and techniques that underpin effective interpersonal communication is thus the key to understanding and identifying what your own strengths and weaknesses are in terms of the interpersonal skills that you possess. The exercise in Table 7.1 is a checklist of the interpersonal skills that are required for effective interpersonal

Table 7.1 Checklist of interpersonal skills

1	Do you usually give others enough time to speak?	Yes	No
2	Do you usually take an interest in what others have to say?	Yes	No
3	Can you spot if you are boring someone?	Yes	No
4	Are you a good listener?	Yes	No
5	Are you sensitive to how others are feeling?	Yes	No
6	Can you usually tell if a smile is real or fake?	Yes	No
7	Are you usually able to see things from the other person's perspective?	Yes	No
8	Are you aware of how others see you?	Yes	No
9	Do you think others see you in the same way that you see yourself?	Yes	No
10	Do you behave consistently across people and situations?	Yes	No
11	Do you usually present yourself to others well?	Yes	No
12	Are you able to communicate clearly and effectively?	Yes	No
13	Are you good at judging others and their motives?	Yes	No
14	Are you good at picking up subtle social signals?	Yes	No
15	Are you good at identifying non-verbal social cues?	Yes	No
16	Are you supportive and encouraging towards others?	Yes	No
17	Do you disclose information about yourself appropriately?	Yes	No
18	Are you able to accept constructive criticism from others?	Yes	No
19	Are you able to resolve conflict situations effectively?	Yes	No
20	Can you negotiate effectively with others?	Yes	No
21	Do you know those you work with very well?	Yes	No
22	Are you usually able to get the best out of others?	Yes	No
23	Are you appreciative of the efforts that others make?	Yes	No
24	Are you able to give negative feedback to others in a constructive way?	Yes	No
25	Do you always exercise good manners in terms avoiding the use of offensive language in public and adhering to social etiquette?	Yes	No
26	Is your physical contact with others always appropriate to the situation?	Yes	No
27	When you talk to someone do you look them in the eye?	Yes	No
28	Would most people you know describe you as cheerful and friendly?	Yes	No
29	Are you tolerant when people do things differently from the way you would do them?	Yes	No
30	Do you always say please and thank you for things?	Yes	No
31	Would you describe yourself as approachable?	Yes	No
32	Do you always make an effort with your dress and personal hygiene before entering social situations?	Yes	No
33	Do you always respect other people's personal space?	Yes	No

Note: This table is available to view and print from the following website: www.routledge mentalhealth.com/9780415671781 communication both at work and in your personal life. This exercise will help you identify how interpersonally skilled you are by highlighting your own strengths and also the areas of weakness which you need to do further work on. Respond to each item in the list by circling 'Yes' or 'No' in the appropriate column.

Developing an action plan aimed at becoming more interpersonally skilled

1 Ensure that you understand the concept of interpersonal skills and the differences between socially unskilled and skilled individuals in terms of their verbal and non-verbal behaviours and attitudes.

2 Identify the areas that you need to work on. If the answer to any of the questions in the checklist in Table 7.1 is 'No', there is work to be done in terms of improving your interpersonal communication skills in that area.

3 For each item you have answered 'No' to, spend a little time reflecting in what ways you feel that this area of your interpersonal skills falls short and in what ways it needs addressing. For example, if you have answered 'No' to question 11 'Do you usually present yourself to others well?', ask yourself 'In what ways do I not present myself well to others?' This process will help you identify specific goals.

4 Make a list of all the situations and people that give rise to problems at work, at home and more generally and include these in your action plan.

5 Refer back to the non-verbal and verbal interpersonal skills outlined earlier in this chapter and use these as the basis for teaching yourself the necessary techniques.

6 Practise your interpersonal skills in real life situations through the use of behavioural experiments and graded (gradual) exposure to a range of scenarios. Also, where possible, make use of techniques such as rehearsal and role-play.

7 Persevere with the goals you have set yourself and use setbacks as an opportunity for further learning rather than self-criticism.

8 Make use of any social skills training groups run by your organization if they are available to you.

9 Identify those aspects of your beliefs, attitudes and behaviours that need to be addressed.

10 Challenge the unhelpful beliefs and attitudes you have identified using the cognitive techniques as outlined in Chapter 9 of this book.

11 Be patient, because changing long-established patterns of thinking and behaviour can take time to change.
12 Reward yourself for your successes.
13 Ask for help and support from work colleagues, family and friends.

Chapter 8

Developing relaxation skills

Introduction

The physical and mental symptoms of stress were outlined in Chapter 1. The result is that the individual remains in a state of 'high alert', being in a constantly overaroused state and unable to switch off either physically or mentally. This is where learning relaxation skills can be helpful. Mentally they can help the individual develop a calmer response towards negative, distracting or worrying thoughts and images. Physically they can help to reduce and ultimately eliminate the bodily symptoms of stress. Being relaxed means being in a 'distress free' state, so any intervention that contributes towards bringing about such a state can be said to have relaxation properties. The relationship between stress and relaxation can be conceptualized as being on a continuum. The aim of relaxation training is thus to create a state of inner wellbeing and peacefulness and bring the individual towards the relaxed end of the continuum, as shown in Figure 8.1.

There are a few possible reasons why people find it difficult to relax. The first of these is that they have been under stress for so long they have simply forgotten how to relax. The second one is that they may never have learned the skills of relaxation. Relaxation training equips them with the tools and techniques to enable them to move from the 'stressed' end towards the more 'relaxed' end of the continuum. However, being too relaxed in a work situation can also lead to problems of its own. For example, the individual may be seen as unmotivated, not working fast enough or not taking their job seriously. So it is important to reach a

Relaxed  Stressed

Figure 8.1 The stress–relaxation continuum

healthy balance. This chapter aims to teach you a range of informal, semi-formal and formal relaxation strategies to help you manage your stress more effectively.

Informal relaxation techniques

It is not advisable to be too prescriptive about what informal relaxation techniques to use, since everyone has their own unique way of relaxing. For example, one individual may enjoy reading a book, or listening to music, whereas another person may enjoy having a hot bath and a warm milky drink and then putting their feet up. Some people enjoy going to the cinema or theatre or to the local pub, or staying in to watching a good film on television. However, relaxation techniques are not only about being physically inactive. A good workout at the gym, swimming, jogging or a game of squash may be just what they need to help them relax. While physical activity may not be relaxing at the time, it is a good stress buster and usually results in a very relaxed state after the physical exertion is over. Broadly speaking, people tend to choose activities which compensate for the stressful work environment in which they work. For example, a person who works largely in isolation from others is more likely to want to engage in social activities outside of work than someone who has extensive contact with people at work. A person who has a physically very demanding job is more likely to want to engage in restful activities outside of work than someone who has a very inactive and sedentary job. A person who has a mentally very demanding job is less likely to want to engage in mentally demanding activities and hobbies outside of work than a person who has a mentally undemanding job. Because of the hectic pace of modern working life, it is more common for people to choose informal relaxation strategies that involve slowing down rather than speeding up. Ultimately, however, the method of relaxation chosen will also depend on the specific interests and hobbies of the individual concerned and these can vary enormously. For example, one individual will find spending hours going through their stamp collection a relaxing pastime, whereas another individual might find such an activity incredibly boring or even stressful. Therefore, the important thing when choosing an informal relaxation strategy is to decide the right one for you personally.

Semi-formal relaxation techniques

The introduction of informal relaxation techniques may be sufficient to help many people manage their stress more effectively. However, for some they are not and where this is the case, slightly more structured relaxation techniques may be required to help them become more relaxed. These are known as semi-formal relaxation techniques and there are numerous kinds of such techniques. Some of the most popular ones include massage, yoga and Tai Chi.

Massage

Receiving a full body massage is an excellent way of getting the muscles in your body into a state of deep relaxation. As your body relaxes, so does your mind, so a massage can have beneficial effects both mentally and physically. Two of the most common types are Swedish massage and Shiatsu massage. The techniques they use are different: Swedish massage is a soothing one but Shiatsu massage manipulates the body's pressure points. Although such forms of massage can be beneficial, the downside is that you generally have to pay for them. However, there are other inexpensive and enjoyable techniques you can use. For example, if you have a partner you can take turns in massaging each other. There are also a range of self-massage techniques that you can use and some examples of these are described below.

Releasing your shoulder tension

The shoulders can get particularly tense as a result of stress. One way of reducing tension in the shoulders is to reach one arm across the front of your body to your opposite shoulder and using a circular motion press firmly on the muscle above your shoulder blade. You need to press quite firmly but not so hard that it hurts you. Continue massaging in a circular motion for a couple of minutes and then move to the other shoulder and repeat the exercise on that one.

Soothing your scalp

Place your thumbs behind your ears and spread your fingers over the top of your head. Then move your scalp back and forth gently while making circular movements with your fingertips for 30 seconds or so.

Relaxing your eyes

Close your eyes and place your ring fingers directly under your eyebrows near the bridge of your nose. Then slowly increase the pressure for 10 seconds and then release. Repeat this exercise three or four times.

Yoga

Yoga involves learning a range of moving and stationary poses and combining these with deep breathing exercises. Perhaps one of the most enjoyable and sociable ways to learn and develop your yoga skills is to join a yoga class. Basic yoga for beginners involves learning slow, gentle movements, stretching exercises and relaxed breathing. It is important that you do not attempt some of the more strenuous forms of yoga until you have developed the right level of fitness, since you could do yourself physical damage if you are not fit enough. If you are unsure about what is best for you, check this out with a yoga instructor to ensure that you are starting at the right level for you. If you have a medical condition you may also need to check with your doctor that it is all right to do yoga exercises. It is safest to learn yoga by attending a group with a professional instructor to ensure that you get the basics right. Make sure that you learn at your own pace and do not feel tempted to try exercises that you do not feel ready to do because others are pressurizing you to do so. You should stop doing any exercise if it is painful. Once you have learned the basics, you can then practise alone or with others without necessarily having to go to the expense of attending yoga classes.

Tai Chi

Tai Chi is usually practised in groups and consists of learning a series of slow, self-paced, non-competitive and flowing body movements. These exercises require concentration, relaxed breathing and focusing attention on the here and now. Tai Chi is a safe and low impact option for people of all ages and levels of fitness. Once you have learned it, it can be practised anywhere, either on your own or with others. As with yoga it is best to learn the basic techniques from a professional instructor. If you have any health or mobility concerns, check with your doctor and instructor.

Formal relaxation techniques

Where an individual is experiencing severe and chronic stress related tension, informal and semi-formal relaxation techniques may be insufficient to break the habit and more formal relaxation techniques may be required. These may consist of physical or mental exercises, or a combination of both. Some common examples of formal relaxation techniques which have been demonstrated to be effective include deep breathing exercises, progressive muscular relaxation, meditation, mindfulness, imagery and visualization exercises. Learning the basics of these exercises is not difficult, but it takes regular practice to master the skills involved and gain maximum benefit from them. They need to be practised at least daily until the individual is able to use them effectively. It is no good trying to fit them in to a spare few minutes in your schedule. You need to set aside time to practise them once or twice daily and not to rush them. Also they are not intended simply as exercises to help you get to sleep at night. It is important to learn how to become relaxed in the fully waking state since you will get the most out of them in this way. There is no one technique that has been proven to be best for everyone, so it is important that you choose the one that suits you, your preferences and lifestyle best. Some of the most common techniques used are described below.

Deep breathing exercises

When people are stressed their breathing is affected. The muscular floor across the abdomen (the diaphragm) and the muscles between the ribs (intercostal muscles) become rigid and do not allow the lungs to expand freely within the rib cage, so the chest feels tight. Breathing thus becomes shallower and more rapid in order to get sufficient oxygen into the body. It is analogous to trying to inflate a balloon within the confined space of a small cage. Relaxed breathing involves learning to breathe more deeply and slowly from the abdomen rather than shallow fast breaths from the upper chest. This is known as 'diaphragmatic' breathing and is the starting point for many other forms of relaxation such as yoga and Tai Chi mentioned earlier, as well as the meditation techniques described later in this chapter. It can also be combined with other elements such as aromatherapy and relaxing music. An example of a deep breathing exercise which you can practise to help you relax is outlined below.

A deep breathing exercise

1   Sit comfortably with your back straight. Check your breathing by placing one hand on your upper chest and the other on the top of your stomach. If your breathing is correct, when you breathe in, your stomach and lower ribs should move out before your chest, which should move very little. If this is not the case, you need to learn how to breathe correctly.
2   Breathe out through your mouth, pushing out as much air as possible while at the same time contracting your abdominal muscles. Try to do this in a slow and controlled way rather than a sudden exhale. One way of doing this is to imagine that you have a lighted candle

6 inches away from your mouth, that you do not want to blow out. This will ensure that you release the air from your lungs slowly.

3 Breathe in through your nose slowly counting to 3 or 4 seconds as you breathe in, taking the air right down into your lungs. Notice the hand on your abdomen moving out as your lungs expand fully. Hold the air in for 3 or 4 seconds.

4 Continue to breathe in slowly through your nose, holding the air in and then exhaling slowly through your mouth. Notice the lower abdomen rising and falling as you do this. If you are breathing correctly, the hand on your chest will move very little.

5 If you find it difficult to breathe from your abdomen while sitting up, try doing the exercises while lying on the floor.

Progressive muscular relaxation

Progressive muscular relaxation training teaches the individual to develop advanced muscular skills which allow them to recognize and release even small amounts of tension. With regular practice the individual develops an intimate familiarity with what tension as well as complete relaxation feel like in different parts of the body and how to achieve deep levels of muscular relaxation. Also there is thought to be a powerful feedback loop between the muscles in the body and mental activity in the brain. It has been found that when a person's muscles are relaxed they are also more likely to report feeling calmer mentally. There are different types of muscular relaxation techniques but the one which is most commonly used is the 'contrast' technique. This involves learning a series of step-by-step muscle tensing and releasing exercises in different muscles groups in the body. The aim of these exercises is to teach the individual the difference between the feeling of tension and relaxation in each group of muscles around the body. So, ultimately, with lots of practice the individual learns to be able to spot and counteract the first signs of muscular tension that accompany stress and can relax these muscles at will.

Most progressive relaxation practitioners start at the feet and work their way up to the head and follow a sequence of muscle groups as they progress through the body. Learning this skill takes practice and in order to learn relaxation techniques properly you will need to set aside about 20 minutes a day to go through the exercises. If you do not make this level of commitment on a daily basis, you are unlikely to gain benefit from the training. There is a range of CDs on the market that can help you learn the techniques which are outlined below. It is important that you do the training only when there is no immediate time pressure.

For example, it is no good trying to fit it in 15 minutes before you rush off to work. This is likely to lead to skipping steps in the process or having your mind on other things rather than relaxation and ultimately experiencing the training as ineffective.

Once you have decided on the best time of day to do the relaxation training, prepare yourself by creating the right environment. Start by finding a room which is quiet and where you are unlikely to be disturbed. If necessary, inform others in the house that you are doing the exercises and do not wish to be disturbed. You do not want the distraction of someone walking into the room to get something or telling you there is a telephone call for you halfway through the exercises. Also, make sure that the room is not too hot or too cold and the lighting is dimmed if possible. You may need to close the curtains if it is too bright. Make yourself comfortable by either lying on a bed or sitting in a comfortable armchair. Loosen any tight clothing such as a belt, tie or the top button of a shirt. Take off your shoes and get yourself comfortable. Take a few minutes to concentrate on your breathing using the breathing exercises described earlier. Once you are breathing in and out in slow deep breaths, you are ready to start the progressive muscular relaxation routine outlined below.

A progressive muscular relaxation exercise

1 Focus your attention to your right foot, squeezing it as tightly as possible to the count of ten.
2 Relax your right foot. Notice the difference between tension and relaxation in the muscles of your right foot. Enjoy the feeling of your foot loosening up and the feeling of warmth as the blood returns to the muscles in the foot. Wiggle your toes around gently and notice the cooler air circulating around them.
3 Stay in this relaxed state for a moment, breathing deeply and slowly.
4 Shift your attention to the left foot and repeat the exercise.
5 Stay in this relaxed state for a moment, breathing deeply and slowly.
6 Move slowly up through your body contracting and relaxing the muscle groups as you go – right calf, left calf, right thigh, left thigh, hips and buttocks, stomach, chest, back, right arm and hand, left arm and hand, neck, shoulders, face, eyes and head.
7 Periodically return to your breathing to ensure that you are breathing slow, deep breaths.
8 Once you have gone through the full routine, spend a few minutes simply enjoying the relaxed state that you are in before returning to your everyday tasks.

9 Repeat this exercise daily until you feel that you have fully mastered the techniques involved.

10 If you notice that the tension is worse in particular muscle groups in the body, tailor the exercise routine to spend extra time on these muscle groups and less on those where it is not such a problem.

11 Once you have learned and are comfortable with the relaxation exercises, you can then begin to use them to combat stress in real life situations, for example when you are stuck in your car in a traffic jam or during your coffee break at work.

A brief relaxation exercise for the neck and shoulders

For many people who are stressed, muscular tension is most severe in the neck and shoulder muscles. Below is a relaxation exercise which takes very little time to do and specifically focuses on the neck and shoulders. It consists of exercises aimed at adopting the correct posture, relaxing the shoulders and relaxing the neck muscles.

1 *Find the correct sitting position*: stand up straight with your arms at your sides about six inches in front of a chair. Move the left leg back so that the back of the knee touches the chair. In one swift movement stick your bottom out and sit back in the chair. Allow yourself to slide into position in the chair with both feet flat on the ground and your back straight.

2 *Neck rotation*: sitting in an upright position looking straight ahead of you, slowly rotate your head to the left until your chin is parallel to your left shoulder. Hold your head there to the count of ten before slowly returning your head to look straight ahead of you. Repeat the exercise, moving your head to the right. Go through the full routine a few times.

3 *Neck elongation*: imagine that you are a puppet with a string attached to the top of your head and someone is pulling the string upwards. You will experience an 'elongation' feeling in the vertebrae (bones) of the spine in your neck. Do not resist this but simply allow it to happen for a count of ten. Then relax and notice a 'sinking' feeling as you relax. Repeat the exercise again after a 30 second gap. When repeated, the action should feel like there is a 'spring' in your neck.

4 *Shoulder exercises*: slowly and gently hunch your shoulders up tightly and move them upwards as if you are trying to touch your ears with them. Hold the position for the count of ten and then relax your shoulders. Repeat the exercise a couple of times.

Note: do not do the neck and shoulder exercises more than three times in one session but do them regularly, especially when you are feeling tension in your neck.

Mental relaxation techniques

So far in this chapter the relaxation exercises described have focused on physical relaxation. However, there are a range of mental relaxation exercises that have also been demonstrated to be effective in reducing stress. Generally speaking they work by reducing the 'mental chatter' that people who are stressed are bombarded with on a daily basis and inducing an inner sense of calm and peacefulness. Some of the best-known techniques include meditation, mindfulness, mental refocusing and visual imagery and these are outlined below.

Meditation

Meditation is often equated with Eastern mysticism and something that The Beatles did in the 1960s while on drugs. However, there is nothing intrinsically mysterious about meditation. It is simply a set of techniques aimed at helping the individual relax mentally. There is a wide range of meditative techniques but generally they involve sitting in a quiet comfortable environment, doing some preliminary muscle relaxation and breathing exercises to ensure a physically relaxed state and then practising a mental exercise which induces a passive attitude to the internal mental activity and external distractions that are being experienced. Meditation uses a 'neutral' focal device to engage the attention of the individual, such as a mental image (picture) or a 'mantra' (a chant or repeating a word or number over and over again). Focusing one's attention on to the neutral focal device allows all other information to drift in and out of the individual's consciousness without paying much attention to it at all. One example of a focal device is to imagine a translucent blue pyramid shape floating in three-dimensional space. Another is to imagine the word 'RELAX' in large bold three-dimensional letters revolving slowly in three-dimensional space. In some ways these examples are comparable to a screen saver on a computer, in that the image moves or rotates slowly on the screen while all other programs are shut down. An example of a mantra would be to the sound 'Oommh' over and over again. The result of paying attention to a neutral focusing device is to induce an inner sense or peacefulness and calm.

Mindfulness

Mindfulness is a particular kind of mediation derived from the Buddhist philosophy. It is based on the observation that when we are in a tense or distressed state, our mind is usually somewhere other than the present moment in time. For example, anxious people tend to live in the future. They spend much of their time worrying about what might happen tomorrow, next week or some time in the future. They predict that disaster and catastrophe are just round the corner. Depressed people on the other hand spend much of their time focusing on the past, missed opportunities and losses. Mindfulness meditation techniques, however, involve teaching the individual how to be fully engaged in the present moment without excessively analysing or over-thinking the experience. So rather than worrying about the future, or dwelling on the past, mindfulness meditation switches the focus of attention to what is happening in the here and now. There is a range of techniques that can bring about a state of mindfulness and some examples of these are outlined below. Give them a try and see what it feels like.

MINDFUL EATING

How often do you sit there at work eating your lunch while your mind is elsewhere? You may be worrying about the meeting that you have to go to later that afternoon, or you may be focusing on the memory of some event that has happened in the past. Because your attention is elsewhere it is likely that you have not even noticed the taste, touch or texture of the food that you are placing in your mouth. You may even be gulping the food down because you are in a hurry. Mindful eating involves paying full attention to the meal that you are eating. Try to eat slowly, taking time to fully enjoy the tastes, smells, colour and textures of the foods you are eating. Notice what it feels like when you chew and swallow each bite of your food.

BODY SCAN

In some respects body scanning is similar to progressive muscular relaxation in that you focus your attention on various parts of your body, starting with your feet and then working your way up the body. However, it is different from progressive muscular relaxation in that in mindfulness you are simply noticing 'what is' rather than tensing and relaxing your muscles, or labelling sensations as good and bad. It is about observing all the sensations you are experiencing in your body without trying to change anything. For example, you may observe that the muscles in your neck are particularly tense but instead of trying to change the sensation, mindfulness is about accepting that this is the way your neck is feeling at the present moment in the here and now.

MINDFUL WALKING

As for eating, how often do we simply rush from one place to another with our mind somewhere else? Mindful walking involves focusing your attention on the physical experience of every step that you take. Notice the sensation of pressure on your feet and in your shoes as your feet touch the ground. Experience the changes when you walk on different kinds of surface. Observe your body movements and sensations in your muscles. Notice the rhythm of your breathing and the feeling of the wind, rain or sunshine against your face. Soak up the sounds, sights and smells impinging on your senses as you progress on your journey.

Mental refocusing

Research has shown that humans have quite a limited attention span. It amounts on average to approximately seven 'bits' of information. So, for example, if we are asked to remember a series of digits in a telephone number, the average person can usually remember seven. Some people can remember one or two more than this and others fewer, but on average it is seven. This is important since although we are constantly being bombarded by hundreds of bits of information from all sensory modalities (sight, sound, taste, touch and smell), we can selectively and consciously pay attention to only a small number of them. The ones that we select are those which we perceive to be most important or relevant to us and the rest are processed unconsciously and go by unnoticed. To illustrate an example of selective attention, imagine that you are at a party and deep in conversation with someone. You are so engrossed that you do not notice what else is going on around you. However, you suddenly hear your name mentioned in a conversation nearby and immediately you switch your attention to that conversation. Why and how can this happen? It happens because your brain is geared up to selectively pay attention to those bits of information that are most relevant and important to you. However, your brain must have been unconsciously processing lots of other incoming information in order to be able to switch attention in this way.

When people are under stress they are hypervigilant to incoming information that signals threat or danger and get into the habit of focusing most (if not all) their conscious attention span to such stimuli. Mental refocusing techniques can be used to train the individual to shift their focus of attention away from the distressing stimuli to neutral or positive ones. One example of mental refocusing is the attention shift exercise. For example, some people experiencing stress may show an attention bias towards internal bodily sensations and symptoms rather than stimuli in their external environment. The purpose of attention training in this context would thus be to shift attention away from focusing on the self towards external, more neutral environmental cues. This change of focus can ultimately result in a reduction in stress in that individual. Exercises can also focus on shifting attention between the five sensory modalities (i.e., sight, sound, smell, taste and touch), or between tasks within a particular sensory modality. To illustrate this you can try the little experiment below for yourself.

A MENTAL REFOCUSING EXERCISE

Begin by focusing your attention on the ticking of the clock in your room. Before being instructed to do this, you may not have even noticed that the clock was ticking. It does not have to be a clock since any sound source will suffice for this experiment. You will notice that once you pay attention to the sound, it seems to get louder. Do this for a couple of minutes before switching your attention to another sound in the room such as the hum of the refrigerator, the fluorescent light or the boiler. While you are paying attention to the second sound source, you will no longer be able to listen to the first one (i.e., the clock). Do this for a couple of minutes. Now notice the sounds coming from outside of the room such as people talking, cars passing by or perhaps the sound of an ambulance siren in the distance? And pay attention to one of these. If you practise these attention training exercises regularly over a period of time, you will become more skilled at shifting your attention. Research has found that attention training can be effective in reducing stress if practised at least twice a day over a period of six months.

Visual imagery

Visual imagery (sometimes called visualization or guided imagery) is a variation on traditional mediation that can have powerful relaxation properties. It involves imagining a scene which makes you feel at peace. You can choose whatever scene you wish. This might be a favourite place from your childhood, an image from a relaxing holiday that you once had, or even a picture by your favourite artist. The main point of the exercise is to find an image, scene or setting which is the most calming to you. You can do the imagery exercise with a therapist, on your own, or with the use of an audio recording. There are lots of CDs on the market which can be used for this purpose. For example, the 'rose garden' takes you in your imagination through a beautiful garden of roses and asks you to savour the experience through all your sensory modalities. Another one is called the 'enchanted forest', which takes you on a magical journey through a very beautiful and peaceful forest. Others create the sounds that you might hear while lying on a beach, for example including the gentle lapping of the waves on the shore or the sound of seagulls flying above you, and ask you to relax in the presence of these sounds.

The important thing about doing imagery successfully is that you imagine a setting that is most relaxing for you personally. To gain maximum benefit from an imagery exercise, you need first of all to do it somewhere comfortable and when you are not in any hurry and unlikely to be disturbed. Start by closing your eyes and clearing your mind of any mental chatter. Focus on deep breathing for a few minutes before commencing the imagery exercise that you have chosen. Picture the images as vividly as you possibly can in all the sensory modalities. Imagine in great detail the sights, sounds, smells, tastes and touch of the setting you have placed yourself in. You could try the following exercise.

A VISUAL IMAGERY EXERCISE

Imagine you have chosen the setting of a Christmas Eve long ago in your childhood at a time when you felt happy, safe and secure. Try to imagine the room you are in, the lighting of the room, the patterns on the wallpaper, the pictures on the wall, the colour schemes, who is there with you, where you are in the room, the way in which the Christmas tree has been decorated, the smell of cooking from the kitchen, the smell of the freshly cut pine tree, the sounds of excited children and Christmas carols coming from the radio, the feeling of warmth on your face from the roaring log fire, the texture of your brand new dressing gown, the taste and sensation of eating a warm mince pie, the reflections from the fire light on the wall and the sight of snow flakes gently fluttering past the window.

This example may of course be a very romantic version of your actual childhood experiences of Christmas Eve. However, it does not really matter if the scene that you imagine is a real memory of a time in the past when you have felt particularly happy and safe, or a product of your imagination. The main thing is that it is a restful image and creates a sense of peace and mental wellbeing in you.

Summary and main learning points

- Stress and relaxation can be conceptualized as being at opposite ends of a continuum.
- Individuals who are experiencing stress either have forgotten how to relax or may have never learned the art of relaxation in the first place.
- There is a range of practical tools and techniques that can help the individual move from the stressed to the relaxed end of the continuum.
- The interventions described in this chapter are at three levels, namely informal, semi-formal and formal relaxation skills.
- For many people informal relaxation strategies are all that are needed to help them manage their stress effectively.
- It is not possible to be too prescriptive with respect to which informal relaxation techniques are best for you personally, since everyone has their own different way of relaxing informally.
- Examples of some of the most popular informal relaxation strategies include reading, listening to music, having a hot bath, going to the cinema, theatre or pub, or watching television. Alternatively, some people prefer to use a physical activity such as swimming, jogging, squash or a vigorous workout at the gym.
- The important thing when choosing an informal relaxation strategy is to decide which one is the right one for you.
- Where informal relaxation strategies are insufficient to help an individual cope with their stress, then semi-formal relaxation techniques may be required.
- Semi-formal interventions consist of slightly more structured relaxation techniques than informal relaxation strategies.
- There are numerous kinds of semi-formal relaxation techniques and some of the most popular ones include massage, yoga and Tai Chi.
- Where an individual is experiencing more chronic stress related tension, informal and semi-formal relaxation techniques are insufficient to break the habit and more formal relaxation techniques may be required.
- Formal relaxation may consist of physical or mental exercises, or a combination of both.
- Some common examples of formal physical relaxation techniques which have been demonstrated to have beneficial effects include deep breathing and progressive muscular relaxation exercises.
- Some common examples of formal mental relaxation techniques which have been demonstrated to have beneficial effects include meditation, mindfulness and visual imagery exercises.

- Deep breathing is of key importance in terms of relaxing and is the starting point for many forms of physical and mental relaxation including progressive muscular relaxation, yoga, Tai Chi and meditation.
- Learning the basics of these more formal physical and mental exercises is not difficult but it takes regular practice to master the skills involved and gain maximum benefit from them.
- Relaxation exercises need to be practised at least daily and preferably more frequently than this until the individual is able to use them effectively.

In conclusion, there is no one technique or level of intervention that has been proven to be best for everyone, so it is important that you choose the technique and level that most appropriately meets your needs, preferences and lifestyle. Once you have decided on the intervention which is best for you, you need to practise it at least daily. Practice is essential when learning a new skill and without it, it is unlikely that you will gain maximum benefit. If in doubt about what is the best level to start, it is preferable to begin with informal interventions, since often these are sufficient to produce the desired effect. It is only if you find the informal techniques to be ineffective that you will need to progress on to the more formal level of interventions as outlined earlier in this chapter. If you are unsure about what interventions to start with, try experimenting with some informal interventions that you think might work for you. If they have the desired effect, that is great. However, you may not get it right first time and it is important that you do not give up at the first hurdle. Treat it as an experiment in which you may try a number of interventions before you find the right one for you. Once you have started putting the relaxation techniques you have learned into practice, you should experience a reduction in your stress levels and a corresponding increase in the feeling of relaxation over time as you move to the more relaxed end of the continuum. You can monitor your progress in this respect by readministering the stress checklist found in Chapter 1 on a regular basis and notice how your scores on the symptoms of stress reduce over time. The range of tools and techniques found in this chapter may not be sufficient to overcome more severe, clinical levels of stress. Where this is the case, the interventions for overcoming stress syndromes outlined in Chapter 10 are likely to be more beneficial.

Chapter 9

Changing the way you relate to your work

Introduction

The beliefs and attitudes that we hold about ourselves, others and the world are formed by our early life experiences and consolidated by subsequent experiences in later life. Each of us is unique in this respect. For example, some of us are more positive in our thinking whereas others may be highly self-critical. Some of us are self-sacrificing in our attitudes whereas others believe they are entitled to special treatment. Some people are very trusting of other people, whereas others find it difficult to trust others at all. It is not helpful to describe a particular set of beliefs and attitudes as being right or wrong. It is, however, reasonable to describe them as being helpful or unhelpful to the individual. The utility of beliefs held can also change over time. For example, beliefs about not being able to trust others may have been adaptive in the context of an early childhood environment where those around you were actually untrustworthy. However, such beliefs could then become problematic later in life in the context of a marital relationship where mutual trust is crucial to the survival of the marriage, or at work where team working is crucial to the success of a project. At the same time, the belief that others cannot be trusted could be adaptive and have survival value for someone who is in a hostile environment such as a war zone or prison.

Our pre-existing beliefs and attitudes can therefore determine whether or not we find a situation stressful. Research has also shown that the experience of stress itself can alter the way we think. The capacity for rational and objective thinking can be impaired in individuals experiencing stress and the resulting irrational appraisals can serve to maintain or even exacerbate stress reactions. The camera analogy outlined in Chapter 1 (p. 9) likened an individual's appraisal of a particular situation or event to taking a snapshot. The settings of the camera (e.g., lens, focus, speed and aperture settings) all determine what the eventual picture obtained will look like. In a similar way, the cognitive settings of an individual's mind will determine the meaning that they attach to a situation or event and these settings themselves can become altered when an individual is under stress.

Recent research in the field of cognitive therapy has shown that it is possible to change unhelpful thinking patterns associated with stress and replace them with more rational, healthy positive ones, leading to reduced stress levels. The aim of this chapter is to teach you to identify, label and challenge your own unhelpful thinking patterns and learn alternative healthier ways of thinking about yourself, others and your environment in order to reduce the stress you are experiencing. In the context of work, this can be particularly helpful, since the working environment itself is not always readily amenable to change. Thus, learning to think differently about a situation can help you cope more effectively with it and make the best of what may be an objectively poor working environment. Up to this point in the book, the interventions described have focused mostly on identifying and changing unhelpful patterns of behaviour with relatively little reference to cognitive strategies. However, the cognitive skills learned in this chapter can also be applied to earlier chapters in this book. For example, positive thinking forms an integral part of a healthy lifestyle (Chapter 4) and healthy thinking patterns are also central to being assertive, socially skilled and managing one's anxiety effectively (Chapters 5 to 8). Four steps to developing these cognitive skills are identified in this chapter. Briefly summarized, these are:

*   understanding the links between thoughts, feelings, behaviours and bodily reactions;
*   identifying unhelpful patterns of thinking;
*   labelling dysfunctional thinking styles;
*   challenging dysfunctional patterns of thinking.

Each of these is covered in detail below.

Understanding the links between thoughts, feelings, behaviours and bodily reactions

Aaron T. Beck, who is seen by many as the father of modern cognitive therapy, used the vignette technique to illustrate the links between thoughts, feelings, behaviours and bodily reactions. Vignettes are essentially little stories which highlight the importance of cognitive interpretations and how these affect emotions and behaviours. One well-known example that Beck used was the cat vignette. This exercise is outlined below, so have a go at doing this for yourself now.

The cat vignette exercise

> Imagine it is the middle of the night and you are fast asleep. Suddenly you are woken up and startled by a loud noise downstairs. You look at your clock and it is 2am. What thoughts are going through your head? How does it make you feel? What do you actually do?
>
> Then, suddenly you remember that you forgot to put the cat out. You usually put the cat out because it has a tendency to climb up on furniture and knock things off. What are your thoughts? What are your feelings? What do you do?

The basic learning point from this exercise is that thoughts are not reality but interpretations that colour our feelings and guide our behaviours. It is likely that before you realized it was the cat, your thoughts, feelings and behaviours were those associated with anxiety and fear. However, once you realized it was the cat, your thoughts, feelings and behaviours were likely to be more relaxed ones. This vignette neatly illustrates the links between thoughts, feelings, behaviours and physical (bodily) reactions to the triggering event of hearing a noise in the middle of the night. It also demonstrates that thoughts are interpretations and not unquestionable truths.

Thus, while on the face of it we may feel we are at the mercy of our thought processes, in reality we do have choices about the interpretations we make of events and situations. Unhealthy (negative) thinkers have a habitual bias towards selecting negative and irrational interpretations of events, whereas healthy (positive) thinkers have a habitual bias towards making more positive and rational interpretations of events. The aim is thus to break the unhealthy habitual biases in thinking displayed by negative thinkers and replace them with more positive and healthy ones. However, before an individual can begin to successfully challenge their dysfunctional thinking patterns they must first be able to identify what these are and what triggers them.

Identifying unhelpful patterns of thinking

The most common technique used to help the individual explore and identify their unhelpful thinking patterns is self-monitoring using a thoughts diary. The thoughts dairy can be used to identify the specific situational triggers that lead to unhelpful thoughts and feelings. The typical format for a thoughts diary sheet is given in Table 9.1.

Table 9.1 Example of a typical thoughts diary

Date/time	Situations	Emotions	Negative automatic thoughts (NATs)	Rational response	Outcome

Note: This table is available to view and print from the following website: www.routledgementalhealth.com/9780415671781

In the 'Situations' column of Table 9.1, the actual triggering event leading to the unpleasant emotions and thoughts is described. The trigger does not have to be an event in the here and now but can equally be a thought, a daydream or recollection leading to the unpleasant emotion. For example, the individual may have just been sitting looking through the paper and read an article which triggers an unpleasant memory. Once an unpleasant emotion has been triggered, the individual is required to identify the emotion (for example, sadness, anxiety or anger) and the strength of the emotion as a percentage from 1 per cent (minimum) to 100 per cent (maximum) in the 'Emotions' column. In the next column the individual is required to identify the distressing thoughts that are associated with the unpleasant emotion and to rate the strength of the belief as a percentage (again from 1 per cent to 100 per cent). These are referred to as negative automatic thoughts (NATs) in this diary example but are also sometimes referred to as irrational or dysfunctional thoughts. At this stage in the process the final two columns ('Rational response' and 'Outcome') are left empty until the individual has learned the techniques for challenging the NATs and identifying outcomes. We will return to the two final columns later in the chapter once these techniques have been covered. Over a period of time the individual will accumulate a number of specific diary examples. From these examples it is usually possible to identify one or a few common 'themes' emerging across the range of situations recorded. Each theme is indicative of a particular dysfunctional thinking style. There are numerous common dysfunctional thinking styles and the task for the individual is to identify and label the one(s) that are relevant to them. Some examples of these thinking styles are outlined below.

Labelling dysfunctional thinking styles

The list of dysfunctional thinking styles below is by no means an exhaustive one. However, it covers some of the most common ones which are encountered in everyday life.

Catastrophic thinking

Catastrophic thinking is characterized by making excessively negative predictions about the future in the absence of evidence to support these predictions. It is about overestimating the chances of disaster, which is seen as being imminent and just round the corner. For example, an individual who makes a relatively minor mistake at work worries that they might lose their job ... if they lose their job they will not be able to pay the mortgage ... they will end up on the street ... their family will leave them ... they will have no job, no money, no family ... end up 'on skid row' and so on. It can be seen that the original trigger event leads to a whole chain of disastrous predictions that are way out of proportion. While most of us make a guess at what is going to happen in the future, this is usually a balance of positive and negative predictions. However, catastrophic thinking is a kind of fortune telling which predicts only bad things happening.

Jumping to conclusions and mind reading

These are specific manifestations of catastrophic thinking. Jumping to conclusions involves making negative predictions (fortune telling) about the future such as 'I know I'll make a mess of things' or 'I know this treatment won't work'. When an individual mind reads, they imagine that they know what people are thinking instead of finding out what they are really thinking. Both jumping to conclusions and mind reading involve making predictions in the absence of evidence to support them and rarely result in successful outcomes. People are notoriously bad at making such predictions.

Overgeneralization

Overgeneralization involves using one small part of an experience or situation to describe a whole experience. Conclusions are drawn on the basis of this very limited information and applied across a broad range of situations. One small bit is used to describe the whole. For example, someone who slightly overcooks the vegetables proclaims that 'the whole meal is ruined'. A single isolated failure is interpreted as part of a never-ending pattern of defeat. It is often accompanied by overgeneralizing statements such as 'never' or 'always', for example, 'I never have any success' or 'I always upset people'.

Magnification

Magnification refers to the tendency to exaggerate the importance of negative events and blowing them out of proportion. It involves focusing one's thinking on and attending only to the negative parts of one's life, while ignoring all the positive things that happen. The person thinks that the mistakes that they have made are more important and significant than they actually are: they selectively attend to one negative aspect or detail while dismissing the broader context. For example, an individual who makes a single bad business deal spends a disproportionate amount of time 'beating himself up' about it rather than focusing on all the other deals that have been successful. Other examples include 'I got question nine wrong' without reference to the fact that they got all the other questions right, or 'Last Tuesday evening was awful', without acknowledging that the other six days of last week were enjoyable.

Minimization

Minimization is in some ways the 'mirror image' of magnification. It refers to playing down the significance of positive events and achievements. The person thinks that the good things that they have done are less valuable than they actually are. With minimization the individual readily attributes positive events to merely 'luck', pure 'chance' or 'the skills and expertise of others' but never their own skills. However, at the same time they readily attribute all the negative events and failures that happen to their own incompetence (as in magnification).

Personalization

Personalization refers to the tendency to see oneself as the 'cause' of some negative events, for which they are not necessarily responsible and when there is no rational basis for doing so. Neutral events are interpreted as having negative significance to the individual. For example, a friend cancels an evening out and you think it's because they don't like you, or your children behave badly and you think it must be your fault. Similarly, someone might 'snap' at you and you blame yourself, thinking 'I must have deserved it'.

Black and white thinking

Black and white thinking is a form of dichotomous thinking, which refers to the tendency to place experiences in one of two discrete categories rather than on a continuum. Shades of grey do not seem to exist for black and white thinkers. It is sometimes referred to as 'all or nothing' thinking. For example, the world is seen in terms of dichotomies, such as people are either 'all good or all bad', '100 per cent successful or a complete failure', 'perfect or rubbish', 'strong or weak', 'loved or hated' and so on. It ignores the middle ground and leads to polarized thinking.

'Should' and 'must' statements

Should and must statements are examples of what are called moral imperatives. Moral imperatives refer to setting rigid and often unrealistic rules and standards about one's own or others' conduct and being particularly harsh and unforgiving towards oneself (or others) for not meeting these. It involves living by fixed rules and fretting about how things ought to be rather than how it actually is. Sometimes these imperatives are used by the individual to motivate them to achieve more. However, in reality they end up making them feel guilty or demoralized as a result of not meeting these expectations or resentful towards others who do not meet them. Some examples of moral imperatives include 'I must help everyone who needs it', 'I must please everybody all of the time', 'I should always be a nice person' and 'I should always put others first'.

Challenging dysfunctional patterns of thinking

Once the individual has learned to become aware of their own dysfunctional thinking style(s), the next step is to evaluate them and look for more helpful and realistic alternative ones to replace them. There are a number of well-established techniques used to challenge the negative automatic thoughts identified in the thoughts diaries. These include 'Examining the evidence', 'Exploring the alternatives' and 'Identifying the advantages and disadvantages' of thinking in such a negative way. Other useful techniques, which can help the individual come up with more positive and plausible alternatives and test them out, include 'The friend technique', 'Checking it out', 'Estimating probabilities', 'Reattributing meaning' and 'Conducting behavioural experiments'. All these techniques are presented below.

Examining the evidence

The examining the evidence technique involves asking oneself the questions: 'What is the evidence for and against the negative thought(s) I am having? Do the facts of the situation back up what I think, or do they contradict it?' It requires the individual to become their own lawyer and to cross-examine themselves. Evidence does not only have to come from the present moment in time; it can also be gathered from an individual's historical experiences. The two column technique shown in Table 9.2 can be useful in this exercise.

Table 9.2 The two column technique for examining the evidence

Evidence for the belief	Evidence against the belief

Note: This table is available to view and print from the following website: www. routledgementalhealth.com/9780415671781

Exploring the alternatives

The exploring the alternatives technique involves asking the following questions: 'Are there alternative ways of looking at the situation which are more positive?', 'How would someone else view this situation?', 'How would I have viewed this situation in the past?' There are usually many different alternative ways to look at any experience. The individual brainstorms as many alternative and less negative explanations as they can. They then examine the evidence for and against each one and try to decide objectively which alternative is most likely to be correct.

Identifying advantages and disadvantages

Another cognitive technique which is commonly used is to identify the advantages and disadvantages of holding the belief. It involves asking the question 'Does holding this belief help me or hinder me from getting what I want?' The individual is encouraged to explore how their negative thinking influences the way that they feel and establish the pros and cons of continuing to hold on to the belief as opposed to changing it. The two column technique can be a useful one in terms of identifying the advantages and disadvantages of holding the belief (see Table 9.3).

Table 9.3 The two column technique for identifying advantages and disadvantages

Advantages of this belief	Disadvantages of this belief

Note: This table is available to view and print from the following website: www.routledgementalhealth.com/9780415671781

The techniques outlined in Table 9.3 are used to challenge the systematic errors in thinking and the dysfunctional thinking styles identified earlier in this chapter. The aim of doing these exercises is to find some alternative, more positive, rational and balanced ways of thinking which reduce distress and are more helpful to the individual.

The friend technique

In the friend technique, the individual is asked to consider how they think their best friend might react in the situation that they are confronted with and also to imagine what advice their best friend might give them if they were here to advise them now. A variation of this technique involves swapping roles. The individual is asked to consider what advice they would give to someone about the best way to react in this situation if they came to them with their problem. People often find that they can give very rational and sensible advice to others but often cannot do this for themselves. The friend technique is thought to work by allowing the individual to stand back a little from their situation and hence adopt a less emotional and more rational stance.

Checking it out

The checking it out technique is particularly useful when an individual is uncertain about what another person is thinking. This can done by simply asking people what they are thinking rather than jumping to conclusions about their motivations or mind reading. Checking things out can provide an immediate and very effective way of challenging negative assumptions.

Estimating probabilities

Estimating the probability of both negative and positive interpretations of an event is a particularly powerful technique for challenging anxious predictions. By assessing both interpretations it does not reject the original negative interpretation, unlikely as it might be, but contrasts it with more likely interpretations. This approach trains the individual to consider thoughts as interpretations of reality rather than reality itself and helps them reach more rational conclusions, the outcomes of which can then be subsequently evaluated. For example, if someone is anxious about flying, it is possible to compare the probability of having an accident while flying, to the probability of having an accident in a car, and get a sense of proportion about the risk involved.

Reattributing meaning

The technique of reattributing meaning is particularly helpful for challenging beliefs about guilt and blame. Rather than blaming oneself, the reattribution technique encourages the individual to consider external environmental factors as causes for negative outcomes rather than just internal personal factors. Also, even if the individual was responsible to some extent, they are encouraged to ask the question 'Are the consequences of this really as bad as they seem?' and consider how might they feel about these events in one day, one week, one month or six months' time.

Conducting behavioural experiments

Challenging cognitive distortions need not take place only at a cognitive level. The process can be greatly enhanced by the use of some more empirical behavioural strategies such as conducting behavioural experiments for example. This involves the setting up of 'mini experiments', whereby the patient's original negative thoughts and the new alternative positive ones are treated as two possible alternative hypotheses predicting an outcome. The patient is then encouraged to test these out in a real life situation and to establish which of the two alternatives is more accurately predictive of the outcome.

Case study: Sarah

This case study has been included to illustrate the use of the cognitive techniques described above to identify, label and challenge dysfunctional thinking patterns.

Sarah was a 32-year-old nurse who had just been promoted to a post as a nurse in charge of an intensive care unit. It was the week before she was due to start in her new job and she was feeling particularly anxious about it. As a result of her early life experiences and upbringing, Sarah was not a very confident individual and was prone to experiencing quite a lot of self-doubt and worry about her own capabilities, even though she was in reality quite a high achiever. As the start date got nearer, she became increasingly anxious, verging on panicky. Sarah was encouraged to commence a thoughts diary in order to identify the unhelpful thinking patterns which were leading to her feeling anxious and panicky. A copy of one of the entries in her thoughts dairy is provided in Table 9.4.

The example in the thoughts diary reported that Sarah had experienced an anxiety attack in a shoe shop and had to leave the shop because of it. The triggering event was identified as attempting to buy a pair of shoes for starting her new job the following week. The triggering thought which led to her anxiety was 'Gosh, this time next week I will have started in the new job'. Through the process of self-monitoring her thoughts using a thoughts diary, Sarah was able to identify and rate a number of dysfunctional thoughts associated with her anxiety. These included 'I will not be able to cope' (80 per cent), 'I will make a mistake' (75 per cent), 'I will show myself up' (80 per cent), 'I will get the sack' (80 per cent) and 'People will think that I am not up to the job' (90 per cent). She labelled these distortions as examples of catastrophic thinking, jumping to conclusions and mind reading. By looking at the evidence for and against each of the NATs listed, Sarah was able to identify alternative more positive and rational beliefs to challenge them. As a consequence of successfully challenging her anxious thinking patterns Sarah's overall level of anxiety reduced considerably and she felt more able to cope.

In addition, Sarah set up a behavioural experiment to test her positive and negative predictions about her new job. Her positive predictions were those beliefs she had reached through the process of challenging her NATs that she would be able to cope, would not get sacked, would not make a mistake or show herself up, and that people would think that she was capable of doing the job. Her negative predictions were that she would not cope, that she would get the sack, make a mistake or show herself up, and people would think she was not up to the job. She tested out the accuracy of these predictions two months after commencing her new job and the outcome was that the evidence completely supported her positive predictions and invalidated the negative ones. Not only had she settled well in her new job, but also she had not made any significant mistakes and had received lots of positive comments about her performance at work from her manager, colleagues and patients. For Sarah, the behavioural

Table 9.4 An example of Sarah's thoughts diary

Date/time	Situations	Emotions	Negative automatic thoughts (NATs)	Rational response	Outcome
Monday 2 March	In a shop trying on a pair of shoes for work.	Felt anxious (80 per cent)	'I will not be able to cope' (80 per cent)	'These are just examples of catastrophic thinking. They would not have given me the job if they thought I could not cope with it'	Reduced anxiety (40 per cent)
	Thought 'Gosh, this time next week I will have started in the new job'	Felt panicky (95 per cent)	'I will make a mistake' (75 per cent)	'I will be able to cope' (70 per cent) 'I have never made a mistake before and there is no reason why I should make one now' (90 per cent)	No longer felt panicky
	Had to leave the shop	Felt embarrassed and ashamed of myself (70 per cent)	'I will show myself up' (80 per cent)	These are two examples of jumping to conclusions	No longer felt ashamed of myself
			'I will get the sack' (80 per cent)	There is nothing to suggest this will happen. 'I will not show myself up or get sacked' (90 per cent)	
			'People will think that I am not up to the job' (90 per cent)	This is an example of mind reading. 'They do not even know me yet, so how can they think this?' (80 per cent)	

experiment had provided evidence that she was more capable than she had initially believed and it disconfirmed her original negative beliefs about herself and others. As a result of the positive outcome of the experiment, she began to feel more confident and relaxed at work.

Challenging work dysfunctions

The term 'work dysfunction' refers to a significant impairment in the capacity to work caused by a dysfunctional relationship between the individual and their job. Two main types of dysfunctional relationships between an individual and their job have been identified. These are over-commitment and under-commitment to work. Some common patterns of over-commitment include perfectionism and workaholism. Common patterns of under-commitment include underachievement and procrastination. The cognitive techniques described earlier in this chapter can be used to help the employee change the way they relate to their job and develop a healthier and more functional attitude towards it. The application of these techniques to some of the most common work dysfunctions is outlined below.

Challenging patterns of over-commitment

Modifying perfectionism

Perfectionism involves the setting of extremely high and unrelenting standards of performance. Two types of perfectionism have been reported. These are healthy perfectionism, where the attitude is positively reinforced by the rewards and goals attained, and unhealthy perfectionism, where an individual is striving to prevent an unwanted outcome such as failure or disapproval by others. Unlike those with 'normal' high standards, people with unhealthy perfectionism are unable to accept even a minor flaw in their work. However, perfectionists are not necessarily efficient people, since their excessive focus on getting things just right reduces their productivity. Perfectionists believe that no less than 100 per cent is good enough (the 'all or nothing' thinking style mentioned earlier) and strive to avoid making mistakes at all costs. They adopt these unrealistic expectations not only for themselves but also for others and become irritated when others fail to meet the standards set. However, because being perfect is an unachievable ideal, the perfectionist is constantly giving themself the message that they have failed and others have let them down. In the work context this can create high levels of stress for the individual concerned and also for those around them.

Cognitive interventions for modifying perfectionism involve identifying and challenging the dysfunctional attitudes associated with it. The advantages and disadvantages of perfectionist thinking can be explored. In particular, the disadvantages are highlighted, in that while striving for perfectionism can produce some high quality work, generally it leads to constant feelings of tension and anxiety. It can also on occasions result in the employee becoming paralysed with the fear of failure, constant self-flagellation and lead to poor relationships with others who are unable or do not wish to live up to their unrelenting standards. Alternative ways of thinking are introduced, such as 'It is all right to make mistakes sometimes', 'Everyone makes mistakes', 'No one is perfect', 'We can learn from our mistakes' and 'It's all right to achieve less than 100 per cent on most occasions'. These new rules for living can then be tested out using behavioural experiments. The outcomes monitored by the individual can be used as evidence that in most situations less than perfect performance does not result in the catastrophic consequences feared. Also, the individual needs to challenge their 'all or nothing' dichotomous thinking style and rather than seeing situations as 'win-lose', 'good-bad' or 'success-failure', see more of the middle ground and rate their achievements on a continuum. For example, they may start to rate their performance as 70 per cent successful on a continuum rather than in one of two categories. They are also encouraged to try out new activities, which previously they may have avoided because of their fear of failure. Overall, the aim of these interventions is to help the individual learn that it is acceptable to accomplish less and accomplish it less perfectly, that it is acceptable to be average at some things, and that the feared catastrophic consequences of dropping their unrelenting standards do not materialize. This should also help them to realize that the benefits both socially and occupationally of adopting a more relaxed and easygoing attitude to life are well worth it.

Modifying workaholism

Workaholism is an 'addiction' to work, which results in a noticeable disturbance on the rest of the individual's life. The workaholic employee typically presents with a Type A personality profile. Such individuals are highly competitive, hostile, impatient, always in a hurry, take on too much work and feeling guilty about relaxing. Many Type A individuals argue that they just do not want to change, or that everything would be fine if other people would stop being so inefficient. However, research has shown that Type A individuals are more prone to stress related illness and burnout than more relaxed and easygoing Type B personalities. Unfortunately, Type A attitudes and behaviours are very much rewarded in our Western culture in terms of financial rewards, career advancement and status. They are also encouraged by many employers since they lead to higher productivity. Workaholics also have a tendency to over-identify with their work. Over-identification means that a major part of a person's identity and sense of self-worth is derived from the job that they do. They believe that their 'self-worth is proportional to their achievements at work', that they 'can only earn the right to be happy through hard work' and that 'success at work is the only route to self-esteem'. As a result of these beliefs they can become a slave to their work. Such individuals dedicate very little time to non-work activities and tend to see themselves personally and their social status in terms of a job label. This is potentially a risky thing to do since having all one's eggs in one basket, so to speak, means that if that basket is dropped (i.e., they lose their job), their whole life is shattered. Problems can also arise in the workaholic's personal life, since it is likely that their partner may eventually get fed up with their unavailability and inability to get the balance between work and home life right. This can result in marital disharmony and ultimately even divorce.

Modifying workaholism involves identifying and challenging the dysfunctional attitudes associated with Type A personality traits and over-identification. The workaholic's relationship to their work needs to be changed from one of continual striving to achieve at an unrelenting pace, to a more relaxed one. The link between work and self-worth also needs to be challenged. The first step is to self-monitor using thoughts diary sheets in order to identify examples of the workaholic attitudes that need to be challenged. The standard cognitive techniques outlined earlier in this chapter can be employed to identify and challenge their dysfunctional beliefs and assumptions about the workaholic's relationship with their work. They need to consider alternative ways of thinking such as 'It is possible to be happy without all the trappings of success such as wealth, possessions and high job status', 'Success and happiness are not the same thing', 'My world will not fall apart if I take my foot off the pedal', 'Type A behaviour can be physically and psychologically damaging to my health' and 'There are other roots to self-worth and happiness apart from work'.

Behavioural experiments can also be an effective way of disconfirming the dysfunctional beliefs and attitudes associated with workaholism. The individual needs to be prepared to take the risk of trying new ways of relating to their work and life outside work. For example, the Type A individual needs to practise speaking deliberately more slowly, becoming less competitive and hostile, giving in now and again, going the long way round when travelling somewhere, hiding their watch, scheduling a rest period in the middle of a busy day, focusing more on quality than speed or quantity and taking time to observe others and listen to them. The over-identifier needs to take the risk of finding alternative roots to status and self-esteem outside of work. The outcomes of such behavioural experiments should serve to disconfirm and weaken their dysfunctional beliefs by demonstrating that their worst negative fears and predictions do not materialize.

Challenging patterns of under-commitment

Modifying underachievement

Under-commitment to one's work usually manifests itself as underperforming in a significant aspect of one's work role and a failure to achieve one's full potential. Underachieving is associated with two main avoidant coping styles, namely failure avoidance and success avoidance. The failure avoidant individual fears failure relative to their peers in areas of achievement such as career, status, income and educational attainment. They are thus unwilling to compete with others to improve themselves. Failure avoidant individuals can be quite bright intellectually and may make claims that they are wasted in their present job and are capable of better things. Yet they seem unable or unwilling to make the effort to improve themselves, for example by enrolling at college, or doing further training. In contrast, success avoidant individuals display a persistent tendency to avoid behaviours associated with achievement, such as decision making, taking responsibility, using their initiative or going for promotion. They fear that they will not be able to cope with the responsibilities demanded of them if they are successful and may find face-saving ways of not taking on new responsibilities.

When an individual adopts an avoidant coping style, they are trying to prevent their underlying negative beliefs and emotions from being activated by avoiding any situation that may trigger them. It is likely that failure avoidant and success avoidant individuals may have learned to believe as children that they were untalented and lack what it takes to succeed. As a consequence they live in fear that exposure of their incompetence is imminent. Cognitive interventions thus focus on challenging dysfunctional assumptions relating to the underlying beliefs that they are 'incompetent', 'unable to cope', 'unable to take responsibility' or 'likely to fail'.

Challenging patterns of underachievement involves identifying and challenging the dysfunctional attitudes associated with failure. The underachiever's relationship to their work needs to be changed from one of procrastination and avoidance to one of confronting challenges in a timely way. The link between work and fear of failure needs to be challenged. The first step is to self-monitor using thoughts diary sheets in order to identify examples of the attitudes associated with avoidant behaviours that need to be challenged. The standard cognitive techniques outlined earlier in this chapter can be employed to identify and challenge their dysfunctional beliefs and assumptions about the underachiever's relationship with their work. They need to consider alternative ways of thinking such as 'I am as good as anyone else', 'I am capable', 'I am competent', 'I am able to cope', 'I can be successful' and 'I can handle responsibility'. These alternative beliefs can then be tested out through behavioural experiments.

The use of behavioural experiments to disconfirm dysfunctional beliefs can be particularly effective where avoidance is a maintaining factor. Underachievers particularly need to confront situations in which they believe there is a risk of failure. For example, the failure avoidant employee is to be encouraged to carry out behavioural experiments in which they come out of their comfort zone and put themselves more in situations where there is a risk of failure. This could, for example, be through enrolling at college, doing further training or going for promotion. Similarly, success avoidant employees could be encouraged to confront situations where they could be successful. This may involve taking on greater responsibilities, practising more autonomous decision making, or going for promotion, in order to confront their fear of success.

Modifying procrastination

Both failure avoidant and success avoidant individuals may also engage in the maladaptive coping strategy of 'procrastination'. This form of avoidance essentially involves 'putting off until tomorrow what one should do today'. Procrastinators repeatedly avoid the timely initiation and completion of assignments that need to be completed by a certain deadline. This often results in a surge of last minute effort, considerable anxiety and a lower quality of work due to the task being rushed.

As with underachievers, individuals who procrastinate need to consider alternative ways of thinking such as 'Don't put things off' and 'Do it now'. Procrastinators should be encouraged to stop putting things off and do them as soon as is practically possible, plan ahead, do tasks in manageable chunks and aim to meet deadlines set. The outcomes of such behavioural experiments should serve to disconfirm and weaken their dysfunctional beliefs by demonstrating that their worst negative fears and predictions do not materialize.

Summary

This chapter has introduced you to a range of cognitive tools and techniques for identifying, labelling and challenging unhelpful patterns of thinking associated with stress. The importance of conducting behavioural experiments has also been emphasized. Finally, some strategies for improving your relationship with your work have also been discussed. You are encouraged to make use of all these tools to identify your own unhelpful thinking patterns and to challenge and change them to more healthy, rational and adaptive ones.

Chapter 10

Overcoming stress syndromes

Introduction

While the primary and secondary level interventions outlined earlier in this book have been demonstrated to be effective in tackling mild to moderate levels of stress, they may not be effective in alleviating the more severe and disabling levels of stress, which are associated with stress syndromes. These can impact on the individual's capacity to carry out their work effectively and ultimately to even remain at work. Where this is the case, more formal tertiary level interventions are required to help the individual overcome the stress they are experiencing. These are typically accessed through the family doctor and delivered by mental health specialists, such as counsellors or psychologists. However, there are a number of practical self-help tools and techniques which can be employed before seeking specialist professional help. Three main stress syndromes have been identified, namely the anxiety or fear syndrome, the depression syndrome and the hostility syndrome. This chapter outlines a range of self-help interventions for treating each of these. These interventions are mainly cognitive behavioural in approach, since research has demonstrated that the evidence base for the effectiveness of cognitive behavioural therapy in treating stress syndromes is strong.

Treating anxiety syndromes

Anxiety syndromes are characterized by chronic feelings of fear and the desire to flee, escape and avoid perceived dangers and threats. Anxiety is a general term for a range of anxiety disorders, which include 'situation specific' anxiety disorders, panic attacks and phobias. In the work context, situation specific anxiety most commonly revolves around the employee's performance on given tasks in a particular work setting and has this been given the term 'performance anxiety'. The presentation and treatment of each of these manifestations of the anxiety syndrome are outlined below.

Performance anxiety

Performance anxiety is driven by an individual's persistent fear that they will fail to achieve the required level of performance in a situation where they are under public scrutiny. Most of us have experienced at least some anxiety when, for example, taking an exam or test (test anxiety), public speaking (public speaking anxiety), having an interview or doing a presentation in a meeting (presentation anxiety) but it is not disabling. At optimal levels it can even enhance performance and is a normal and adaptive experience. However, at higher levels of anxiety, it can be extremely distressing and disabling for the individual. One might imagine that performance anxiety is highest in employees with the least training, knowledge and experience but this is not the case. There is in fact a high incidence of performance anxiety in experienced professionals who have achieved high status, have considerable knowledge, skills and years of formal training to do the job. Such individuals may be generally well adjusted to their work and in interacting with their peers but experience 'stage fright' in a particular area of their work such as making a presentation, or when talking in larger groups. It is as if the higher that the individual has climbed up the career ladder, the more they fear the fall from that ladder. The higher levels of public scrutiny, higher expectations and a greater number of opportunities to expose their 'incompetence' may be contributory factors. Such individuals often live in fear of being publicly exposed as being 'incompetent' and much time is spent worrying that failure is just 'one miserable performance away'.

People with performance anxiety see themselves in a very negative and self-critical way. They imagine that they are coming across to others as socially incompetent and make negative self-evaluations of their own performance and what they believe others are thinking about them. Three processes then maintain and worsen this distorted self-image. These are an 'internal focus of attention' on physical and mental symptoms of anxiety, 'anxious thoughts' about themselves and how others see them, and the use of 'safety behaviours' to prevent their feared consequences from coming true. Physical symptoms of anxiety include sweating, shaking, palpitations, tension, hot flushes, nausea, dizziness, over-breathing, light-headedness and so on. Cognitively they may experience difficulty concentrating and the mind racing. Common examples of anxious negative thoughts about oneself in performance anxiety include 'I am not up to the job' ... 'I will fail' ... 'I will look stupid' ... 'show myself up' ... 'won't be able to cope' ... 'what if I start to shake' ... 'what if my mind goes blank' ... 'what if I look stupid' ... 'come across as strange' ... 'collapse in front of others' ... 'blush' ... 'sweat excessively' ... or 'stammer'. Examples of negative cognitions about evaluation by others include 'others will see that I am incompetent' ... 'think I am stupid' ... 'see how weak and inept I am'. As a result of experiencing the physiological and cognitive components of anxiety, the individual then adopts what are called 'safety behaviours'. Examples of 'safety behaviours' displayed in performance anxiety include avoiding eye contact, sitting near an escape route, talking too little (or sometimes too much), talking faster, keeping quiet in meetings, folding their arms, fidgeting, trying not to make themselves the centre of attention and keeping out of the spotlight. They believe that these safety behaviours are helping them cope more effectively with their anxiety, but unfortunately they inadvertently have the effect of maintaining it. The following case study illustrates performance anxiety.

Case study: Philip

Philip first realized that he had a problem when he had been unable to do a brief presentation in front of his peers as part of his management training course. He felt comfortable in most informal situations such as social gatherings and indeed saw himself as the 'life and soul' when mixing with others at a party. He just had an excessive fear of doing formal presentations. He would begin experiencing anxiety weeks before a presentation and was aware that the day before he gave a presentation, he experienced marked physiological symptoms of anxiety, particularly shaking, hot flushes, a churning stomach, a dry mouth and an increased heart rate. His strategy for coping with this anxiety was to spend a great deal of time preparing for the presentation, often for weeks in advance. He spent many hours rehearsing what he was going to say by going through his script dozens of times and repeatedly making minor changes. He also arrived early at the venue to familiarize himself with the room in which he was due to present. However, his anxiety never seemed to reduce.

On a few occasions Philip had managed to complete the presentations with great difficulty by employing a number of safety behaviours which he felt helped him to cope. These included, for example, drinking lots of water before and during the presentation to stop his mouth from drying up, wearing lots of anti-perspirant and opening all the windows to keep the room cool to reduce his sweating. He also began wearing loose-fitting clothing and keeping his hands in his pockets to hide the fact that he was shaking, wearing a high neck jumper to hide the blotches on his neck and positioning the furniture in the room to move himself out of the spotlight. While actually doing the presentations he would avoid eye contact with people, speaking quickly and not allowing time for any questions. He simply wanted to get it over with as soon as possible.

Even when he had finished the presentation, Philip would do a 'post-mortem' by ruminating on how he had come across to his peers and convincing himself that the event had been a complete disaster. He began to develop a dread of doing presentations and knew in himself that unless he did something to address the problem he would soon be unable to do them and would end up calling in sick. This would have a disastrous effect on his ability to meet the assessment requirements of the course and subsequently his opportunities for career advancement. He knew that he needed to overcome this fear if he was going to make a success of his career.

On reflection, Philip recalled that he had experienced some embarrassing incidents at school when he had been made to stand up in front of the class to read and had stumbled on his words. This had resulted in being teased by his peers and a rebuke from his teacher. After that time he had tried whenever possible to avoid doing public speaking or presentations and had managed to do so quite successfully for a number of years. His experiences at school of having to read out loud seemed to have contributed to the development of beliefs that increased his vulnerability to social anxiety problems in his later life. However, he was no longer able to avoid doing this in his management training because it was a part of being assessed for the course.

Treating Philip's performance anxiety

As mentioned earlier in this chapter, treatment interventions for this problem focus on Philip shifting his focus of attention on physical and mental symptoms of anxiety from an internal to an external one, challenging and modifying his anxious thinking and dropping his excessive use of safety behaviours. The techniques used to treat Philip's performance anxiety are outlined below.

SHIFTING THE FOCUS OF ATTENTION

Philip was so preoccupied with how bad he was feeling when 'performing' that he rarely sought any additional information from the reactions of his peers to his presentation. He concluded that if he felt so bad, his performance must be equally bad. However, by shifting his focus of attention from an internal to an external direction, he was able to reduce the confirmatory evidence from his internal state and increase the opportunity to disconfirm evidence from the environment. By scanning his social environment he was able to see that his peers were listening and interested and it took his attention away from all the negative physical and cognitive events that he was experiencing internally.

CHALLENGING NEGATIVE THINKING

Philip began keeping a record of his thoughts and feelings in a thoughts diary (as described in Chapter 9). By doing so he was able to identify and label the unhelpful thoughts relating to how badly he imagined he would perform in front of his peers. For example, he imagined that he would 'go to pieces', 'shake uncontrollably', 'sweat', 'blush', make a 'complete fool' of himself and show everyone that he was 'not up to the job'. He was able to use the techniques outlined in Chapter 9 to challenge his negative thinking and set up behavioural experiments to test out his new predictions. Also, by shifting his attention externally he was able to access external evidence that he could use to weigh up how likely it was that his feared consequences would occur, i.e., that people would notice his anxiety and judge his performance as poor.

DROPPING SAFETY BEHAVIOURS

Philip dropped his safety behaviours in an incremental way and used behavioural experiments as a way of establishing if his feared outcome would come true or not. For example, he practised speaking more slowly, making more eye contact, wearing less anti-perspirant, drinking less water and wearing tighter clothing to establish if making these changes really did have the catastrophic consequences that he had imagined they would. He found to his surprise that his fears never materialized.

In addition to using the techniques described above, Philip also introduced forms for people to give him feedback about his performance and video recorded a couple of his sessions. Both of these provided further evidence to disconfirm his beliefs about his poor performance since the written feedback given was positive, and from observing himself on video he was able to see himself in the way others did. He also realized that his tendency to avoid situations involving public speaking served to maintain his problem and thus decided to offer to do more presentations in order to confront and overcome his fear. In the short term this was difficult but in the longer term it assisted him to make further progress in terms of building his confidence.

What can we learn from the case study of Philip?

Although Philip's problem of performance anxiety did lead to him experiencing high levels of anxiety on occasions, he was able to successfully overcome his problem by confronting his fears directly. However, many people get into a vicious circle in which things can deteriorate quite rapidly. This is because becoming anxious about one's performance can actually reduce the quality of one's performance. This deterioration in performance can draw the individual to the attention of their line manager, supervisor or colleagues, who may notice for example that they have little to say, appear withdrawn, contribute little to meetings, volunteer infrequently or appear to have few ideas. This in turn is likely to lead to increased scrutiny and criticism of their observed poorer performance. This scrutiny and criticism then leads to even greater anxiety and further impairs their performance. This invites even more criticism and a downward spiral of decreasing performance, negative feedback and increasing anxiety is created. If this downward cycle continues unabated, the employee's anxiety can become increasingly disabling and they may begin to experience panic attacks.

Panic attacks

A panic attack is defined as a 'sudden onset of intense fear or terror, often associated with feelings of impending doom'. In the most extreme cases the symptoms experienced can be so powerful that the individual suffering them can actually believe that they are dying. Physical symptoms of panic include increased breathing, dizziness, blurred vision, shaking, hot flushes, sweating, tingling in the hands and feet, chest pains and palpitations. The increased rate of breathing disrupts the balance of oxygen and carbon dioxide in the bloodstream and this causes the individual to experience further 'odd' bodily sensations associated with hyperventilation, such as feelings of light-headedness, dizziness and feeling faint (see Figure 10.1).

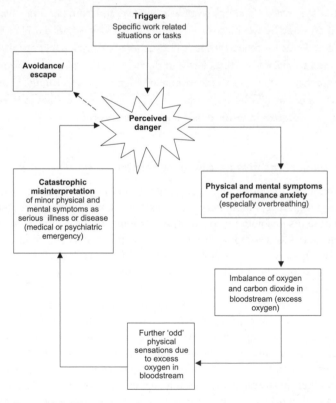

Figure 10.1 The panic cycle

Case study: Andrew

This case study of Andrew illustrates the treatment of panic attacks based on the conceptualization outlined in Figure 10.1.

Andrew was a 32-year-old school teacher with no previous history of mental health problems. He had ten years' experience of teaching at the local secondary school and had always been proud of his ability to cope with the demands of the job. However, in the few months prior to experiencing panic attacks, he had been experiencing a lot of pressure at work. There had been a visit to the school by an Ofsted official (Ofsted inspects schools in the UK and assesses their quality and performance against national standards). The Ofsted inspector had made some damning criticisms of the quality of teaching in the school. In addition, one of the parents had made a complaint about Andrew's treatment of their son, who was a pupil in his class, which was being investigated formally. Andrew took both of these events very much to heart since he had always been proud of both the quality of his teaching and his positive attitude towards his pupils. He began to feel very tense generally and one day while teaching, he experienced a full-blown panic attack in front of his pupils. Physically, he experienced his heart pounding, felt very weak, a tight chest, dizziness and difficulty getting enough air (suffocation). He described it as the worst feeling he had ever experienced and had really believed that he was going to collapse or even die. He felt so bad that he was unable to complete the lesson. The experience eroded his self-confidence and he began to worry about having another attack. He went on sick leave and began to wonder if he would ever be able to return to the job.

Treating Andrew's panic attacks

The treatment of panic attacks usually begins with educating the individual about the cognitive, emotional, physiological and behavioural symptoms of anxiety and the 'fight-flight' mechanism (as outlined in Chapter 1). It also involves developing an understanding of the way in which the different components in the 'panic cycle' interact to produce an escalation of anxiety, ultimately leading to panic attacks (as described in Figure 10.1). This can be a very useful starting point in terms of helping the individual gain a better understanding of how anxiety can escalate into panic.

Using this conceptualization of panic and by keeping a thoughts diary (as illustrated on p. 158), Andrew was able to identify that he was catastrophically misinterpreting the symptoms of his own anxiety as a medical emergency. When he began to feel anxious, he really believed that he was going to suffocate and die. This in turn led to further physical symptoms of anxiety, particularly those related to over-breathing. This escalation of symptoms then convinced Andrew that his catastrophic beliefs were about to come true and he really was going to suffocate and die.

Andrew was taught some anxiety management techniques including progressive muscular relaxation exercises, relaxed breathing and some meditation exercises (as outlined in Chapter 8). He was then taught some cognitive techniques for challenging his catastrophic thinking (as outlined in Chapter 9). These essentially focused on challenging his catastrophic belief that his anxious pattern of breathing would result in suffocation and dropping dead. With the permission of his doctor, Andrew did an exercise, which resulted in a reattribution of the meaning of the symptoms for him. This entailed deliberately over-breathing. When Andrew deliberately hyperventilated, he found to his surprise that he began to experience all the symptoms he usually experienced when he had a panic attack. This exercise resulted in Andrew becoming convinced that if he could stop catastrophizing about his bodily symptoms, control his breathing and try to relax more, he could overcome the problem.

Andrew began practising a positive internal self-dialogue, in which he told himself that his bodily reactions were normal ones associated with anxiety, and although they felt unpleasant, they were not harmful. He also tried not to add frightening thoughts or imagine unpleasant consequences. If he did, then he used the cognitive techniques he had learned to challenge these anxious thoughts. He also made use of attention shift exercises (see pp. 150–151), which encouraged him to focus his attention away from internal bodily sensations and mental events, towards 'scanning' his external environment and away from the future of 'what might be' to the here and now of 'what is'. Over a period of time Andrew felt able to control his anxiety more effectively and was no longer experiencing panic attacks. Eventually he felt able to attempt a 'staged' return to work and was gradually reintroduced to the teaching role. After a few weeks back at school Andrew felt that he had regained his confidence to teach his pupils again. He also was far more aware of the need to adopt a different attitude to his job and to make more time in his life for relaxation.

Phobic avoidance

Because of the extremely distressing nature of panic attacks, it is not unusual for the individual experiencing them to want to avoid the situations that trigger them altogether, for fear of experiencing another panic attack. In the case study of Andrew, it can be seen that as part of his recovery plan he needed to participate in a staged return to work in order to regain his confidence. Andrew had developed a very mild phobic reaction to his work situation and needed some support to overcome it and get back to work. However, in more extreme cases, the fear and avoidance can become so persistent and excessive that the condition is described as a phobia. In such cases the phobic avoidance is so severe that the individual is unable to return to work without engaging in a more intensive and structured treatment regime. More severe presentations of phobic avoidance are often rooted in a traumatic experience and form part of a post-traumatic stress reaction. However, the treatment is the same as for other causes.

Treating phobic avoidance

Phobic avoidance is best treated using the behavioural technique of systematic desensitization. This involves the individual identifying and making a comprehensive list of all the situations that they are currently avoiding. They then rate each situation in the list on a scale from 0 to 10 on how anxiety provoking it would be for them to confront that situation (where 0 is no anxiety and 10 is maximum anxiety). Once all the situations on the list have been rated, they are then placed in a hierarchy with all the most difficult situations scoring highest on distress (10) at the top and then the scores of 9 and so on right down to the lowest scores of 1 and 0 (the easiest to confront). The individual then confronts the lowest one in the hierarchy and moves on to confront the next step in the hierarchy only when they feel confident that they have overcome the previous one. Eventually, the individual works through all the stages of this graded exposure hierarchy. The case study of Maxine illustrates the technique of systematic desensitization.

Case study: Maxine

Maxine was a supermarket manager who had developed a phobia of working in her own supermarket after being the victim of an armed robbery at the store when she was on duty. This had resulted in Maxine feeling terrified to return to work and going on long-term sickness absence. The systematic desensitization technique was used to help her overcome her phobic anxiety about returning to work. The graded exposure hierarchy used can be found in Table 10.1. Although

Table 10.1 A systematic desensitization hierarchy for Maxine

Week 1
Commence flexible and informal visits to other branches of the supermarket in the area. These visits to be facilitated and supported by the managers of each store.

Week 2
Undertake more formal store visits dressed in the company uniform with the aim of working half a day in each store.

Week 3
Work one full day in one of the stores (not own store) in a non-managerial role.

Week 4
Work two full days 9am to 5pm in the same store (not own store) in a non-managerial role.

Week 5
Work three full days 9am to 5pm in the same store (not own store) in a non-managerial role.

Week 6
Gradually take no more managerial responsibilities and commence shift work (not own store).

Week 7
Commence working full time doing shift work and taking on managerial responsibilities (not own store).

Week 8
Commence working at own branch of the supermarket one day a week from 9am to 5pm.

Weeks 9–10
Increase the number of days working at own branch and commence shift working.

Weeks 11–12
Increase to full-time shift work, taking full managerial responsibilities at own branch.

the actual anxiety ratings are not included in Maxine's programme, they can be deduced from the order in which tasks are introduced (i.e., the least anxiety provoking tasks first). This programme was carried out on a week-by-week basis over three months, with the support of her managers and occupational health advisers.

Over a period of three months Maxine was able to return to all of her former managerial duties. She was assisted in doing this by a very supportive management team and occupational health service. Without this structured help and support, it is unlikely that Maxine would have been able to return to work, leading to negative consequences for both her and her employer. Maxine went on to get promotion to an area manager post two years after returning to work and needless to say was very sympathetic to the welfare needs of her staff.

Treating the depression syndrome

The depression syndrome is characterized by feelings of sadness, negative thinking and the desire to withdraw, give up, surrender and accept defeat. When people are depressed, they feel low in mood, tearful, troubled by thoughts and feelings of low worth, guilt and self-reproach. They may be more irritable than usual, have little energy or motivation, lose interest in things that they previously enjoyed and everything seems like a big effort. They become less active, lose their appetite, and experience sleep problems and loss of sexual desire. In severe cases of depression, there is a risk of suicidal behaviour. In the context of this chapter, depression refers to the less severe end of the spectrum. If the individual is feeling 'suicidal', it is essential that they seek expert help immediately through their doctor. The treatment of choice for depression is cognitive behavioural therapy. The CBT approach teaches the individual to identify and change the unhelpful patterns of thinking and behaviour associated with the depressive syndrome. The techniques used to challenge depressive thinking and behaviours are outlined below.

Challenging depressive thinking

Depressive thoughts are identified through the use of a thoughts diary (see pp. 157–159). The negative thoughts identified are then systematically challenged using a range of specific cognitive techniques (as outlined in Chapter 9). To recap briefly, these include looking at the evidence for and against the negative thoughts being true (rather like a jury in a court of law), coming up with more balanced and realistic alternative (less distressing) explanations for distressing situations, looking at the advantages and disadvantages of thinking in that way and challenging their distortions. If the individual learns to successfully challenge their negative automatic thoughts and replace them with more positive and healthy ones, this leads to a corresponding improvement in their mood state.

Challenging unhelpful behaviours

The two main techniques used to challenge the unhelpful behaviours associated with depression are activity scheduling and conducting behavioural experiments.

Activity scheduling

When an individual is depressed, they tend to withdraw from and stop doing the activities that previously they used to enjoy. They become unmotivated and inactive, which in turn provides even more time to ruminate on their negative thoughts. This creates a downward spiral of inactivity, which tends to make their mood even worse. Activity scheduling involves keeping a daily timetable of activities, which prevents the depressed individual from being inactive and spending too much time ruminating. It allows the individual to structure their day better and also to plan a gradual increase in activity. They are also asked to rate these activities on 'mastery' (how good they are at it) and 'pleasure' (how much they enjoy it) using a ten point scale (where 0 = lowest on mastery or pleasure and 10 = maximum mastery or pleasure). Rating the activities they do enables them to identify which ones they are good at and also which ones they find most enjoyable. Once they have identified these, they can then introduce more of the enjoyable activities into their daily schedule.

Conducting behavioural experiments

The behavioural experiment (see p. 165) can be an extremely useful technique in the treatment of depression, since it provides additional evidence to challenge depressive predictions through the process of hypothesis testing. The individual is encouraged to challenge their negative predictions about future events with more positive alternative hypotheses. They are then encouraged to find out exactly what the outcome was to that given situation and how it compared with the predictions made. Invariably, because the predictions made are excessively negative and gloomy, as one would expect in depression, the outcome is more positive than the individual's predictions and can be used as evidence to disconfirm their depressive thinking patterns. Consequently, most behavioural experiments will have the effect of weakening the individual's original negative view of situations and events and at the same time strengthening alternative more positive explanations.

A note on the burnout syndrome

The burnout syndrome has been included here because there are a number of researchers who argue that burnout is basically work related depression. However, others argue that burnout differs from depression because in classical depression, a person's symptoms appear to manifest across all situations, whereas a person who is 'burned out' in the work sphere may function well in non-work spheres. Whatever the stance taken, the research literature indicates that there is a considerable overlap between burnout, depression and various elements of job satisfaction and that it is related to greater absenteeism, increased staff turnover and detrimental effects on work performance. Thus, burnout deserves a mention in the context of work related stress syndromes and it is most closely linked to the depression syndrome. It is found in occupations where there is a large amount of direct face-to-face contact with clients, particularly where resources are limited and inadequate. Some of the most common signs and symptoms of burnout include a high resistance to going to work every day, a sense of failure, anger and resentment, discouragement and indifference, isolation and withdrawal, feeling tired and exhausted all day, clock watching, loss of positive feelings towards clients, avoiding client contact, a more cynical and blaming attitude towards clients, avoiding discussion of work with colleagues, frequent colds and flu, frequent headaches, high absenteeism, poor sleep and increased use of drugs and alcohol.

The burnout syndrome is characterized by three main symptoms of emotional exhaustion, depersonalization and low personal accomplishment. It is thought to develop in three stages corresponding to these symptoms, the first being emotional exhaustion. As feelings of emotional exhaustion set in, the worker's perception of their clients change. There is a gradual withdrawal of emotional involvement with them and an increasing perception that they have caused their own difficulties and are therefore less worthy of help. They often feel that they are being exploited by their clients and experience an increasing sense of depersonalization. As emotional exhaustion and negative attitudes towards clients increase, the worker becomes increasingly dissatisfied with themselves. They begin to feel that they do not understand the clients or accomplish much with their work with them. As the feeling of low personal accomplishment takes hold, the employee feels that they are not up to the job and ultimately experience a lowering of self-esteem.

Treating burnout syndrome

Treatments for burnout syndrome incorporate both cognitive and behavioural components. These include stress reduction programmes and general stress management techniques such as physical exercise and relaxation training. It is also associated with patterns of over-commitment to work such as perfectionism, unrelenting standards, workaholism, over-identification with work and a Type A behavioural pattern (described in Chapter 9). Modification of these patterns of over-commitment can help reduce the symptoms of the burnout syndrome.

Treating the hostility syndrome

The hostility syndrome is characterized by feelings of chronic anger, irritability, frustration and the desire to fight perceived injustices. In the work context, overt displays of aggression are usually not tolerated and are channelled into alternative displacement behaviours, which collectively may be called letting off steam. Examples of such displacement behaviours include banging the desk, raising one's voice, slamming a door to vent angry feelings and the proverbial 'kicking the cat'. The person may verbalize a desire to punch someone on the nose, engage in sarcasm directed towards the perpetrator or become increasingly cynical about their work or those they work with. However, of greater concern is the possibility that workers may find more destructive outlets through which they can displace their angry feelings onto their work colleagues or onto others in their personal life (family, partner or children). In one's personal life this could take the form of physical abuse and domestic violence. In the workplace it could manifest itself in more subtle forms of aggressive behaviour, such as bullying, harassment, humiliation, inter-personal conflicts, passive aggression and acts of rebellion, which are more difficult to quantify.

The experience of anger is usually triggered by the perception that one has been treated unfairly. This results in a number of systematic biases in thinking, which lead to demonizing or monsterizing the perceived perpetrator. They condemn the whole person, magnify all the negative aspects of the other person, mentally filter out all the positives, polarize and blame the person to whom they attribute the injustice. The key point is that the negative distortions about the alleged perpetrator are often very much exaggerated. Physiologically the angry individual experiences a heightened state of arousal, which may be experienced as a range of bodily symptoms such as the body tensing up and the heart thumping.

Treating the hostility syndrome involves the individual learning a number of anger management strategies. Most anger management training packages consist of a number of components such as relaxation training and breathing techniques to reduce physiological arousal, coping skills such as social skills training, assertiveness skills, effective communication and negotiation skills, which are all aimed at broadening the individual's repertoire of coping responses (see Chapters 6 to 8). In addition, cognitive therapy techniques are used to help the individual address their dysfunctional assumptions of justice, fairness and moral codes of right and wrong, which underlie aggressive reactions and serve to perpetuate the problem. These include techniques such as looking at the evidence for and against, alternative ways of seeing the situation, advantages and disadvantages and correcting distortions as outlined in Chapter 9. The individual practises these techniques in real life situations in order to consolidate the skills learned.

If the individual is still having difficulties in managing their anger after going through their anger management routine, they need to learn to exit themselves from the triggering situation in order to ensure that they do not act upon their aggressive inclinations and only to return to the situation once they have calmed down. They should then be able to deal with it in a more rational and objective way than they would when they were in a state of heightened arousal.

Summary

This chapter described a range of tertiary level interventions for individuals who are suffering from clinical levels of distress associated with stress syndromes. Specifically, a number of cognitive and behavioural interventions aimed at managing the anxiety, depression and hostility syndromes were described. The aim of this chapter has been to encourage the individual to develop their own self-help programme before resorting to seeking more specialist help. The range of self-help resources and references listed in the Appendix can also be utilized to assist the individual with this process. However, if the self-help approach proves to be ineffective, the option of seeking specialist help through one's doctor or occupational health service still remains. It is emphasized that if as a result of the severity of their symptoms the individual feels that they may be at risk of harming themselves or others, they should seek expert professional help immediately and not attempt to try to deal with this on their own.

Part III

Pulling it all together

Chapter 11

Developing a self-help plan

Introduction

Simply reading about stress does not necessarily equip you with the skills required to put what you have learned into practice. Many people report feeling stuck when it comes to applying what they have read about in the literature to their own real life problems. The aim of this chapter is to bridge that gap between theory and practice by taking you step by step through a structured self-help plan to overcome your occupational stress.

The eight stages of a self-help plan

The eight stages of the self-help plan, which are described below, are as follows:

1   Make a problem list.
2   Prioritize your problems.
3   Set your goals.
4   Establish the criteria of success.
5   Plan your interventions.
6   Develop a self-help treatment plan.
7   Monitor and review your progress.
8   Prevent relapse.

Make a problem list

Perhaps you have been identifying and making a note of the problem areas that apply to you as you have been progressing through each chapter. If this is the case, get a sheet of paper and make a list of all the problem areas you have identified. If you have not been making notes as you have been going along, you will need to review each chapter and highlight the problem areas that you think need to be addressed. Once you have done this, make a list of them. For example, you might identify that you are not living a healthy lifestyle, or lack certain time management, assertiveness, or social skills. Alternatively, you might identify that you have difficulty relaxing, or a tendency to think negatively. Whatever the problem is, put it on the list.

Prioritize your problems

Where more than one problem area has been identified, they need to be prioritized. The ones that you consider to be the most important and urgent ones to address should be placed at the top of the list and the less important ones lower down the list. This creates a hierarchy of problems: those placed at the top of the hierarchy should be tackled first.

Set your goals

Starting with the problem at the top of the list, identify the specific unhelpful behaviour(s) and/or thinking pattern(s) that need to be addressed. For example, if you identify that you are 'living an unhealthy lifestyle', you need to be specific about what aspects of your lifestyle are unhealthy and need changing. You need to ask yourself some basic questions such as 'Do I need to take more exercise?', 'Do I need to reduce my alcohol intake?', 'Do I need to get more sleep?', 'Do I need to eat a healthier diet?' If the answer to any of these is 'Yes', it needs addressing. Reflecting on the problem in this way allows you to identify the specific aspects of it which need changing and clarifying the goals you need to set yourself.

In a similar way to the lifestyle example above, other problem areas can be explored in order to identify the specific goals you want to set yourself. For example, if you identify that 'poor time management' is a problem, you should explore which specific aspects of managing your time are problematic and need to be addressed. For example, ask yourself 'Do I need to overcome a tendency to procrastinate?', 'Do I need to learn to delegate more?', 'Do I need to learn to prioritize tasks more effectively?', 'Do I need to develop my planning skills?', 'Do I need to develop my organizational skills?' You need to specify each problem area at this level of detail in order to identify a specific goal.

If you identify that your social and interpersonal skills are lacking, you need to be specific about what aspects of your social skills are lacking in order to identify the goals for that particular problem area. For example, ask yourself 'Do I need to focus on changing some of the "non-verbal" aspects of my behaviour? such as "body posture", "facial expression", "eye contact" or "personal space", or "verbal" aspects such as "paraphrasing", "summarizing", "asking open questions", or "appropriate self-disclosure"?'

If you identify that assertiveness is a problem for you, you need to identify what specific aspects of your behaviours and attitudes are unassertive and require changing. For example, 'Do I need to learn to manage conflict more effectively?', 'Do I need to learn to "say no" more often?', 'Do I need to learn to stand up for my rights more?' Similarly, if you identify that you are prone to negative thinking then you need to identify the specific dysfunctional thinking style(s) that you need to change. For example, 'Am I catastrophizing?', 'Jumping to conclusions?', 'Mind reading?', 'Overgeneralizing?', 'Magnifying?', 'Minimizing?', 'Personalizing?' or 'Thinking in black and white terms?'

Identifying your goals is therefore about deciding exactly what unhelpful patterns of behaviour and thinking you want to change. The relevant questionnaires and checklists presented in this book should assist you in this task.

Establish the criteria of success

Deciding which specific unhelpful patterns of behaviour and thinking you want to change does not in itself tell you very much. You also need to decide what criteria you are going to use to determine when you have successfully achieved the goals you have set yourself. A problem solving approach can be helpful in deciding on your criteria of success. This essentially involves acknowledging where you are at now in terms of the problems that you have identified (Point A) and where you would ideally like to be at some point in the future (Point B). After all, if you have no vision of where you want to be in the future, how do you expect to get there? Point A is the present unacceptable state of affairs or the current mess that you find yourself in and Point B is your preferred scenario at some time point in the future. It is no good just hoping that when you wake up one day, everything will be sorted out. You need to have a clear idea about what changes you want to make, how you are going to get from Point A to Point B and what the shorter-term targets on the way to achieving this are.

The goals and criteria of success that you set yourself should be 'SMART'. That is, they should be Specific, Measurable, Achievable, Relevant and Time bound. Some illustrations of this are given below. For example, if 'leading an unhealthy lifestyle' is at the top of your problem list and your goals are to 'take more exercise' and 'reduce your alcohol intake', these objectives are not 'SMART', since they are too vague. However, specifying that you will increase your exercise from its present level to half an hour per day within four weeks, or reduce your alcohol intake from forty to ten units of alcohol per week within four weeks would constitute 'SMART'. This is because you are identifying specific, measurable, achievable, relevant and time bound goals.

Plan your interventions

The decision making tree presented in Figure 11.1 should be helpful to you in terms of deciding which level of intervention is the most appropriate one for you to use for the problems that you have identified. Before planning which interventions to use, you need to decide if the stress you are experiencing is primarily triggered by factors in the work environment. If you assess that the stress you are experiencing is a direct consequence of the work environment, then this would indicate that primary level interventions, aimed at reducing or eliminating stressors in the workplace (as outlined in Chapter 3) should be selected. You may of course decide that even though the job itself is a cause of the stress you are experiencing, the options for changing things in the workplace are very limited in the context of the organization that you work in. Where this is the case the secondary level interventions (outlined in Chapters 4 to 9) which aim to enhance your coping skills to help you cope more effectively with the stressors present are the appropriate option. If, however, you are suffering from more severe levels of stress associated with stress syndromes, the tertiary interventions (outlined in Chapter 10) are indicated. Where secondary or tertiary interventions have been ineffective, referral for more specialist help may be an option to consider. However, not all workplace occupational health services or health insurance companies are willing to fund this level of intervention. Ultimately, where all interventions to manage your work related stress have been exhausted, it is worth considering redeployment or as a last resort changing your job altogether. However, it is acknowledged that in the current climate of the job market, finding alternative employment is not always easy.

Develop a self-help treatment plan

Write your 'treatment plan' down on a sheet of paper. Table 11.1 is an example of a treatment plan which contains all the components of a self-

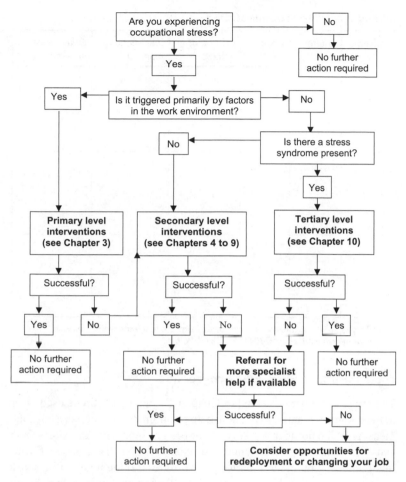

Figure 11.1 A decision making tree

help plan. In the first column you can list all the problem areas that you have identified. In the second column these can be numbered in order of priority. The goals and criteria of success for each problem can be recorded in columns three and four and the specific interventions that you have chosen to use can be reported in column five. The outcome column can be completed only once the outcome of the intervention is known.

Table 11.1 A 'self-help' treatment plan

Problem	Priority	Goals	Criteria of success	Interventions planned	Outcome of interventions
1					
2					
3					

Note: This table is available to view and print from the following website: www. routledgementalhealth.com/9780415671781

Monitor and review your progress

The stress checklist presented in Chapter 1 (Table 1.2) can be used prior to the commencement of your self-help programme to establish a baseline measure of the number and severity of the symptoms of your stress. You can then readminister the checklist at intervals in the course of your treatment programme to monitor your progress. If the interventions you are using are helpful, this should be reflected in lower scores being obtained on the stress checklist.

The questionnaire aimed at identifying the main causes of stress in your working environment which can be found in Chapter 2 (Table 2.1) will help you identify and monitor the stress specifically related to your work environment. Again this can be readministered at intervals during your treatment programme to establish whether or not the causes of stress in your working environment are reduced as a result of the interventions you are using.

However, you do not have to just use questionnaires and symptom checklists to monitor your progress. Other criteria can be helpful in terms of monitoring your progress. For example, the criteria for living a healthy lifestyle found in Chapter 4 can be helpful in terms of monitoring your progress towards achieving a healthy lifestyle. Some illustrations of this are given below. With respect to exercise, for example, it is recommended that ideally you want to build up to approximately 30 minutes of moderate intensity exercise a day and a combination of 80 per cent stamina and 20 per cent flexibility exercises. Your progress with respect to exercise can thus be measured by how close you are to achieving these criteria. Similarly, in terms of dietary intake the recommended calorie intake for an adult woman of average build is approximately 2,000 a day and for adult men it is approximately 2,500 calories a day. A maximum of no more than 20 grams of saturated fat, 90 grams of sugar and 6 grams of salt per day is recommended. The recommended safe limits for alcohol intake for men is 21 units a week and no more than 4 units per day. For women it is 14 units a week and no more than 3 units a day. It is also estimated as a rough guide that having more than 600 milligrams of caffeine a day may cause problems. There is no safe level for smoking and it is recommended that you stop as soon as possible. The criteria outlined in Chapter 4 for living a healthy lifestyle can thus be used as a set of targets for you to aim for.

If you wish to monitor your progress in terms of assertiveness or inter-personal skills, the questionnaire in Chapter 6 (Table 6.1 on assertiveness) and the checklist in Chapter 7 (Table 7.1 on interpersonal skills) can be used respectively. Your progress with respect to identifying, labelling and challenging unhelpful thinking patterns as outlined in Chapter 9 can be monitored through the use of thoughts diaries, which provide a record of how your patterns of thinking change over time.

With respect to measuring clinical levels of distress associated with the stress syndromes outlined in Chapter 10, there is a range of more formal psychometric tests available to assist in this process. Indeed, there is a whole industry built around the publication of psychometric assessment tools. These more formal assessment measures are usually copyright protected and need to be purchased through the companies that specialize in publishing them. The use and interpretation of these tests is generally restricted to accredited and approved specialist practitioners such as clinical psychologists. However, it is helpful to know that these measures do exist and can be accessed via specialist practitioners in the field. It is recommended that self-report measures are used to measure stress, since the individual's appraisal of their situation is of primary importance in the stress reaction.

So, in conclusion, there is a wide range of measures which can be incorporated into your treatment plan to enable you to monitor and review the progress you are making towards achieving the goals that you have set yourself. At the end of the self-help programme you can compare the first (pre-treatment) and the last (post-treatment) measures to identify how successful the outcome of the programme has been.

Prevent relapse

As you progress towards achieving the goals you have set yourself, it is not uncommon to have worries about relapsing and ending up where you were at the beginning of therapy. When people are doing well, they often do not want to tempt fate by focusing on the possibility of a relapse. However, it is important that you do consider your contingency plans in the event of a setback and how you are going to get back on course again. The 'relapse prevention' exercise provides a structured way of doing this and involves asking yourself a series of questions and finding answers to them. These include: 'What gains do you feel you have made to date?', 'What has changed as a result of the interventions you have carried out?', 'What have you learned about yourself?', 'What have you learned as a result of conducting a self-help programme?', 'How can you continue to put into practice what you have learned in your everyday life?', 'What outstanding goals do you still have to achieve?', 'What are your future plans for self–help?', 'How might you deal with any setbacks?', 'What are the likely high risk situations for a relapse?' and 'What contingency plans do you have in place to deal with such a lapse?' Write your answers down and keep them somewhere safe where you can refer to them at a later date if necessary.

Case study: Helen

This case study is used to illustrate how the framework described in this chapter can be used to deliver the range of interventions covered in this book in a logical and systematic way.

> Helen was a 27-year-old administrative assistant who had been working for an accountancy firm since leaving school at the age of 16 years. She was very able academically, having obtained ten GCSEs at school but had decided not to do her A levels. She was also a very able worker who had been encouraged to go for promotion by her boss on several occasions, but on each occasion that she had the

opportunity for promotion, she had decided not to apply for the job. The problem for Helen was that she had been doing the same job for many years and was feeling dissatisfied and unfulfilled by it, yet at the same time she lacked the confidence to go for promotion. Although she longed for career advancement, she was paralysed by fear at the prospect of having to do anything that involved making decisions, using her own initiative or taking responsibility. She had a great fear of failure and because of this, felt unable to compete with her peers in areas of achievement. Helen had a dilemma in that she felt panicky even at the thought of taking additional responsibility and yet was depressed at the prospect of spending the rest of her working life in a boring and unfulfilling job. She also lacked the confidence to assert herself with her colleagues at work and as a result some of her peers would take advantage of her by giving her a disproportionate amount of work to do. As a result of her unhappiness she began comfort eating and putting on weight, which further reduced her self-esteem. Helen realized that this could not continue and that she needed to do something about her situation. The framework described in this chapter was used to address her problems and the stages in achieving this are presented below.

Making a problem list and prioritizing the problems

Helen was helped to identify her main problems. She then ranked them according to what she considered to be the order of priority (1 = highest priority and 6 = lowest priority). These were:

1 Comfort eating and weight gain.
2 Avoidance.
3 Procrastination.
4 Unassertiveness.
5 Anxiety.
6 Poor self-image.

Setting the goals and establishing the criteria of success

Having identified and prioritized her problems, Helen moved on to the next stage of setting the goals and was assisted to identify the criteria of success for each goal that she had set herself.

Comfort eating and weight gain

With respect to her comfort eating and subsequent weight gain, Helen was helped to realize that she needed to tackle the problem both by reducing her food intake and by increasing her activity levels. She therefore set herself the goals of losing weight and doing more exercise. Her criteria of success were over a period of four months to lose 2 stones (about 12.7 kilos) in weight and through a graded exercise programme work up to doing half an hour of vigorous physical activity three times a week.

Avoidance

Helen was encouraged to spend some time reflecting on the things she was actually avoiding and to make a list of these. The main ones she identified were avoidance of going for promotion at work, taking responsibility and making decisions at work. She then put the list of avoidant behaviours into a hierarchy with the most difficult ones at the top. The goal she set herself was to confront her avoidance in a systematic way by tackling the behaviours lowest in the hierarchy first and then moving up to the more difficult ones. Her criteria of success were by the end of therapy to be able to take more responsibility and make decisions. Ultimately she wanted to feel able to go for promotion when the opportunity arose but she acknowledged that it was unlikely that a post would become available during the course of her therapy.

Procrastination

Helen also identified that she had a tendency to put things off and delay doing tasks (especially difficult ones) wherever possible. These included making telephone calls to people, filing papers and keeping up to date with the typing. She acknowledged that this was not a helpful coping strategy and that set the goal of addressing these tasks in a more timely way by 'doing them now rather leaving them until tomorrow'. Her criteria of success were within the next three months to make 80 per cent of the phone calls and do 90 per cent of the filing and typing the same day, rather than putting them off until later.

Unassertiveness

Helen realized that she had a tendency to take the line of least resistance at work and as a result of this, some of her colleagues would take advantage of this by giving her a disproportionate amount of work to do. She was assisted to identify some specific goals related to assertiveness. These were to get to know what her rights were and to learn more assertive attitudes and behaviours. The criteria of success she set were that within three months she would be able to say 'No' to extra work from her colleagues when she felt that they were taking advantage of her and to stand up for her rights more rather than simply taking the line of least resistance.

Anxiety

Helen was helped to realize that although her anxiety was not too problematic at the moment, this was because she was avoiding rather than confronting her fears and that it was likely to escalate if she were to address her avoidance. With respect to her anxiety she was encouraged to set the goals of learning some formal and informal relaxation exercises. Her criteria of success were that within three months she would be able to deal with stressful situations such as taking responsibility, making decisions and asserting herself in a calmer and more relaxed way.

Poor self-image

Underlying all of the problems identified above was Helen's longstanding low self-esteem and negative self-image, which she was helped to recognise was being maintained by underlying negative beliefs and assumptions of inferiority, inability to cope, failure and incompetence. Helen identified that her goal was to learn the techniques to enable her to challenge the unhelpful negative beliefs and assumptions associated with her poor self-image and replace them with more positive healthy ones. She identified her criteria of success as being able to successfully challenge her negative beliefs about her self and having developed a more positive self-image. Specifically she wanted to be able to believe that she was 'good enough', 'competent', 'able to cope', 'able to take responsibility', 'able to make decisions' and 'no more likely than anyone else to fail'. Helen realized that it might take longer to achieve these goals than some of the others mentioned earlier so set herself a six month timescale to achieve these goals.

Planning the interventions

Helen was encouraged to make use of a range of the problem specific secondary level interventions found in this book; as described below.

Interventions for comfort eating and weight gain

With respect to the priority problem of comfort eating, Helen was directed to the interventions for 'developing a healthier lifestyle' (see Chapter 4). More specifically, the interventions for eating more healthily and taking more exercise were incorporated into her intervention plan. With respect to her diet, she decided to limit her calorie intake to the recommended intake for a woman of average height and build (i.e., 2,000 calories a day), restrict her fat intake to 70 grams per day (a maximum of 20 grams of this being saturated fats), a maximum of 90 grams of sugar and 6 grams of salt a day, and a diet consisting of a variety of fibre rich and high energy (carbohydrate) foods.

Helen also established a graded exercise programme. She set herself targets that were achievable and built up gradually. She began by doing 10 minutes of exercise in the morning and repeating it again in the afternoon. This consisted of taking a brisk walk twice a day. Over a period of a few months, she built this up to approximately 30 minutes of moderate intensity exercise a day, which included cycling to and from work and going swimming a couple of times a week. She also built some exercise into her daily routine, such as taking the stairs rather than the lift and going for a walk during her lunch break.

Interventions for avoidance

Helen made use of the behavioural technique of systematic desensitization as outlined in Chapter 10 (pp. 183–184) to help her confront her avoidance behaviours. This involved identifying and making a comprehensive list of all the situations that she was currently avoiding. She then rated each situation in the list on a scale from 0 to 10 on how anxiety provoking it would be for her to confront that situation (where 0 is no anxiety and 10 is maximum anxiety). Once all the situations on the list were rated, Helen placed them in a hierarchy with all the most difficult situations scoring highest on distress (10) at the top and then the scores of 9 and so on right down to the lowest scores of 1 and 0 (the easiest to confront). Her plan was to begin by confronting the one lowest in the hierarchy and move up through the hierarchy as her confidence grew, until she had eventually worked through all the stages of this 'graded exposure' hierarchy.

Interventions for procrastination

Helen decided that the only way that she was going to overcome the habit of procrastination was to make a concerted effort to change her behaviour. This involved the decision to do things in a more timely way and not to put off things she could do today until tomorrow. Her slogan became 'do it now' and she aimed to do the identified tasks as soon as was practically possible. She also aimed to plan ahead more, to break bigger tasks down into manageable chunks and aim to meet the deadlines that she had set herself.

Interventions for unassertiveness

With respect to becoming more assertive, Helen was directed to the range of cognitive and behavioural interventions outlined in Chapter 6. These included learning what her rights were, how to ensure that she got these met and developing more assertive attitudes and behaviours. Assertive behaviours include both non-verbal and verbal aspects and Helen identified that she needed to practise some non-verbal skills such as maintaining good eye contact and a more confident posture as well as verbal skills such as communicating in a confident, firm and steady tone of voice and being able to say 'No' to people more often without feeling guilty.

Interventions for anxiety

Helen made use of some of the informal and formal relaxation techniques outlined in Chapter 8. Informal techniques included reading a good book and having a hot bath at the end of each day. She also learned some more formal relaxation techniques including deep breathing exercises and progressive muscular relaxation training to help her manage her anxiety more effectively.

Interventions for poor self-image

With respect to challenging her poor self-image, Helen made use of a range of interventions outlined in Chapter 9. These included making a thoughts diary to help her identify the specific situational triggers that lead to the unhelpful thoughts and the feelings associated with her low self-esteem and poor self-image. She also learned the techniques for labelling and challenging unhelpful patterns of thinking and how to set up behavioural experiments to test out negative predictions. This involved setting up 'mini experiments', whereby her original negative thoughts and the new alternative more positive ones could be treated as two possible alternative hypotheses predicting an outcome. She was then able to test these out in real life situations in order to establish which of the two alternatives was more accurately predictive of the outcome.

Developing a self-help treatment plan

Table 11.2 summarizes Helen's problems together with the goals and criteria of success that she set herself and her planned interventions in the form of a comprehensive treatment plan. This is a particularly clear and structured way of outlining a treatment programme.

Monitoring and reviewing progress

It can be seen from Table 11.2 that the goals and criteria of success for the therapy Helen set herself were 'SMART' (Specific, Measurable, Achievable, Relevant and Time bound). Because Helen's treatment plan was SMART and sufficiently detailed, she was able to make use of a range of measures to monitor and review her progress towards achieving her goals:

• With respect to her goal of adopting a healthier eating programme, Helen was able to monitor her progress using a number of measures.

Table 11.2 Helen's treatment plan

Problem (in order of priority)	Goals	Criteria of success	Interventions planned
1 **Comfort eating and weight gain**	(a) Eat more healthily	Lose 2 stones in weight over a period of four months	Healthy eating programme: Max. 2,000 calories Max. 70 grams fat Max. 90 grams sugar Max. 6 grams salt (per day) High fibre and high energy diet
	(b) Increase activity levels	Half an hour of vigorous physical activity per day within four months	Graded exercise programme: Brisk walk twice a day building up to 30 minutes of moderate exercise a day over a period of four months Cycle to and from work Go for a walk at lunchtime Use the stairs rather than the lift
2 **Avoidance**	Confront avoidance	Feel comfortable taking more responsibility Feel comfortable taking decisions To achieve these goals within four months Go for promotion if/when the opportunity arises at work	Confront fears in a systematic hierarchical way Practise taking more responsibility Practise more autonomous decision making

(Continued)

Table 11.2 Helen's treatment plan (Continued)

Problem (in order of priority)	Goals	Criteria of success	Interventions planned
3 Procrastination	Overcome procrastination	Get rid of the backlog of tasks Do tasks in a timely and responsive way Meet deadlines set To achieve these goals within four months	Practise not putting tasks off, do it now Break tasks down into manageable chunks Plan ahead more
4 Unassertiveness	Be more assertive with work colleagues	Know rights and be able to assert these effectively Be able to say no to colleagues at work who try to force extra work onto me To achieve these goals within four months	Get to know my rights Learn more about assertive attitudes and behaviours Practise using the techniques learned
5 Anxiety	Be more relaxed	Be able to successfully deal with stressful situations in a calmer and more relaxed way To achieve these goals within four months	Introduce some informal relaxation techniques into daily routine Do deep breathing exercises Do progressive muscular relaxation training
6 Poor self-image	Be able to successfully challenge dysfunctional beliefs and assumptions as they arise and consider alternative more positive ways of interpreting situations	Have a more positive self-image and believe that I am 'good enough', 'competent', 'able to cope', 'able to take responsibility', 'able to make decisions' and 'no more likely than anyone else to fail' To achieve these goals within six months	Learn standard cognitive techniques for labelling and challenging dysfunctional beliefs and assumptions related to poor self-image Use of thoughts diaries Use of behavioural experiments

These included monitoring calorie, fat, sugar, salt and fibre intake as identified in the treatment plan, as well as weight loss.

- In order to achieve her goal of increasing her activity levels, Helen identified that she needed to build up to 30 minutes of moderate physical exercise over a period of four months and so was able to monitor her progress towards achieving this in the timescale set. The fact that she was also able to begin cycling to and from work, began to use the stairs rather than the lift and go for walks at lunchtime provided further evidence to Helen that she was achieving her targets with respect to increasing her activity levels.

- In terms of the goal she set herself to overcome her avoidance, Helen was able to monitor the extent to which she was taking more responsibility and making more decisions over a four month timescale. She was also able to monitor the extent to which she was overcoming her problem of procrastination by achieving deadlines set and by the reduced amount of time she was taking to do tasks set.

- Helen made use of the assertiveness questionnaire in Chapter 6 (Table 6.1) to monitor her progress in this area by assessing her score at regular intervals during the programme.

- She made use of the stress checklist presented in Chapter 1 (Table 1.2) to monitor her progress with respect to learning to relax more. A lowered score indicated that she was becoming more relaxed.

- She also made use of a thoughts diary to monitor the change in her unhelpful thinking patterns over time.

At the end of her treatment programme Helen was able to compare the first (pre-treatment) and the last (post-treatment) measures in all of the areas described above to identify how successful the outcome of her programme had been. So, in conclusion it can be seen that there is a wide range of relatively simple measures which can be incorporated into a treatment plan to enable one to monitor and review the progress being made towards achieving the goals that have been set. However, in order to be able to do this the goals set must be 'smart'. As Helen progressed towards achieving the goals that she had set herself, she was encouraged to do a relapse prevention exercise, which helped her consider her contingency plans in the event of a setback. At the end of the therapy she was encouraged to continue practising and improving the skills she had in a proactive way to promote positive mental health rather than simply using them to tackle mental health problems.

Summary

In this chapter a step-by-step guide to developing a self-help plan was introduced, aimed at helping you tackle and overcome your work related stress. Eight stages of developing a self-help plan were identified. These were: making a problem list, prioritizing your problems, setting your goals, establishing the criteria of success, planning interventions, developing a self-help treatment plan, monitoring and reviewing your progress, and preventing relapse. Each one of these stages was described in detail and a decision making tree (Figure 11.1) was included to help you decide which level of intervention to use. A case study (Helen) was presented to illustrate the practical application of the framework described in this chapter. It should be noted, however, that in the case study, Helen's situation was slightly different from your own in that she did not have the benefit of this self-help manual to draw upon when addressing her problems. However, she was given some support and guidance by a therapist to compensate for this. The interventions employed in Helen's case were exactly the same as those covered in this book. In conclusion, it is anticipated that having read this chapter, you will feel better equipped with the necessary tools and techniques to develop your own self-help plan, review your progress with the goals you have set yourself and essentially become 'your own therapist'.

Chapter 12

Summary and conclusions

Occupational stress is a major problem of pandemic proportions, affecting millions of people across the world. This is in part due to the ever increasing pressures being placed on workplace organizations to remain competitive in the context of a global economy. Generally speaking there are many more people looking for work than there are job vacancies, so employers are often in a strong position to dictate the terms and conditions of work and demand a flexible workforce that is able to work around the clock. In our 'must have' consumer society expectations are high and many people are working long hours to pay for goods and services that previous generations would have simply perceived as being unobtainable. These are just some of the many factors which can create a pressure on employees and ultimately lead to occupational stress. The traditional wisdom was that occupational stress is a problem resulting from a deficit in coping skills on the part of the individual employee and not the business of the employer. This attitude is summarized by the saying 'if you can't stand the heat then stay out of the kitchen', meaning that if you cannot take the pressure, you should get out of the job. However, more recently there has been a growing realization among employers that occupational stress is an issue not only for the employee but also for employers. It is costing employers billions of pounds each year through increased sickness absence, staff turnover, recruitment problems, low staff morale, decreased productivity, poor timekeeping, impaired decision making, increased industrial conflicts, increased accident rates, premature retirement due to ill health, redeployment, retraining, replacement costs, grievance procedures and litigation costs. Thus, the new wisdom is that tackling stress in the workplace is worthwhile not only on humanitarian grounds but also because it makes sound economic sense to do so.

When reading the literature on stress, it is easy to jump to the conclusion that all stress is bad for us. However, it is important to realize that this is not the case. In fact a certain amount of stress is a natural and unavoidable part of life and at low to moderate levels can actually be a positive thing. It acts as a motivator to the individual experiencing it and at optimal levels can enhance performance. However, prolonged high levels of chronic unmitigated stress are potentially harmful and can lead to serious physical and mental health consequences. One might argue that if an individual is experiencing harmful stress, then why don't they simply leave the job? After all, few jobs are worth suffering ill health for. However, for many people it is not that straightforward, and there may be numerous reasons why an employee is unable to just walk away from the problem. For example, they may have invested many years training to do the job, might lack the training to do any other kind of work, or be trapped in 'golden handcuffs', meaning that they cannot afford to take a drop in salary. They may be tied to a particular geographical area through personal and family commitments. Also, even if none of these things were applicable, there may not be the jobs out there to go to when times are tough economically. Also, it is worth remembering that even though being in work may be stressful, being unemployed can be even worse for your mental health.

The purpose of this book is to equip the employee who is experiencing occupational stress with a range of strategies to help them cope more effectively. It is a user friendly self-help manual which provides a step-by-step guide to learning a range of practical tools and techniques, advice and suggestions for managing stress in the workplace. It aims to help you not only to understand the causes and consequences of occupational stress but also to utilize a detailed and comprehensive self-help programme based upon the clinically proven techniques of cognitive behavioural therapy. It deliberately steers clear of the jargon and copious references that would typically be found in an academic textbook. However, it is intended to retain a sufficient level of in-depth analysis of the subject matter to keep the intelligent lay person stimulated, without taking the patronizing or superficial stance found in some self-help books.

The book has been presented in three parts. Part I (Chapters 1 and 2) promoted your understanding of the stress concept. It also outlined the main causes of occupational stress and identified the consequences of stress for both the individual and the employer. Chapter 1 introduced the transactional model of stress, in which stress was conceptualized as being the result of an interaction between an individual and their environment.

The sequence of physical, emotional, cognitive and behavioural changes associated with the emergency response was outlined. The central importance of the appraisal or meaning of an event or situation to the individual in the causation of stress was emphasized and an overview of the emotional and physiological changes triggered in the stress reaction was also presented. Chapter 2 focused on identifying the main causes of occupational stress. The individual causes of stress covered included a range of genetic/inherited, acquired/learned and personality/trait factors. Environmental causes of stress were identified in the demands of the job itself, the physical working conditions, amount of control and autonomy over the job, supports available, quality of working relationships, role clarity and the way change is managed. The interface between work and home life is also a potential causal factor. The transactional model of occupational stress introduced in Chapter 1 was elaborated upon and applied to the work situation. Occupational stress was conceptualized as being the consequence of a mismatch between the individual employee's resources (capabilities and needs) and their work environment, sometimes referred to as a poor person–environment fit.

Part II (Chapters 3 to 10) outlined a range of interventions for tackling occupational stress. Researchers in the field have identified three levels of interventions for managing work related stress more effectively, known as primary, secondary and tertiary level interventions. Primary level interventions aim to change the sources of stress in the work environment itself. It was acknowledged, however, that sometimes it is not possible to change the work environment because either it is uneconomical for the employer to do this, or there are aspects of the job itself that are inherently stressful. Where this is the case and the sources of stress cannot be readily removed, secondary level interventions are considered to be more appropriate. Secondary level interventions aim to teach the employee a range of coping skills or strategies to help buffer them against an inherently stressful environment and to assist them to develop the confidence to look after themselves more effectively in situations that would in actual fact be stressful to anyone. Tertiary level interventions are aimed at more severe levels of clinical distress which are impacting on the individual's capacity to be productive in the work setting, or even to remain at work and where secondary level interventions are assessed as being unlikely to be effective on their own. These involve more formal psychological therapy to assist the individual to return to their previous normal levels of productivity.

Chapter 3 presented a range of primary level interventions aimed at providing a healthy working environment. These included creating the right organizational culture and climate, providing the necessary resources, equipment, training, supervision and supports to do the job effectively, ways of reducing workload, job enlargement and enrichment, improving physical working environment, increasing control, improving working relationships, tackling bullying, role clarification and managing change. Some strategies for improving the home–work interface were also included. Chapters 4 to 9 presented a range of secondary level interventions. These included developing a healthy lifestyle, effective time management, assertiveness, interpersonal/social skills, relaxation training and cognitive coping skills aimed at changing the way that an individual relates to their environment. Chapter 10 presented a range of tertiary level interventions aimed at helping the individual overcome the symptoms associated with anxiety, depression and hostility syndromes.

In Part III, Chapter 11 outlined the tools and techniques to essentially 'become your own therapist'. A step-by-step guide to enable you to develop your own self-help plan to overcome occupational stress was provided. The eight steps outlined were: making a problem list, prioritizing your problems, setting your goals, establishing the criteria of success, planning your interventions, developing a self-help treatment plan, monitoring and reviewing your progress, and preventing relapse.

A range of resource materials has also been provided to help you assess and monitor your progress in terms of developing the knowledge and skills required to manage your stress more effectively. For example, Chapter 1 contained a stress quiz (Table 1.1) to enable you to test your knowledge of stress. The subsequent list of answers provided were aimed at dispelling some commonly held myths and misconceptions about stress. The chapter concluded with a stress checklist (Table 1.2), which allowed you to identify the symptoms and assess the severity of your own stress. Chapter 2 contained a questionnaire to help you identify the main causes of stress in your own work environment (Table 2.1). Chapter 4 contained a checklist of lifestyle habits (Table 4.2) aimed at helping you to identify the changes that need to be made in order to adopt a healthier lifestyle. Chapter 6 contained an assertiveness questionnaire (Table 6.1) aimed at helping you to identify and address those areas in your life in which you need to become more assertive. Chapter 7 contained a checklist of interpersonal skills (Table 7.1) to allow you to identify how interpersonally skilled you are and the areas you need to do more work on. These resources were supplemented by numerous case studies and lots of tools, tips and techniques intended to help you manage your work related stress more effectively.

Consistent with the conceptualization of stress being a product of the interaction of the individual with the environment, this book also addressed environmental causes of stress. In particular it highlighted the employer's 'duty of care' to ensure that they provide a healthy and stress free working environment as far as possible for their workforce. In the UK the Health and Safety Executive (HSE) has identified a number of management standards with respect to managing stress in the workplace, which employers are expected to comply with. Each management standard spells out good management practice in each of six areas relating to job demands, control, support, relationships, role and the way that organizational change is managed. In the UK employers in any organization with three or more employees have a legal duty under health and safety legislation to do a risk of stress assessment on their own workplace based on the six management standards. They are also required to make every effort they can to ensure that these standards are being met within the teams that they manage. Although not adopted internationally in every country, the management standards approach has generated a significant amount of interest in many countries around the world. It is also flexible enough to be accommodated within the range of different regulatory systems present in these countries, so it should become the norm.

One of the main responsibilities of UK employers in reducing occupational stress is to create the right working conditions, which maximize the chances of the employee being effective in achieving their work related goals. Some of the main interventions aimed at changing the working environment were outlined in Chapter 3. However, the employer's responsibilities do not stop there. Where employees are identified by their work organization as being psychologically more vulnerable, there is also an obligation on the part of the organization to assist them to develop the necessary coping strategies to work more effectively in the job they do. This is not merely a moral or ethical argument but, as argued in Chapter 1, it makes sound economic sense to do so. However, despite the legislation there still remains a major challenge for many workplace organizations in terms of 'normalizing' psychological support in the workplace. There is still a prevalent attitude among many employers that showing stress is a sign of weakness and it is not the responsibility of the employer to rescue those who become victims of stress. The reality of course is that virtually anyone under sufficient pressure will start to display the symptoms of stress.

Despite the progress made to date, there is still some way to go, if stress is to be further eradicated from the workplace. There needs to be a culture shift in workplace organizations, from one that sees psychological support for employees as an optional extra to one that sees it as an integral part of the normal culture of the organization. There needs to be a culture in which stress is no longer stigmatized and senior members of the organization lead by example. These are some of the major challenges, which workplace organizations and occupational health service providers need to jointly address if they are to successfully optimize the health of the workforce. Comprehensive packages of interventions at the primary, secondary and tertiary levels need to be provided by workplace organizations and their occupational health services, aimed at reducing occupational stress. However, until this becomes a reality, in many organizations individual employees are left to their own devices.

In conclusion, this chapter has summarized some of the key learning points about occupational stress and its management to be found in this book. It has also highlighted the responsibilities of the employer for supporting the employee, not only for moral and ethical reasons but also because it makes sound economic sense to do so. The importance of the individual taking responsibility for their own occupational stress is also emphasized, particularly when there is an absence of supports in the workplace. A wide range of self-help interventions for managing work related stress has been introduced in this book. However, if you wish to study any specific topic covered in this book in more depth, resource materials and references can be found in the Appendix.

Useful books and contacts

This book has been written in a way that allows it to be easily read and understood without being punctuated by numerous references that disrupt the flow of the text. However, you may want to follow up specific topics covered in the book in more detail. This Appendix provides information on resources in the form of books, websites, postal addresses and telephone numbers, which enable you to follow up a subject area in more depth.

General books

Butler, G. and Hope, T. (2007) *Manage Your Mind: The Mental Fitness Guide*, 2nd edn. Oxford: Oxford University Press.
Fontana, D. (1997) *Managing Stress*, 5th edn. Leicester: British Psychological Society.
Williams, C. (2009) *Overcoming Anxiety, Stress and Panic: A Five Areas Approach*. London: Hodder Arnold.

General websites

Glasgow STEPS
Gives advice and information on how to manage common stress problems:
http://glasgowsteps.com

Living Life to the Full: Helping You to Help Yourself
A computer based life skills course which aims to equip the user with the key knowledge necessary to tackle the demands of everyday life stresses:
www.livinglifetothefull.com

MoodGYM

A free computer based self-help programme to teach cognitive behavioural therapy skills to people vulnerable to anxiety and depression: www.moodgym.anu.edu.au

Net Doctor

Gives advice on a range of mental health problems including stress: www.netdoctor.co.uk

Organizations specifically addressing workplace stress

ACAS (Advisory, Conciliation and Arbitration Service)

Provides information on stress, employer and employee rights in the workplace:
www.acas.org.uk

American Mental Health Foundation (AMHF)

Promotes scientific research and seminars in the field of mental health and related areas:
http://americanmentalhealthfoundation.org

Amicus

The Amicus publication *Stress–An Amicus Guide for Members* is available free on the Amicus Union website:
www.amicustheunion.org/pdf/stressguide.pdf

Health and Safety Executive (HSE)

HSE has a stress home page:
www.hse.gov.uk/stress/index.htm

Healthy Work Matters

Provides information and guidance for employers and employees on stress:
www.healthyworkmatters.org.uk/stress/stress_employer.htm

International Labour Organization (ILO)

Provides information and guidance on stress in the workplace:
www.ilo.org/safework/lang—en/index.htm

Mind (UK)
Mind (formerly National Association for Mental Health) offers advice on a wide range of psychological difficulties:
Granta House, 15–19 Broadway, Stratford, London E15 4BQ
Tel: 020 8519 2122
www.mind.org.uk

NHS Direct
Run by the UK National Health Service, it provides help and guidance on health matters:
Tel: 0845 4647
ww.nhsdirect.nhs.uk

Trades Union Congress (TUC)
The TUC publication *Tackling Stress at Work* is available from TUC Publications:
Congress House, Great Russell Street, London WC1B 3LS
Tel: 020 7467 1294
www.tuc.org.uk/publications/index.cfm

World Health Organization (WHO)
The WHO publication *Work Organization and Stress* is available on its website:
www.who.int/occupational_health/publications/en/oehstress.pdf

Lifestyle

Alcohol

Alcohol Focus Scotland
Provides information on alcohol-related issues:
166 Buchanan Street, Glasgow, G1 2LW
Tel: 0141 572 6700
www.alcohol-focus-scotland.org.uk

Alcoholics Anonymous
Provides help for people with drinking problems:
PO Box 1, 10 Toft Green, York YO1 7ND
Tel: 01904 644026
Helpline: 0845 769 7555
www.alcoholics-anonymous.org.uk

Drink Aware
Provides facts and figures about alcohol:
www.drinkaware.co.uk

Drinkline
Available Monday to Friday 9pm to 11pm, Saturday and Sunday 6pm to 11pm:
Calls are free and confidential: Tel: 0800 917 8282

Diet

Cooper, P. (2009) *Overcoming Bulimia Nervosa and Binge Eating: A Self-Help Guide Using Cognitive Behavioural Techniques*. London: Robinson.

Sleep problems

Espie, C.A. (2006) *Overcoming Insomnia and Sleep Problems: A Self-Help Guide Using Cognitive Behavioural Techniques*. London: Robinson.

Smoking

Carr, A. (2009) *Allen Carr's Easy Way to Stop Smoking: Be a Happy Non-Smoker for the Rest of Your Life*. London: Penguin.

Time management

Fontana, D. (1993) *Managing Time*. Leicester: British Psychological Society.

Assertiveness

Adams, A. (1992) *Bullying at Work: How to Confront and Overcome It*. London: Virago.
Back, K. and Back, K. (2005) *Assertiveness at Work*, 3rd edn. London: McGraw-Hill.

ACAS
Provides information on bullying, including information on your rights:
www.acas.org.uk

Dignity at Work Partnership
Provides information and guidance on bullying in the workplace:
www.dignityatwork.org

Interpersonal skills

Edelmann, R.J. (1993) *Interpersonal Conflicts at Work*. Leicester: British Psychological Society.
Fontana, D. (1994) *Social Skills at Work*. Leicester: British Psychological Society.

Relaxation

Fraser, T. (2003) *The Easy Yoga Workbook: The Perfect Introduction to Yoga*. London: Duncan Baird.
Kabat-Zinn, J. (2006) *Mindfulness for Beginners* (audio book and CD), unabridged edn. Louisville, CO: Sounds True Inc. Also see www. soundstrue.com
Kennerly, H. (1997) *Managing Anxiety: A User's Manual and Tape on 'How to Relax'* (also available as a CD). Oxford: Oxford Clinical Psychology.
Lam, K.C., Mathews, S., Morgan, P., Hilton, J. and Munro, P. (1994) *Step by Step: Tai Chi*. Stroud, UK: Gaia Books.
Shakti, G. (2003) *Meditations: Creative Visualization and Meditation Exercises to Enrich Your Life*. Novato, CA: New World Library.

Healthy thinking

Burns, D. (1999) *Feeling Good: The New Mood Therapy*. New York: Avon.
Greenberger, D. and Padesky, C.A. (1995) *Mind Over Mood: Change How You Feel by Changing the Way You Think*. New York: Guilford.
Young, J.E. and Klosko, J.S. (1998) *Reinventing Your Life: How to Break Free from Negative Life Patterns*. New York: Penguin Putnam.

Managing anxiety

Kennerly, H. (1995) *Managing Anxiety: A Training Manual*. Oxford: Oxford Medical Publications.
Kennerly, H. (2009) *Overcoming Anxiety: A Self-Help Guide Using Cognitive Behavioural Techniques*. London: Robinson.

Coping with depression

Gilbert, P. (1997) *Overcoming Depression: A Self-Help Guide Using Cognitive Behavioural Techniques*. London: Robinson.
Williams, C. (2009) *Overcoming Depression and Low Mood: A Five Areas Approach*. London: Hodder Arnold.

Depression Alliance
Provides information and support services:
20 Great Dover Street, London SE1 4LX
Tel: 0845 123 2320
www.depressionalliance.org

Managing anger

Davies, W. (2009) *Overcoming Anger and Irritability: A Self-Help Guide Using Cognitive Behavioural Techniques*. London: Robinson.

Coping with panic

Silove, D. and Manicavasagar, V. (1997) *Overcoming Panic: A Self-Help Guide Using Cognitive Behavioural Techniques*. London: Robinson.

No Panic
Provides support to people suffering from panic attacks, phobias and other anxiety disorders:
93 Brands Farm Way, Randlay, Telford, Staffordshire.
Tel: 01952 590005
Helpline: 0808 808 0545
www.nopanic.org.uk

Index